1 MONTH OF
FREE
READING

at

www.ForgottenBooks.com

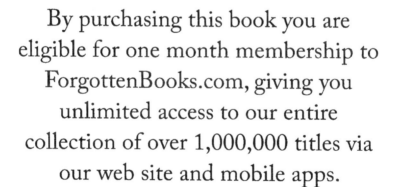

By purchasing this book you are eligible for one month membership to ForgottenBooks.com, giving you unlimited access to our entire collection of over 1,000,000 titles via our web site and mobile apps.

To claim your free month visit:

www.forgottenbooks.com/free1374142

ISBN 978-1-397-32915-8
PIBN 11374142

TWENTIETH ANNUAL REPORT

OF THE

PROVINCIAL BOARD OF HEALTH

OF ONTARIO

BEING FOR THE YEAR

1901.

PRINTED BY ORDER OF
THE LEGISLATIVE ASSEMBLY OF ONTARIO.

TORONTO:
PRINTED AND PUBLISHED BY L. K. CAMERON,
Printer to the King's Most Excellent Majesty.
1902.

WARWICK BRO'S & RUTTER, Printers.
TORONTO.

TWENTIETH ANNUAL REPORT

OF THE

PROVINCIAL BOARD OF HEALTH.

CONTENTS.

PART II.

ANNUAL REPORT OF BOARD OF HEALTH.

PART II.—*Continued.*

PART III.

TWENTIETH ANNUAL REPORT

OF THE

PROVINCIAL BOARD OF HEALTH.

INTRODUCTION.

To *His Honour the Honourable* SIR OLIVER MOWAT, K. C. M. G., *Lieutenant-Governor of Ontario.*

MAY IT PLEASE YOUR HONOUR :

The Provincial Board of Health respectfully begs to present for approval its Twentieth Annual Report of work done under the Act respecting its organization passed in 1882.

Not only does the Board take pleasure in reporting the general and, indeed, unusual freedom of the Province from any death-dealing epidemic disease during the past year, but would also recall to your attention the noticeable improvement manifest in the general condition of the public health during the past twenty years as illustrated in the interesting summary of twenty years of sanitation in Ontario in Chapter I of the Secretary's Report to the Board, and in Chapter IV, in which municipal development in sanitary matters during the period is referred to. As expressed by the Secretary, after illustrating the establishment of public water supplies in the newer towns of Ontario, "this again illustrates the truth that the extent of sanitary, as of other improvements, is the measure of the mental and moral status of any people."

The extent to which the knowledge of the causation as well as well of the means for the prevention of the several diseases known to be contagious has grown during this period may well be said to mark an era in the history of the world ; for during it the knowledge of the cause of tuberculosis has been gained and much practical information regarding its modes of prevention and cure have been received. To-day its diagnosis in the very earliest stages is discoverable by the wonderful biological discovery of antitoxin, tuberculin, while a distinction between it and other chronic pulmonary ailments is readily discoverable by the microscope. Beyond this, however, the clinician and sanatorium have gone, and to-day there is seen a world-wide movement for the removal of sufferers from tuberculosis at an early stage in the disease from the impure atmosphere of workshops and crowded tenements, wherein the infection is so readily spread, to the pure air of the country, where in sanatoria, practically open-air pavillions, the tuberculized may live in the fresh air in sanitary surroundings, and at the same time, under strict medical regimen, be taught the principles of personal hygiene, under which he is to improve, and through which he is alone to expect permanent recovery from the infection. The next twenty years, we may fairly hope, will see the practical application of this knowledge by the reduction notably of the mortality at present caused by tuberculosis in its varied forms. What this reduction means has been fully illustrated in the Secretary's summary, and it may in general terms be said that cholera is removed from the list of diseases which need be feared n Canada, that the plague whose origin and means of prevention are known cannot readily become a menace to this country, that smallpox has not caused more than two hundred deaths in twenty years in Ontario, and even with its presence to-day in a mild form

[3]

in the Province is preventable to the degree that vaccination is promptly practised and thorough isolation and disinfection are carried out, that diphtheria, of all diseases during these twenty years, the dread and plague of our people, has been greatly robbed of its terrors owing to the discovery of its cause and of its antitoxin, and that the several other common contagious diseases have taken on so mild a form in general or are so promptly dealt with that the mortalities resulting from this large class of acute contagious diseases has during these years been lessened by more than fifty per cent., indeed to the extent of almost two-thirds. Were such alone the record of these years, fruitful in scientific results, your Government might very well be congratulated on such an outcome of the establishment of the Provincial Board of Health ; but, as has been pointed out in the *resumés* in the Secretary's Report, progress has been in many diverse directions. Municipal development in the work of sanitary improvement has been marked by very large expenditures upon public waterworks ; it is estimated that at least $11,000,000 have been expended in the 110 cities, towns and villages of Ontario on this work and each succeeding year sees a notable extension of this inestimable convenience and source of health to the people. Along with it sewerage systems have been instituted in many cities and towns, some 50 in all, and while slower in being installed more systems are yearly now being constructed.

The extent to which governmental assistance in educating and encouraging municipalities to enter upon sanitary improvements, as upon other municipal works, ought to go might, as a matter for academic discussion very well have come up twenty years ago, but to day the experience of such a period must largely have convinced economists and legislators of the most extreme *laissez faire* school, that an enormous gain has resulted to the public by the assistance at an almost nominal cost which the Provincial Board has given to the various municipalities in Ontario. As in England and elsewhere, it has been found that in such scientific work, exact knowledge is not the common possession of the people and that the smaller municipalities, who deem themselves unable to pay for expert advice, may be greatly encouraged by an officer who will point out to them that the scientific and correct way of doing such work always means economy in the end. Besides this method of assistance the government has encouraged in various ways the carrying on of experimental work, whereby the Provincial Board of Health may not alone supply itself with more accurate information, but be further in a position to advice action to the various municipalities, based upon such knowledge. This has been seen in the bacteriological examinations of specimens of diseased tissues from patients suffering from supposedly contagious diseases, made to assist Local Boards of Health in taking prompt and efficient measures for suppressing outbreaks, and also in the examination of suspected waters from polluted wells, and from altered or proposed sources of public supplies. The new work now being undertaken for the systematic experimental investigation of sewage disposal works is one peculiarly demanded in a Province, whose industrial development is moving along with surprising rapidity, and where the disposal of the industrial wastes which have been a problem for practical sanitarians in England for fifty years is forcing itself upon Ontario, as it did there and is demanding a solution. Fortunately science has equipped us to-day with means not then to hand in England, and we are in this particular, fortunate in being " heirs of all the ages."

The work of the Provincial Board of Health is expanding in every direction, keeping place with the needs of the people; and there is every reason to look forward into the new century and another twenty years of the Board's work with confident hope, anticipating the still greater triumphs of Sanitary Science, which has now taken so prominent a part in governmental work everywhere under the title of Public Medicine.

Respectfully submitted,

H. E. VAUX, M.D.,
Chairman.

Annual Report of the Provincial Board of Health of Ontario.

PART I.

REPORT OF THE SECRETARY.

CHAPTER I.

SUMMARY OF PUBLIC HEALTH WORK IN ONTARIO DURING TWENTY YEARS.

In presenting the summary of work for the year 1901 to the members of the Provincial Board, it becomes my pleasing task to recall not only the events of the past year, but also those which present the more salient features of public health work in Ontario during the past twenty years, of which this is the Twentieth Annual Report. It is a comparatively easy thing to set down side by side the statistics of the several contagious diseases in the several quinquennia of the period, and to draw more or less obvious conclusions from them ; but it is not quite so easy a matter to present in a short chapter a picture of the outbreaks of diseases of different character, the circumstances under which they have prevailed, whether of a particular class in an unusual season, and of the available means at hand for its suppression, or to indicate those more potent, yet occult, psychological influences, due to social, religious or scientific causes, which play their part in the daily life of the individual, as regards personal habits, occupations and modes of living, and which influence in the most distinct manner the morbility and mortality rates of a country.

In old communities, in what might be termed a statical condition, where the social customs of generations are a part, as it were, of the very religion of a people, where few emigrants, whether to or from a country, influence. the lives of its people, it would be a simple and easy matter to compare then and now ; but when it is remembered that Ontario during the past twenty years has sent out of her children 150,000 to plant the standard of agricultural progress on the plains of the Northwest and Manitoba, has carried the industrial instincts of her larger manufacturing centres to British Columbia and the Yukon, or has sent settlers to the number of 150,000 to carry the ideals begotten of a superior educational system and social life to the neighboring States of the Union, and has transferred of her rugged rural population —— to her own urban centres, it will be clear that no mere comparison of county with county, and of city with city, or township with city, can adequately illustrate the influence of public health work in a community, so little stable either in its population or influences, acting upon its individuals. In a paper printed in the Report for 1900, the influence of periods of settlement in Ontario counties upon the mortality from tuberculosis was studied, and certain untoward results, attaching to the aging of a community with lengthening periods of settlement were indicated. . In the Annual Report of the Registrar-General for 1900 it has been pointed out how there must of necessity be an annually increasing mortality in an old county, whose population has lessened, as that of many of those in Ontario has done, if the proportion of young to old lives is not duly maintained; while in the report of the Department of Education the following figures, taken from the assessment returns, indicate similarly how in such a relatively stationary population must necessarily decrease :

Year.	Population at school ; age 5-21.
1887	611,212
1892	595,238
1897	586,350
1900	580,105

This seems closely in keeping with facts. since the difference between this population in 1887 and 1900, of 31,107 is almost exactly paralleled by the registered attendance in schools which had fallen in 1900 by 29,984. In addition to these facts, illustrating a condition which actually has taken place in Ontario, we add the fact that with the imperfectness of registration in earlier years the births in Ontario were high, it is plain that a cause lying at the bottom of these facts and conditions, and indeed influencing all phenomena dependent upon life, has been at work, viz., that of a definitely decreasing birth-rate. In figures elaborated elsewhere the fact is beyond dispute that a steady decline in birth-rates has gone on since 1862, since taking 500 persons insured in the largest Canadian insurance company, in 1862, and comparing them with 500 insured in 1900, it is found that the number of brothers and sisters in the families of the insured in the first period averaged 7.8 and 6.7 in the latter; while the children born to those married in each group having an average age almost the same in both, is 54 per cent. less in the latter.

These preliminary remarks have seemed essential in order that the results of sanitary influences during the period may be properly estimated. For instance, the number of school children to be affected by sickness in 1900 is 5 per cent. less than in 1887. With this in mind, it becomes of interest, however, to find from a table published by the Registrar-General in the report for 1900, that the following results, as regards total deaths, have been obtained during the school ages, 5-15, during which most contagious diseases occur :

Table of Deaths from Contagious Diseases in Ontario.

—	From 5-9 years.	From 10-14 years.	Total.
In 1891	1,544	722	2,262
In 1900	803	563	1,366

The character of this reduction is explained by reference to tables which are found scattered in the Annual Reports of different years of this period.

From these illustrations it would seem apparent that during the past twenty years there has been, on the whole, a very remarkable change in the habits of thought amongst the people of Ontario as regards disease prevention. Up to twenty years ago smallpox was commonly treated by the family physician, who, exerting more or less care, continued to attend at the same time his other patients. To-day the public will practically boycott any physician who is willing to attend smallpox. The reasons which have produced this situation are the direct result of sanitary education. and on the whole are to be commended. Not to the same extent is the physician feared who attends scarlatina and diphtheria; but the public here too, by sad experience, have at times been taught the extremely contagious character of both of these, and are not slow to remark that it is strange that the members of families are isolated, while physicians seem to go direct from the sick-room with diphtheria to the sick-room of a child with bronchitis or scarlatina. Further, while it has not been possible to carry the idea of family isolation out in cases of whooping cough, measles, and mumps, yet a great step in advance is seen, when health boards are, in some instances, requiring physicians' certificates to be presented to the school authorities before a child from any house where sickness exists is allowed to return to school. The next stage to this is being here and there introduced, at least during an emergency, of having physicians visit the schools to examine for suspects, when an exposure to some sick child had taken place ; and to follow up the absentees to their homes to enquire into the reason for such absence. The fact has been made apparent that along with their physicians the general public have been led on until the contagious nature of all of our ordinary communicable diseases is generally recognized and local health authorities are generally upheld in their action in stamping out any disease. Here and there will be found the physician who, in an anarchistic spirit, assumes still an air of wisdom above that of ordinary mortals, and health laws; an occasional municipal officer who, for cheap popularity, chooses to advocate doctrines of laissez-faire, in dealing with contagious disease; while now and then some citizen with a new zeal, begotten of some self-imposed mission of healing, assumes the non-existence of those organisms whose life history in the bodies of plants and animals has been as well worked out by the slow experimental, but sure methods of science. as have the history, growth and development of the horse or ox, and who carries physical disease into the sphere of moral causation to the utter subversion of all those laws of human government, based upon the accumulated scientific observation and practical common sense of centuries. The general public, hard-working, sane and practical, are always good-natured and tolerant of vagaries, and if the apostle of a new gospel be only fairly clever the public often are even inclined to encourage him in his aberration, whether from the Athenian peculiarity of curiosity or desire for amusement, or at times from the seeming fear that they may be suppressing some spiritual manifestation of truth. But let severe disease appear, such as malignant smallpox, or diphtheria, and take away loved ones then outraged common sense suddenly reassets itself, and demands that the science, which has grown up unobtrusively in their experience, be set to work to correct what they in their folly have listened to from the voice of the enunciator of a new doctrine. We have referred to the wider influences and underlying social conditions in so far as public health progress is concerned, and may now refer to some of the visible signs, which have marked this progress. In 1882 a Provincial Board of Health was established, with a permanent secretary, having well-defined powers and duties set forth by statute. At that time municipal councils were endowed with powers to appoint health committees or Local Boards of Health (under the Act of 1874), and carry out health work under such by-laws as they chose to adopt. Many local investigations were instituted by the Provincial Board of Health during the several succeeding years ; outbreaks of malaria, typhoid, and local nuisances being enquired into as indicated in the following list, under which the detailed reports up to 1897 appear on p.p. 14-18 for that year :

    (1) Machinery of public health work ; (2) collection of sanitary information; (3) dissemination of sanitary information ; (4) health legislation; (5) investigations into causes of disease; (6) outbreaks of disease; (7) food and drink supplies; (8) school hygiene; (9) public institutions.

    As, after much effort during two years, it appeared that the councils had established in 1883 but fifty health committees, the Public Health Act of 1884 was introduced by Sir Oliver Mowat, and became the body of public health law, which has existed to the present, having additions added to it from time to time, as the needs of experience have dictated. Some of the most notable of these are the following amendments to the Act of 1884 :

    1. 1885. For enlarging powers of the Provincial Board for dealing with contagious diseases.

    2. 1886. For expropriation of land for isolation hospitals.

    3. 1887. For notification of school teachers in cases of contagious disease. Remedy for tenant when Board neglects action. Inspection of slaughter houses, dairies and ice supplies.

    4. 1889. Appointment of Stipendiary Magistrates to be health officers in unorganized districts.

    5. 1890. For inspection of meat and milk and animals suffering from contagious disease.

    6. 1891. Appointment of and powers of county health officers.

    7. 1895. Alteration in mode of appointing members of Local Boards of Health. Power given to Provincial Board to approve of all systems of sewerage and water supply in municipalities.

    8. 1896 and 1900. Provisions for licensing and inspecting meat and milk supplies.

    9. 1901. Provisions for sanitation of industries in unorganized territories.

    Smallpox. Under the provisions of the Public Health Act the development of the work Provincial Board has steadily progressed to the present time. First of course has been that of dealing with preventable diseases. In the very year in which the Public Health Act was passed it proved its value in dealing with a severe and extended outbreak of smallpox in Hastings County, which resulted, in Hungerford Township alone, in 203 cases and 66 deaths. This outbreak was stamped out with much rapidity, and left the Board in a position of confidence to meet what proved to be the most serious outbreak ever known in Canada — that of the Montreal epidemic of 1885, when 3,425 deaths occurred in the city, and over 7,000 in that Province, during the year. So complete were the defences in Ontario that only twenty-one deaths occurred in 1885.

DIPHTHERIA.

During this period, and for a number of subsequent years, diphtheria became a very serious plague. The nature of the disease as a true zymotic disease, had been questioned and denied, and Local Boards of Health were seriously in doubt as to what means was best calculated to deal with its ravages. What these were will be gathered from the table of deaths already given. Not, indeed, till 1891, when the experimental work of Yersin and Roux in Paris had shown the bacteriological character of the disease as first had been indicated by Loeffler in 1887, was the truly communicable nature of the disease generally recognized, and a special Order-in-Council for dealing with it along the same lines as smallpox was passed in Ontario in 1891. Since that year the prevalence of the disease as seen in the decreased deaths has notably decreased. Scarlatina had during all the years from 1882 been marked by local outbreaks of a notably mild character, and up to the present it has been treated as a communicable disease and been fairly well kept under control. Indeed it, with measles and whooping cough, has been treated as a less serious disease, than in Europe, where the annual mortality caused by these diseases has been much greater than in America.

Typhoid Fever. This has, as would be expected from the nature of its causation, had relationships to that sphere of work, peculiarly associated with municipal development in matters of public water supplies and sewerage systems. At the time of the formation of a Public Health Department in 1882, there were only twelve public water supplies, and seven sewerage systems in Ontario. In 1901 there were 110 public water supplies and 48 sewerage systems. Under the Public Health Act municipal authorities were required to submit proposed plans and water from proposed sources of supply to the Provincial Board for approval, and were entitled to receive advice, based upon investigation, with a view to securing supplies of water of assured purity. The plans of proposed sewerage systems were similarly revised and advice tendered, with a view to preventing the pollution of streams used as public water supplies.

As experience proved that the Health Act did not insure effective results, the Act was amended in 1895, making the establishment of systems of both public water supplies and sewerage systems dependent upon the approval of the Provincial Board of Health. The Act thus amended has proved of much benefit, and to-day it may be said that scarcely a single public water supply is under any suspicion of pollution, and sewerage disposal works have been instituted in most sewerage systems instituted within recent years.

This branch in the development of public health work became possible only with the institution of laboratory methods, and after some preliminary work by your Secretary, the Provincial Board succeeded in 1890 in obtaining the appointment of a qualified bacteriologist, and the equipment of a small laboratory, the work of which has since then been notably enlarged. The regular examination of public water supplies and waters suspected of causing typhoid fever was begun, and great additions to exact knowledge of the biological relations of water to disease have resulted.

Animal Diseases. The work of the laboratory was soon extended into the field of animal diseases, and valuable studies were made of the causes of hog cholera, actinomycosis, tuberculosis in cattle, anthrax and hydrophobia, and other diseases peculiar to animals.

• Foods. Studies of milk, of vaccines, of antitoxins, of diseases in bees and of insects affecting food, were carried on, and later, when the presence of the bacillus of diphtheria in the throats of patients became recognized as associated with the disease, the laboratory freely extended its aid to all physicians and medical health officers, desirous of assistance in the diagnosis of the disease, and of ascertaining with certainty the freedom of a patient from the disease before being set free from isolation. Some idea of the extent of this work may be obtained from the laboratory statistics which follow.

Tuberculosis. The year 1882, which saw the formation of the Provincial Board of Health, was to witness the announcement of the discovery by Prof. Koch of the bacillus of tuberculosis, a disease which for years had proved to be the *opprobrium medicinae*, whether as regarded its cause or its cure. The manifold manifestations of the disease in different organs, its sometimes rapid, its often chronic cause, had produced theory after theory equally untenable, and had left mankind as the prey of what remains to-day the greatest cause of mortality in man. Statistics of its ravages in Ontario had been year by year set forth, and its relations to insanitary house conditions, to various occupations, and to innutrition illustrated with discouraging iteration. But still the ravages of the disease remained unchecked, and to-day its ravages remain as great as ever in Ontario. To aid in popularizing the idea of its specific characters, the study of it in animals was continued, and a series of diagnostic studies in the use of tuber-culin were made in 1893,and at subsequent periods. But,further,Local Boards of Health were encouraged to have specimens sent through the Medical Health Officers, to promote early diagnosis, and the knowledge of means most useful in lessening the dangers of infection to householders. This work has proved of much interest and utility, as serving to show how frequently the disease has continued for months before its true character has become known, and of how too .other methods than the merely bacteriological are necessary in a certain proportion of cases, if an early diagnosis is to be possible.

Hydrophobia. The appearance of this disease, so frightful in its symptoms and so rapidly fatal in its progress has fortunately been relatively seldom in Ontario ; but the first attempts to prove, by the experimental method of Pasteur, the nature of a suspected case was made by an officer of the Board as early as 1890. Since that time a number of cases have been proved, and patients sent to the Pasteur Institute in New York for treatment.

During more recent years assistance has been given in the diagnosis of cases of suspected typhoid by examining specimens of blood, still further extending the labor-atory work in assisting in the more accurate diagnosis of disease. This work grows year by year with the analysis of suspected well waters, where the disease has cc-curred..

Anthrax. The occasional appearance of this disease in man has been noted during the past twenty years ; but actual outbreaks of the disease in animals were noted as far back as 1886, when a serious outbreak in cattle occurred on the flats along the Speed, at Guelph. Veterinarians had seen the cattle, but not till the second year of its appearance was it brought to the attention of the Board. By the bacteriological method the nature of the disease was promptly diagnosed, and the probable cause in the washings from foreign wool in a factory indicated. Since then a number of out-breaks at different places have been reported, and their relations to the sewage from tanneries importing foreign hides were in practically every case demonstrated. These outbreaks are indicated in the following table :

Table of Anthrax Outbreaks.

Guelph outbreaks	1887	1891	1892
Acton outbreaks	1891	1892	....
Kingston outbreak	1899	....	....
Listowel outbreak	1900	....	....
Whitby outbreak	1900	....	....
Wellesley Township outbreak	1901	...	....

Hog Cholera. Outbreaks of this disease occurred with frequency at the period when the laboratory of the Broad was first instituted, and the utility of the experimental method as compared with the crude veterinary means of diagnosis was promptly demon-

strated. Outbreaks in Toronto and suburbs, in Essex and in Kent were dealt with and assistance given to the local authorities in stamping out the disease. It is remarkable
of how great utility such laboratory work may be and has been in Ontario in dealing
with animal diseases, and how slow the Department, especially detailed to deal with
outbreaks throughout the Dominion, has been to establish means adequate for dealing
with the work has been.

Early in the history of the laboratory the presence of this disease was brought
to the attention of the Board, and it is most creditable that in the laboratory of the
Board some of the first cultures, showing the germ to belong to the group of schizo-
omycetes, were made years before the disease was added to the list of contagious
animal diseases under the Canada Animals Contagious Diseases Act. The disease was
legislated against in Ontario, and an amendment to the Public Health was made in 1890,
for stamping out the disease where it occurred.

Sewage Disposal Works. The growing importance of this work
is becoming yearly more apparent, as the industries of our cities
and towns are increasing. Within recent years actions at law have been instituted against several towns and cities for polluting streams, and the problem of how
to so dispose of sewage as to make it innocuous has become an acute one in such cases.
The complicated nature of the problem has long been recognized, and mechanical and
chemical means of the most varied character have been instituted in different countries
and places, with varied results. Everywhere difficulties have been encountered depending upon the varying nature of the sewage itself, the differences in climate and
soil and, the greatest of all, that due to the fact that municipalities everywhere have
looked upon sewage as a waste to be got rid with as little trouble and expense as possible. It is perhaps too much to expect that it will for years be looked upon in Canada in any other light; but the experience of at least one institution, the London Asylum for the Insane, has shown that the commercial value of house sewage is beyond
question, and has pointed to the direction wherein much progress toward the solution
of the problem may be made. To aid our municipalities in the solution of this problem the Provincial Board may perhaps be expected to lend its energies to an extent
which hitherto has not been possible. At various intervals, however, work has been in-
itiated in the laboratory and during the past three years analyses have been made in
connection with the works at both Berlin and Stratford. The need of a chemist with
greater equipment is a *sin qua non* to progress in this work of the greatest practical
and theoretical importance.

School and factory ventilation. It is a remarkable, but very regrettable. fact
that with the very energetic and practical work done in the question of ventilation of
public buildings during the earlier years of the Board's work, this work of the most
far-reaching character in its practical results has recently almost completely been neglected. There are several reasons for this, the first being the lack of laboratory assistance
in carrying on such chemical work, as marked the progress of this work even forty
years ago in England. Another reason has been that Local Boards of Health having
had no encouragement extended to them in this respect have practically assumed that
the house inspection of institutions, as schools and factories, forms no essential part
of their work, and have apparently assumed that it belongs to the functions of the
officers, acting under the Ontario Factories' Act. While the work done by these officers is valuable in the matter of protecting against accidents from machinery, and
in insisting upon sanitary conveniences, yet the most important work of investigation
through actual chemical and biological methods of the actual air conditions of public
buildings, schools and factories as is provided for in Massachusetts is wholly unprovided for. If ever the fight against tuberculosis is to be seriously undertaken, then this
work must be provided for not in a haphazard or spasmodic way, but systematically
as a part of public health work. London and other English cities, Boston and New
York, have laws definitely providing for the proper construction of buildings; but it
would appear that we in Ontario are allowing this work to go by default, and much will by
and by have to be undone, which now might be easily prevented.

The following summary shows the extent and character of work done in 1901 in the laboratory of the Provincial Board of Health.

Months.	Diphtheria.				Tuberculosis.		Typhoid		Water samples.			Miscellaneous.	To alls for each month
	Diagnosis.		Release.						Bacteriological.	Chemical.			
	+	−	+	−	+	−	+	−					
January............	21	22	9	11	20	50	4	11	10	2		6	166
February	17	18	15	21	31	61	6	7	8	.		8	157
March	18	25	23	26	32	58	6	7	6	1		8	210
April	19	30	12	19	26	62	14	16	..	1		11	210
May	20	20	21	6	45	62	1	22	2	....		11	210
June	35	22	11	15	34	60	4	8	24	6		2	221
July	17	47	50	49	35	69	9	9	21	2		12	320
August	17	26	8	27	26	47	17	14	41	5		11	239
September	13	15	8	9	27	37	32	40	21	2			209
October.........	29	28	9	9	26	42	53	24	12	1			253
November............	20	37	21	31	18	56	23	34	46	10			299
December	23	43	6	20	28	54	13	31	24	8		26	256
	249	333	193	243	348	658	182	233	215	38		98	2780 Grand total.
		1018				1006			405				

Diagnosis positive = + = 582.   Release = − = 436.

1899. There were examined 1,370 specimens.

Sputum 629
Exudate 375
Typhoid 164
B. Water 116
C. Water 29
Miscel 52
Rabies 5
─────
1370

1900. There were examined 1,669.

Sputum....... 703
Exudate 526
Typhoid 221
B. Water 194
C. Water 33
Miscel 25
─────
1669

Illustration of sewages analyzed, Berlin sewage, in parts of 1,000,000.

Oct. 1.	No. of bacteria per 1 c.c.	Free Ammonia.	Alb. Ammonia.	Nitrogen as nitrites and nitrates.	Oxygen consumed.	Chlorine.
Creek 1½ miles below tanks, 5 p.m. Sept. 26.	1.280 000	7.125	4 80	26.250	109.50	240
1½ miles below farm, 10 a m., Sept. 27.	1.915.000	3.975	7 125	2.520	71.55	195
From creek 1½ miles below farm, 12 m. Sept. 27.	420.000	5.5125	5.475	22.6352	47.625	210

Illustration of sewages analyzed, Berlin sewage, in parts of 1,000,000.

Dec. 5.	No. of bacteria per 1 c.c.	Free Ammonia.	Alb. Ammonia.	Nitrogen as nitrites and nitrates.	Oxygen consumed.	Chlorine.
Before septic tank.	220.000	3.50	39.00	2.80	1290.00	400.00
After tank.	38.500	1.75	12.00	3.08	685.00	200.00
After filter bed.	14.000	13.75	7.00	1.029	350.00	600.00
After passing through filter bed.	21.000	17.50	5.00	1.246	340 00	700.00

The following example may be given of work done in the shape of research work.

1st. The examination at Port Stanley and Rond Eau of fishes of fourteen varieties, twenty-three in all, for the presence of the colon bacillus in their intestines. This was undertaken to see if it was possible for fishes to give of themselves the colon bacillus to a water. No colon bacilli were found in any of them. The results of this work are published in the Report of the American Public Health Association for 1901.

2nd. Work was commenced with the object of finding if the bacillus of diphtheria is ever found in the throats of well people. This is being done in conjunction with a committee of the New England Boards of Health Association. One per cent. only has so far been found.

JOHN A. AMYOT, Bacteriologist.

CHAPTER II.

SOME CHARACTERISTICS OF THE RECENT SMALLPOX EPIDEMIC.

In the annual reports of the past two years references, more or less extended, have been made to the outbreaks of smallpox which have appeared in Ontario and in neighboring States; but its reappearance in the first quarter and thereafter in the fourth quarter of 1901 in epidemic form, forces me to again direct the Board's attention to the disease. Its appearance in a widespread outbreak in the lumber camps of the Sudbury district in February was noted last year, and in the first quarterly report printed in the last Annual Report the principal facts relating to it were set forth, and again in a paper in the Report of the Executive Health Officers' Association. and prepared by Dr. C. A. Hodgetts, the chief medical inspector in charge of the district. In the following table have been arranged the counties and municipalities in which district outbreaks occurred, together with their sources, so far as it has been possible to trace the latter :

ALGOMA.

Municipality.	Date.	Source.	New cases of smallpox in March, 1902.	Number at present sick.	Total number of cases since Jan. 1, 1901.
Thessalon Village		Originated	1		11
Howland Township		in			20
Assigmack "		Northern			19
Bruce Mines		Michigan,			
Sault Ste. Marie Town		thence	1		28
Gore Bay Town		from			
Gordon Township		lumber			
St. Joseph's Island		camps.			
Sandfield Township					
Tehkumah "					
Carnarvon "					
Billings ::					
Hilton ::					
Burpee ::					
Joscelyn "					
Johnson "					
Sault Ste. Marie Township					
Dawson "					
Plummer add'l "					1
Balfour ::					
Wells "			1		1
Hallam "			2		2
Nairn Centre Camps					9
Missanabie Township					
Thessalon "					
Little Current Town					
Barrie Island					
Bayfield					
Serpent River					
Day Mills Village					
Cockburn Island					
Nemogosenda					2
Windermere					1
Spanish Mills					5
Creighton Township					1
Superior Mine					1
Blind River					11
Drury, Denison and Graham (Indian Reservations)					15
Goulais Bay					3
Helen Mine					1
Michipicoten					4
Macdonald and Meredith					
Ellen Mine			1		
Maple Camp			2		
Copper Cliff			13		18

BRANT.

Brantford Township					
Burford "	May	Brantford			
Dumfries, South Township					
Oakland "	May	Burford			
Onondago "					
Paris Town					
Brantford City	{ April 23, Sept. 23, Jan.	} Sudbury			6
Tuscarora Indian Reserves					30

2 H.

BRUCE.

Municipality.	Date.	Source.	New cases of smallpox in March, 1902.	Number at present sick.	Total number of cases since Jan. 1, 1901.
Chesley Village					
Tiverton "					
Eastnor Township					
Tara Village					
Albemarle Township					
Amable "					
Arran "					8
Brant ::			2	2	2
Bruce "	December	Kincard'neTp.			12
Carrick ::					5
Culross ::					
Elderslie "					
Greenock ::	February	Bruce Tp.			3
Kincardine "	December	Manitoba			28
Kinloss "					16
Lucknow Village					
Kincardine Town					
Port Elgin Village					
Paisley "	January, 1902.	Kincard'neTp.			2
Southampton Town	March, 1902				2
Saugeen Township					
Walkerton Town					
Huron Township					
Teeswater Village					
Wiarton "					
Lindsay and St. Edmund Townships					

CARLETON.

Fitzroy Township					1
Gloucester "	September	Hull	13	9	56
Goulbourn "					9
Gower, North Township	February, 1902	Ottawa			1
Huntley "					4
Marsh "					
Marlborough "					
Nepean "		Hull			78
Osgoode "	January	Ottawa			4
Torbolton "					
Ottawa City			12	16	233
Richmond Village					
Ottawa East "					8
Hintonburgh "			1	1	32

DUFFERIN.

Garafraxa East Township					
Amaranth Township					
Melancthon "					
Mono "					
Mulmer "					
Orangeville Town					
Shellburne Village					
Luther East Township					
Grand Valley Village					

ELGIN.

Municipality.	Date.	Source.	New cases of smallpox in March, 1902.	Number at present sick.	Total number of cases since Jan. 1, 1901,
Aldborough, Township					
Bayham, "					
Dorchester South, Township					
Malahide, Township					
Southwold, "					
Yarmouth, "					
Aylmer, Town					
St. Thomas, City					
Vienna, Village					
Dunwich, Township					
Port Stanley Village					
Springfield "					
Dutton "					

ESSEX.

Anderson Township	March	Detroit			6
Colchester North Township					
Colchester South "					
Gosfield North "					
Mersea "					
Rochester "					
Sandwich East "					
Sandwich West "	March, 1902				8
Tilbury North "					
Amherstburg Town	March	Detroit			2
Sandwich "					
Windsor "					
Malden Township	March				1
Pelee Island					
Belle River Village					
Leamington "	June	Detroit			4
Maidstone Township					
Kingsville Village					
Essex Town					
Gosfield South Township					
Walkerville	April	Detroit			1
	July 1	Cleveland			
Tilbury West					
Sandwich South					

FRONTENAC.

Barrie Township					
Bedford "					
Clarendon and Miller Township					
Hinchinbrooke Township				1	1	1
Howe Island					
Kennebec Township					
Kingston "					
Loughborough "					
Palmerston "	May, 1902	Shanties	1		1
Pittsburgh "					
Portland "					
Storrington "					
Wolfe Island "					
Garden Island "					
Kingston City					
Portsmouth Village					
Olden Township					
Oso "	June	From shanties	1	1	10

GREY.

Municipality.	Date.	Source.	New cases of smallpox in March, 1902.	Number at present sick.	Total number of cases since Jan. 1, 1901.
Artemesia Township					
Bentinck "					
Collingwood "					
Derby "					
Egremont "					2
Euphrasia "	May	S. St. Marie..			2
Glenelg "					
Hol'and "	Jan. 1902	Toronto			1
Keppel "					
Normanby "					
Osprey "					
Proton "					
Sarawak "					
St. Vincent "					
Sullivan "					
Sydenham "					8
Owen Sound Town					
Meaford "					
Durham "					
Dundalk Village					
Markdale Village					
Thornbury Town					
Hanover Village					

HURON.

Municipality.	Date.	Source.	New cases of smallpox in March, 1902.	Number at present sick.	Total number of cases since Jan. 1, 1901.
Ashfield Township					
Colborne "					
Goderich "					
Grey "					
Hay "					
Howick "					
Hullet "					
Morris "					
McKillop "					
Stanley "					
Stephen "	Jan	Michigan			60
Tuckersmith "					
Turnberry "					
Usborne "					
Wawanosh East Township	Dec	Manitoba			18
Wawanosh West Township	Mar. 1901	London tp.			11
Clinton Town	Jan. 1901	Bay City			1
Goderich "					
Seaforth "					
Brussels Village					
Wroxeter Village					
Wingham Town					
Exeter Village					
Blyth "					
Bayfield "					
Hensall "					

HALIBURTON.

Municipality.	Date.	Source.	New cases of smallpox in March, 1902.	Number at present sick.	Total number of cases since Jan. 1, 1901.
Anson Township					
Minden "					
Stanhope and Shelbourne Township					
Cardiff "					
Monmouth "					
Dysart, etc. "					
Glamorgan "					
Snowden "					
Lutterworth "					
Sherbourne, McClintock, etc					

HALDIMAND.

Municipality.	Date.	Source.	New cases of smallpox in March, 1902.	Number at present sick.	Total number of cases since Jan. 1, 1901.
Canborough Township					
Cayuga North "		Hamilton			2
Cayuga South "					
Dunn "	Mar. 1902				1
Moulton "					
Oneida "					
Rainham "					7
Seneca "	Dec	Jarvis			1
Walpole "			1	1	23
Caledonia Village					
Cayuga "					
Dunnville "					
Sherbrooke "					
Hagersville	Nov	Jarvis			2

HASTINGS.

Municipality.	Date.	Source.	New cases of smallpox in March, 1902.	Number at present sick.	Total number of cases since Jan. 1, 1901.
Carlow Township					
Dungannon "					
Elzevir "					
Hungerford "					
Huntingdon "					
Madoc "					
Marmora and Lake Township	June	Sudbury			1
Monteagle and Hershel Township	Mar	Shanties			1
McClure, Wicklow and Bangor		In Wicklow ..	1	1	
Rawdon Township					
Sidney "					
Thurlow "					
Tudor "					
Tyendinagea "					
Belleville City			1	1	1
Deseronto, Town	Mar. 1901	Sudbury			2
Stirling Village					
Trenton Town					
Madoc Village					
Wollaston Township					
Limerick "					
Faraday "					
Tweed Village					
Mayo Township					

HALTON.

Municipality.	Date.	Source.	New cases of smallpox in March, 1902.	Number at present sick.	Total number of cases since Jan. 1, 1901.
Esquesing Township	Jan. 1902	Manitoba			5
Nassagaweya "		"			1
Nelson "	Feb. 1902	"			4
Georgetown Village					
Milton Town					
Oakville "					
Trafalgar Township	July	Niagara camp.			2
Acton Village	Dec	Manitoba			5
Burlington Village	July	Niagara camp.			3

KENT.

Municipality.	Date.	Source.	New cases of smallpox in March, 1902.	Number at present sick.	Total number of cases since Jan. 1, 1901.
Wallaceburg Town		Dover Tp			2
Camden Township					
Chatham "					24
Dover "		Detroit			399
Harwich ::	Jan. 1902	Dover Tp			10
Howard "					
Orford ::					
Raleigh "	Jan. 1902	Dover Tp			16
Romney "					
Tilbury East Township		Dover Tp			40
Zone "					
Bothwell Town		Dover			
Chatham "					45
Dresden "					
Blenheim "					
Thamesville Village					
Ridgetown Town					
Tilbury Centre Village				1	1

LENNOX AND ADDINGTON.

Adolphustown Township					
Amherst Island "					
Camden, East "					
Denbigh, Abinger and Ashley					
Ernesttown Township,	May, 1901	New York	1		2
Fredericksburgh, North Township					
" South "					
Kaladar, etc. Township	June	Belmont Tp			4
Richmond "					
Sheffield "	June	Belmont			6
Bath Village					
Napanee Town					
Uxbridge Village					
Oso					10

LINCOLN.

Caistor Township					4
Clinton "					
Gainsborough Township	Sept	Buffalo			2
Grantham "					
Grimsby, South "					
Louth "	Feb., 1902	Stephen Tp			2
Niagara Town					
St. Catharines City	July	Hamilton			3
Port Dalhousie Village					
Merritton "					
Grimsby "					
Beamsville "					
Grimsby, North Township					
Niagara Township					

LEEDS AND GRENVILLE.

Municipality.	Date.	Source.	New cases of smallpox in March, 1902.	Number at present sick.	Total number of cases since Jan. 1, 1901.
Augusta Township	Jan	Manitoba	... .	... .	1
Crosby, North Township..............					
" South "					
Edwardsburg "					
Elizabethtown "	Jan., 1902....	Manitoba			4
Elmsley, South "					
Gower, South "					
Kitley "					
Lansdowne and Leeds, Front of					
" " Rear of........					
Oxford Township					
Wolford "	Jan., 1902....	Manitoba			1
Yonge, Front of Township............					
" Rear of "					
Brockville Town.....	Feb., 1902....	Ottawa	3	3	6
Gananoque "					
Kemptville Village					
Merrickville "					
Prescott Town......................					
Newboro' Village					
Cardinal "					
Athens "					

LANARK.

Bathurst Township			1		2
Beckwith "					
Burgess, North Township					
Dalhousie and N. Sherbrooke........					
Darling Township...					
Drummond "					
Elmsley, North Township............					
Lanark "					
Montague "					
Packenham "					5
Ramsay "					
Sherbrooke, South "					3
Almonte Town		Ottawa	3	3	7
Carleton Place Town		"	1	1	4
Lanark Village					
Perth Town........................				1	1
Smith's Falls Town		Ottawa	7	3	10
Lavant Township					

LAMBTON.

Bosanquet Township....					
Brooke "	Feb., 1902....	Chatham			1
Dawn "					
Enniskillen "					
Euphemia "					
Moore "	Feb., 1902....	Sarnia			1
Plympton "					
Sarnia "					
Sombra "					
Warwick "					
Oil Springs Village					
Sarnia Town	Feb., 1902..	{ Detroit .... } { Ekfrid Tp .. }	1	2	8
Petrolia "					
Wyoming Village					
Watford "					
Arkona "					
Thedford "					
Point Edward "					
Alvinston "					
Forest Town					

MUSKOKA.

Municipality.	Date.	Source.	New cases of smallpox in March, 1902.	Number at present sick.	Total number of cases since Jan. 1, 1901.
Chaffey Township					
Bracebridge	February, 1901	Sudbury			2
Brunel					
Cardwell					
Draper					
Gravenhurst					
Huntsville	February, 1902	Whitney			1
Macaulay					
Monck					
Morrison					
McLean and Ridout					
Muskoka					
Madora and Wood				1	1
Oakley					
Port Carling					
Ryde					
Stisted					
Stephenson					
Watt					
Parry Island					1
South River					1
Cooper	March, 1902	Sudbury	1		1

MIDDLESEX.

Municipality.	Date.	Source.	New cases of smallpox in March, 1902.	Number at present sick.	Total number of cases since Jan. 1, 1901.
Adelaide Township					
Biddulph "					
Caradoc "					
Delaware "					
Dorchester N. Township					
Eckfrid "	January, 1902	N.W. Terr.			12
Lobo "					
London "					11
Metcalf "					
Mosa "			1	1	1
McGillivray "		Michigan			2
Nissouri West "			2		2
Westminster "	March, 1901	London			5
Williams East "					1
Williams West "					
London City	January, 1901. November March September January, 1902.	Cleveland Brandon Chicago Detroit Chatham			31
Lucan Village					
Parkhill Town		Michigan			1
Strathroy "					
Wardsville Village					
Newbury "					
Glencoe "					
Ailsa Craig "		Michigan			1
London West "					

NORTHUMBERLAND AND DURHAM.

Municipality.	Date.	Source.	New cases of smallpox in March, 1902.	Number at present sick.	Total number of cases since Jan. 1, 1901.
Alnwick Township					
Brighton Village					
Cartwright Township					
Cavan "					
Clarke "					
Cramahe "					
Darlington "					
Haldimand "	February, 1901	Sudbury			4
Hamilton "					
Hope "					
Manvers "					
Monaghan South Township					
Murray "					
Percy "				1	2
Seymour "	March, 1901 ..	Sudbury			1
Bowmanville Town					
Cobourg "					
Colborne Village					
Newcastle "					
Port Hope Town					
Hastings Village					
Brighton Township					
Millbrook Village					
Campbellford Village	May	Shanties			3

NIPISSING.

Municipality.	Date.	Source.	New cases of smallpox in March, 1902.	Number at present sick.	Total number of cases since Jan. 1, 1901.
Appleby, etc.					
Bonfield					5
Cameron					
Calvin					
Caldwell					
Ferris					5
Field, Badgerow and McPherson					
Mattawa Village					
Mattawan Township					
McKim "		Michigan			20
Nipissing "					
North Bay Town		Michigan			1
Pappineau Township					
Ratter and Dunnett					20
Springer				3	12
Sturgeon Falls		Copper Cliff ..			6
Sudbury		Michigan			25
Temiscamingue, B.					
Widdifield					2
Chisholm					5
Dyment Township					
Copper Cliff				4	2	11
Hazell and Kirkpatrick					5
Beaucage					1
Cache Bay					2
Eau Claire					2
Mono Lake					8
North Bay					1
Warren					20
Whitney					22
Government Tent Hospital	Feb.-J'ne, 1901	Sudbury			170

NORFOLK.

Municipality.	Date.	Source.	New cases of smallpox in March, 1902.	Number at present sick.	Total number of cases since Jan. 1, 1901
Charlotteville Township..........	....	....	....	....	....
Houghton "	....	....	....	.....	.....
Middleton "	... .	....	....	......	.....
Townsend ::	....	....	Burford	....	10
Walsingham South "	....	....	....	....	1
Windham ::	....	... .	Burford	....	44
Woodhouse "	....	....	....	....	7
Simcoe Town	....	....	....	1	1
Port Dover Village	....	....	....	1	.....
Waterford Village...........	....	....	....	.....	....
Walsingham North	....	....	....	....	1
Port Rowan Village	....	....	....	....	.....

ONTARIO.

Beaverton Village	....	....	....	....	1
Brock Township..........	....	....	.....	.....	.....
Mara "	....	....	....	....	2
Pickering "	....	Sudbury	....	....	.....
Rama (:	....	....	Rama	....	.....
Reach ('	....	....	....	.....	.....
Scott ''	....	....	....	.....	.....
Scugog "	....	....	....	....	.....
Thorah "	....	Sudbury	....	....	1
Uxbridge Town..........	....	....	....	.....	.....
Whitby East.......	....	....	....	.....	.....
Whitby West......	....	....	....	.....	.....
Oshawa Town........	....	....	....	.....	.....
Port Perry Village	....	....	....	.....	.....
Whitby Town	....	....	....	.....	.....
Cannington Village......	....	... .	....	.....	.....
Uxbridge Township...	....	....	....	.....	.....

OXFORD.

Blandford Township..............	....	....	....	....	.....
Blenheim "	....	....	....	.....	1
Dereham "	....	....	....	.....	.....
Nissouri East "	....	....	....	.....	1
Norwich North "	....	....	....	.....	.....
Norwich South "	....	....	....	.....	.....
Oxford East "	....	....	....	.....	.....
Oxford North "	....	....	....	.....	2
Oxford West "	....	May	Michigan	.....	20
Zorra East "	....	....	....	.....	.....
Zorra West "	....	....	....	.....	2
Embro Village	....	....	....	.....	.....
Ingersoll Town........	....	....	....	.....	.....
Tilsonburg Village......	....	....	....	.....	.....
Woodstock Town..................	....	....	....	.....	.....
Norwich Village.............	....	....	....	.....	.....

PARRY SOUND.

Municipality.	Date.	Source	New cases of smallpox in March, 1902.	Number at present sick.	Total number of cases since Jan. 1, 1901.
Armour Township					
Bethune and Proudfoot Tp					
Burk's Falls					
Chapman					
Christie					
Carling					
Foley					
Harresin					
Gurd, Pringle and Patterson					
Himsworth, North					
Himsworth, South					1
Hagerman					
Humphry				1	1
Indian Islands					
Joly					
Lount					
Laurier					
Machar					
McDougal					
McKellar					
McMurrich					
Nipissing				3	22
Parry Sound Town				2	6
Perry					
Ryerson					
Strong					
Sunbridge					
French River					2

PETERBOROUGH.

Municipality.	Date.	Source	New cases	Number at present sick.	Total
Asphodel Township	March, 1902	Michigan			2
Belmont, etc., Township		Shanties			5
Douro "		"			1
Dummer "					1
Ennismore "					
Harvey					
Otonabee "	March, 1902	Michigan	1	1	1
Smith "					
Ashburnham Village					
Peterborough Town		Ottawa			2
Galway Township					
Monaghan, North, Township					
Lakefield Village		Shanties			1
Norwood "		"			2
Apsley "					
Havelock "		Shanties			8

PRESCOTT AND RUSSELL.

Municipality.	Date.	Source	New cases	Number at present sick.	Total
Alfred Township			6	6	16
Caledonia "					
Cambridge "	Dec	Ottawa	2		22
Clarence "		"	3		80
Cumberland "		"			30
Hawkesbury East Township		"	3	3	14
Hawkesbury West "					
Longueil "					
Plantagenet North "		Ottawa			26
" South "		Ottawa			11
Russell		Ottawa	3		33
Hawkesbury Village			5	2	16
L'Orignal Town					9
Rockland Village					21
Casselman "			5	3	26
Vankleek "					1

PRINCE EDWARD.

· Municipality.	Date.	Source.	New cases of smallpox in March, 1902.	Number at present sick.	Total number of cases since Jan. 1 1901.
Ameliasburg Township					
Athol, "					
Hillier, "					
Maryborough, North, Township					
" South					
Sophiasburg					
Picton, Town					
Wellington Village					
Hallowell Township					

PEEL.

Albion Township					
Caledon "					
Chinguacousy Township				1	1
Toronto "					
Toronto Gore					
Brampton Township					1
Streetsville Village					
Bolton "					

PERTH.

Blanchard Township					
Downie "					
Easthope, North, Township					
Easthope, South "					
Ellice "					
Fullarton "					
Hibbert "					
Logan "	Feb	Detroit			2
Mornington "					
Ballard "					
Listowell Town					
Mitchell "					
Stratford City					
St. Mary's Town	Mar. 1902	Spokane			1
Milverton Village					

RAINY RIVER DISTRICT.

Rat Portage Town	May				?
Keewatin Township	Feb., 1902	Sudbury			1
Van Horne "					
Regina Mine					
Emo Township					
Alberton and Crozier					
Chapple					
Lac Seul Mission					
McIrvine					
Mikado Mine and Shoal Lake					
Mine'Centre					
Wainwright, Dryden, etc					
Wabigoon and Zealand					
Wabigoon Mission Grant, etc					
Unorganized (Alberta)					
Beaver Mills	May, 1901	Minnesota			11
Golden Star Mine		"			2

RENFREW.

Municipality.	Date.	Source.	New cases of smallpox in March, 1902.	Number at present sick.	Total number of cases since Jan. 1, 1901.
Admaston Township	May, 1901	Sudbury			34
Alice "		Rathbun			1
Bagot and Blythefield Township					
Bromley Township			5	3	5
Brougham "					8
Horton "					
McNab "					6
Pembroke "		Sudbury			2
Pettewawa "					
Rolph, Buchanan and Wylie			1		10
Ross Township					
Sebastopol "					
Stafford "					4
Westmeath "			1	1	1
Wilberforce and Algona Township					
Arnprior Village	Mar., 1901	Sudbury			6
Pembroke Town		Ottawa	23	7	50
Renfrew Town		Sudbury	1		6
Brudenell and Lyndock					
Griffith and Mattawatchen	April 7th		1	1	
Grattan Township					12
Radcliffe and Raglan Township					2
Hagarty, etc. "			1	1	
Eganville Village					1
Head, etc					
Cobden Village					2
Blythefield Township	Mar	Shanty	1		1
Clara "					1
Madawaska "	Dec	Odessa			5
Matcheson	Mar., 1901	Shanty			3
Wylie					2

SIMCOE.

Adjala Township					
Essa "					
Flos "					
Gwillimbury, West, Township					
Innisfil Township					
Medonte "					
Nottawasaga Township					
Orillia "					
Oro "					
Stayner Village	May				1
Tay Township	Mar., 1901	Sudbury			17
Tecumseth "	June				4
Tiny "	May	Sudbury			6
Tossorontio "					
Vespra "					
Barrie, Town					
Bradford Village					
Collingwood Town	Feb., 1901	Sudbury			6
Orillia "	Mar., 1901	Sudbury			2
Alliston Village	July				5
Sunnidale Township					
Midland Town		North Shore			6
Penetanguishene Town					3
Tottenham Village					
Beeton "					
Matchedash Township					
Creemore Village					
Allandale					

STORMONT, DUNDAS AND GLENGARRY.

Municipality.	Date.	Source.	New cases of smallpox in March, 1902.	Number at present sick.	To al number of cases since Jan. 1, 1901.
Charlottenburg Township............	....	....	17	4	51
Cornwall "	....	....	....	1	5
Finch "	....	....	1	1	41
Lancaster "	....	....	....	....	....
Lochiel "	....	....	2	2	over 70
Matilda "	....	.. ..	....	....	....
Osnabruck "	....	....	....	....	....
Roxborough "	... .	....	1	1	....
Williamsburgh "	....	....	....	....	....
Winchester "	....	....	....	... .	1
Cornwall Town...............	....	....	....	....	11
Iroquois Village	....	....	....	....	....
Morrisburgh Village................	....	....	....	....	....
Mountain Township	....	....	....	....	....
Kenyon "	....	....	....	....	13
Alexandria Village	....	....	....	....	2
West Winchester Village	....	....	....	....	1
Chesterville "	....	....	....	....	....
Maxville "	....	....	....	....	....
Lancaster "	....	....	1	1	1

THUNDER BAY.

Oliver Township	....	....	....	....	....
Neebing "	....	....	....	....	....
Port Arthur Town.....	....	....	....	....	8
Fort William "	Jan. 1901	Winnipeg	....	....	1
Nepigon	....	....	....	....	....
Schreiber....	....	....	....	....	.. ....
Shuniah	....	....	....	. ...	....
Strevels' Camp	....	Winnipeg	....	....	11

VICTORIA.

Bexley Township	....	. ...	....	....	....
Carden "	May	Sudbury .	.. . .	....	21
Eldon "	May	Sudbury	....	....	19
Emily "	....	....	....	....	....
Fenelon "	....	....	....	....	.. ..
Laxton, Digby, etc., Township........	....	....	....	....	....
Mariposa "	....	....	....	....	....
Ops "	....	....	....	....	....
Somerville "	....	....	....	....	....
Verulam "	February,1901	Massey St.	....	....	1
Lindsay Town	....	. ...	....	....	....
Bobcaygeon Village......	....	. ...	....	....	....
Omemee "	....	....	....	....	....
Fenelon Falls "	....	....	....	....	....
Woodville "	....	....	....	....	....
Dalton Township	....	....	....	....	....
Sturgeon Point Village............,....	....	... .	.. ..	....	....

WATERLOO.

Municipality.	Date.	Source.	New cases of smallpox in March, 1902.	Number at present sick.	Total number of cases since Jan. 1, 1901.
Waterloo Township					2
Wilmot "			1		3
Woolwich "					
Berlin Town		Michigan			1
Galt "					
New Hamburg Village					
Waterloo Town					2
Hespeler Village					
Dumfries, North Township					
Preston Village					
Wellesley Township					
Ayr Village					
Elmira "					

WELLAND.

Bertie Township					
Crowland "					
Pelham "					
Stamford "					
Thorold Town					
Wainfleet Township					
Willoughby "					
Chippawa Village					
Niagara Falls Town					
Fort Erie Village					
Port Colborne Village					
Thorold Township					
Welland Town					
Humberstone Township					
Niagara Falls Village					
Bridgeburgh "					

WELLINGTON.

Arthur Township					
Eramosa "	Jan., 1902	Manitoba			1
Erin Village					
Garafraxa, West, Township					
Guelph "					
Luther, West "					
Maryborough "					
Minto "					
Nichol "					
Peel "					
Pilkington "					
Puslinch "	Jan., 1902	Manitoba			18
Arthur Village					
Elora "					
Fergus "					
Guelph City					
Mount Forest Town					
Harriston "					
Drayton Village					
Clifford "					
Palmerston Town					
Erin Township					

WENTWORTH.

Municipality.	Date.	Source.	New cases of smallpox in March, 1902.	Number at present sick.	Total number of cases since Jan. 1, 1901.
Ancaster Township.............					1
Barton "					1
Beverley "					
Binbrook "					
Flamboro', East, "		Manitoba			6
Flamboro', West, "					
Glanford "					
Saltfleet "					
Dundas Town					
Hamilton City		Michigan	1	1	21
Waterdown Village					

YORK.

Etobicoke Township.............			1		1
Georgina "					
Gwillimbury, East, "					
Gwillimbury, North. "					
King "		Aurora	3	3	3
Markham "	Mar., 1902 ..	Toronto			1
Scarborough "					
Vaughan					
Whitechurch "					
York "	July	Toronto			7
Aurora Town........................		Ottawa	5	4	8
Holland Landing Village					
Newmarket Town					
Richmond Hill Village.............					
Toronto City			2	2	40
Markham Village...................					
Stouffville "					
Woodbridge "					
Weston "					
Toronto Junction Town.					
East Toronto Village					
North Toronto "					
Sutton "					

With the explosive outbreak of the last three months, December (1901), January and February, practically suppressed, it becomes a matter of some interest both to examine into the causes of so sudden and widespread an outbreak of the disease, and describe the machinery which has now for three successive years proved effective in suppressing the disease.

Sources of the Disease. The several sources of individual outbreaks have been set forth in the preceding table; but speaking generally the outbreak in the Sudbury district, beginning in January, 1901, was directly traceable to several cases, where infected workmen, drifting from the Houghton district of Northern Michigan to the railway construction works at the "Soo" and to the lumber camps, introduced the disease to several centres. Others in the camps, exposed to the disease believed to be "grippe," with a subsequent rash, attributable to the pork eaten in camp, were infected and some of the worst cases, leaving camp went to the railway, and thereby to the nearest town with an hospital or physician; and in some cases were attended in hospital, and in others in hotels and boarding houses, where the disease was not diagnosed as smallpox, and therefore not quarantined. The exposure of many unvaccinated persons, and the neglect to vaccinate those exposed, caused an explosion of the disease of a very widespread character; workmen recovering took trains to their homes in eastern counties on the Ottawa, while commercial travellers in several instances carried the disease to Toronto and other urban centres. Other centres in southwestern Ontario, in Middlesex, Oxford and Brant, came in directly from Michigan and Ohio, but were localized and quickly suppressed. The outbreak caused by the dispersion of the lumbermen was transmitted to the Quebec side of the Ottawa, and became the chief centre from which the smouldering fire was to spread once more to the Sudbury lumber district when operations began again in September. The centres and dates of appearance are given in the tables. But another and unlooked for source made its appearance. In August, after the Ontario harvest, thousands of farm laborers and prospectors went to Manitoba to assist in reaping the enormous harvest. Owing to rains and the great yield operations were long continued and many remained till November and even December. Their return coincided closely with the appearance of the disease in widely separated centres in the rural parts of the Province, set forth in the tables. In some cases it has been found that men had been exposed to the disease in Manitoba and in others, probably more, **that** they were exposed in the three-days' trips either by the Canadian route and yet more by the Minnesota route to either convalescents or to others infected in the colonist cars. Thus in November, December and January there were 15 outbreaks and 81 **cases** directly attributable to this source. Several outbreaks **from Michigan in** Western Ontario again appeared, those in Kent alone from December to the end of March amounting to 537 owing to the character of the community in which it appeared and the failure on the part of one or more physicians to promptly diagnose the **nature of the disease.**

    An Unprotected Population. From these many sources of infection it is apparent that unless first cases were promptly detected and isolated many others exposed would take the disease unless immune. The history of the disease and all recent observation proves that with few exceptions all unvaccinated persons, whether infants or old men, are susceptible to smallpox and will take the disease if exposed. The past year has in a remarkable manner shown the unprotectedness of the great bulk of the rural population of Ontario under 20 years of age, and indeed of many persons much older, even as regards primary vaccination. Many illustrative statistics may be given, which but imperfectly prove the extent to which this neglect has gone during recent years, since many unvaccinated, through prompt quarantine and revaccination, have not had an opportunity to develop the disease.

    Outbreaks in Ottawa, Sudbury, Dover and Burford were especially interesting, and which, owing to the large number under the careful observation of experienced physicians, served to teach the lesson, which is everywhere at present being taught to populations where the absence of dangers has begotten indifference, and the immunity begotten of public health work has developed a contempt or disregard of the lessons of the past century. One is glad to know that the lesson again taught has during the past year been learned by many, but at a large cost.

    The Mild Type of the Disease. This subject was dealt with to some extent in the Report for 1900, and what was then pointed out as contrary to theory as well as most obvious fact, that the disease was mild owing to a transmitted immunity through past generations of vaccinated persons in America, has been unfortunately only too well illustrated by the virulent outbreaks which during the year have appeared in New York, Boston and Philadelphia. What was further pointed out then that the presence of a virulent type of the disease in Great Britain and Italy, only required introduction by American seaports to this continent to show that the absurd theory of an immunity in the people of this continent greater than that of the people of England systematically vaccinated for half a century has during the year been fully demonstrated.

    The continued presence, however, of the benign type in the great area of the United States and Canada west of the Atlantic seaboard demands that in the interests

    .   3 H.

of the public and of the hundreds of physicians in the Province, who still remain unacquainted with the disease from personal experience, I refer somewhat specifically to
the clinical features of the disease as it has appeared during the past three years. In
this I am especially fortunate in having the assistance of Dr. C. A. Hodgetts, who has
been for months constantly engaged in dealing personally with the outbreaks in all
parts of the Province.

When we wish for exact teaching, we naturally turn to those great masters of
medicine who have had the widest experience under the most favorable opportunities
for obtaining knowledge. As regards smallpox, we naturally go back to the years
between 1870-80, when the school of cellular pathology had attained a pre-eminence,
and when in Germany, France and England clinicians had to deal with an epidemic of
smallpox which for virulence, as Sir John Simon has said, exceeded all within histori-
cal recollection.

No pathologist of his time has written with greater precision and perspicuity
than Prof. S. Jaccoud of the Paris Faculty in his "Traité de Pathologie Interne," and
we may therefore turn to his work for some of the broad facts relating to variola.

Having spoken of the zymotic theory of the disease Jaccoud says : "The virulence of the variolous virus is pandemic; but it is subordinated to the organic receptivity, not only as to the degree of its effects but also to their production. The fact
of a natural total immunity is proved by the notable number of persons who escaped
all attack in the epidemics of variola prior to the discovery of vaccine ; the fact
of the partial and variable immunity according to individual receptivity is established by the variable intensity of the effects of the poison in divers patients at the same
time and place. We are not bound to attribute this plurality of forms to the plurality of poisons, because here, as in cholera, the lightest form may transmit the most
intense : The poison is one, the receptivity is various, like the individual. On the
other hand, we cannot impute the mild forms of variola to the common practice of vaccination; that these benign forms may by this means become much more numerous
is quite true, but such existed before vaccine, and the proof is that at the period when
artificial inoculation with variolous virus was practised, they took good care to employ
virus only from the mildest cases. The theoretical idea was erroneous, since the product depends especially upon the soil and not upon the seed; but this practice proves
positively that light forms of smallpox have preceded vaccination." Apropos of this
summing up of facts, it may be stated that Von Swieten in 1759 is quoted by Copeland
as describing a mild or mitigated outbreak of smallpox. It is stated there "that the
primary fever is often little more than a febricula, and the pustules seldom exceed more
than from 1 to 200. These indeed seldom reach a pustular stage, but, having passed
through that of tubercle or papule into that of vesicle on the sixth day or even sooner,
dessicate, shrivel up and crust. The form is so mild that secondary fever is not manifested, and consequently is wanting, convalescence coming on the eighth day of the
eruption."

It is important, however, to note as was remarked last year, when referring to
the increased virulence of the disease at New Orleans amongst the negroes in two successive winters, that Jaccoud states : "Constitutional weakness, bad hygienic conditions, excesses and fatigue of every kind, expose patients to the severest forms of the
malady. The hurtful effect of these circumstances is such that I have seen it several times annihilate the salutary action of a vaccination of which the protective period had not yet elapsed." It might be thought that with these practical considera-
tions pointing to variation in the type of the disease as being both by history and
in theory a part of the natural history of smallpox and of other eruptive and infectious diseases that little more need be said; but experience during the past two years
has made it abundantly apparent that the clinical pictures of the disease which the
present generation of physicians, drawn from the virulent outbreaks of 1870-74, recall
are so fixed in the memory that it seems quite impossible not to have many mistakes
made. As one physician who had seen or treated over one hundred cases last year
said, in defence : "I know it is not chickenpox, but I cannot believe it is smallpox,

although I never saw a case." It may then seem not ill-advised to once more deal with the pathology and varying clinical appearance of the disease as it has appeared during the past two years.

Jaccoud remarks : "The cutaneous features of true smallpox are those of a true suppurative and ulcerative dermatitis disposed in little foci more or less numerous. The initial lessons are circumscribed and isolated hyperemias which occupy the whole thickness of the skin, even to the subcutaneous tissue, but which have their greatest development in the papillae; the papillae appear elongated in consequence of the development of vascular aggregations. This epidermal covering is strongly raised and the rete malphigii is thickened throughout. The pock then presents under the form of a red point slightly elevated, however, circular without trace of cavity or of liquid; it is a papule. Soon exudation supervenes while a serous liquid bathes the deeper layers of the epidermis, dissociates its parts and arrives under the superficial more resistant layer, which arrests it. In this passage the liquid crowds again to the periphery, the cells of the rete malphigii, are themselves engorged with a fluid exudate and these cells are accumulated in a circular zone surrounding the pock, which are taken for a pseudo membrane. The superficial epidermal layer is raised in the centre by the collected liquid; thus the papule has been transformed into a vesicle. In a third stage the fluid becomes turbid from the cellular hyperplasia of the rete malphigii, and the vesicle is changed into a pustule. At length, under pressure of the fluid, the surface of the pustule thins and then breaks down, and after its escape one finds at the base little cup-shaped depressions. These heal without completely restoring the loss of tissue, leaving depressions recalling the form of the previous ulceration. Such is the common history and picture, but Jaccoud goes on to say : "The dermatitis of mild cases is superficial, and several eventualities are possible, the loss of substance only takes place in some of the pocks; in others it is hardly recognized, and after healing there is only a small number of depressed cicatrices, the others are so slightly marked that they can only be discovered by close inspection. In other cases the inflammation loses its essential character or at least the exudation is eliminated by dissociation without loss of tissue. There is no loss of substance at all; the contents of the pustule dry up and it is transformed in situ, with the skin covering it, into a crust of a yellow more or less brown, and whenever these crusts fall off there remain no depressions, but only round elevations of a dusky red, due to the persistent tumefaction of the papilla. Little by little these elevations ·lessen, the redness disappears and the skin retains no trace of the eruption. This variety often coincides with one of the preceding, and one there finds again some few cicatrices, which recall the existence but not the abundance of the pustulation. "The pocks do not always have a special appearance, the centre is often umbilicated, as if the raising of the skin had been prevented at this point by retraction or by adherence. This umbilication, which has been wrongly given a distinctive character, is not constant; it is bound to no particular shape, and it is produced sometimes from the presence of a hair follicle at the orifice of which the raising of the epidermis is held down, or from the adhesion between the deep and superficial layers of skin being maintained. The umbilication only becomes real at the beginning of desiccation, which commences from the centre."

In these several paragraphs we find set forth in the most precise language the clinical phenomena, which are present under varying conditions in the disease, affected both by the type of the germ and the personal element in the patient, whether dependent upon relative natural immunity or that acquired through vaccination, inoculation or a previous attack of smallpox.

With such teaching from a master in pathology it becomes easy for us to understand how a type of the disease, such as that which has prevailed in Ontario during the past three years and which has been the occasion of most frequent and serious doubts as to its true nature, may occur. With a view to presenting some of those clinical variations, which have caused so much uncertainty, the following illustrative characteristics are set forth both from personal observation and from the much larger experience obtained by Dr. C. A. Hodgetts, medical inspector of the Board, who has been personally engaged in field work both in the unorganized districts of Northern Ontario, directly under the supervision of the Board, and in the assistance rendered to the Local Boards of Health, which have asked for assistance. Probably not less than 2,000 cases have thus come under the personal observation of officers of your Board. Speaking in notes supplied regarding the difficulties of diagnosis and varlation in the signs and symptoms of the disease, Dr. Hodgetts states : "Yet the infection of smallpox pervades the whole, and there can in my opinion be no doubt as to its true character. As others of the group of communicable diseases, e.g., scarlatina and diphtheria, with which the medical profession of the Province is more familiar, may present in different individuals exposed to the same source of infection, symptoms and signs, both subjective and objective, entirely different in character and appearance, so I desire to demonstrate such is the case with smallpox." "This mild type of smallpox is no respecter of persons, whether as regards age or condition. Those past four score years, equally with the child of a few weeks, male and female, if unvaccinated, have suffered. On the other hand, the vaccinated have in most instances proved immune or have had the disease in a modified form. A father or a mother with a good scar or a child fortunate enough to have been successfully vaccinated have escaped in multiplied instances; the only exceptions in those exposed to infection amongst the unvaccinated being in persons who had previously had smallpox. In houses where the disease appeared and the sick were treated at home, and where other inmates refused to be vaccinated, I have never known an unprotected person escape, even though partial isolation had been carried out; whilst, in similar cases when vaccination has been practised, it has given either complete or partial immunity."

"Inasmuch, however, as departures from the normal have been so numerous in many of the earlier outbreaks in first cases, many practitioners not finding such to conform to the disease described in the textbooks, have believed, indeed, that it must be something else—some new and undescribed disease—and hence it has been called 'Cuban itch,' 'Philippine rash,' 'pine knot itch,' 'swine pox,' 'yaws.' 'grippe,' 'chickenpox,' 'impetigo contagiosa,' etc., etc." Such attempts at diagnosis, while in most instances not creditable to the professional skill or education of the practitioner, do nevertheless illustrate the many abnormal qualities of the disease; but when wide experience as well as the literature of the subject shows that the disease may abort at any of its several stages, the conclusion is easily and naturally arrived at that it simply proves once more that smallpox follows the variations common to parasitism in all diseases of the class, whether affecting plants or animals.

Dealing with the disease in its various stages, while the incubative period has never in the experience of Dr. Hodgetts, been found less than 13 days, yet there have been frequent cases when it has extended to 16, 17 or 18 days after exposure. Prudence dictates that unless successful revaccination has been practised with no rise of temperature being present, the quarantine should be extended to this length of time.

"The onset of the disease has in many cases been found to be indistinct and illmarked, the rigor or distinct chill being absent. In a few instances, when the initial chill had been well marked, the case has subsequently proved mild. The greater number of adults describe the disease as 'grippe.' referring especially to such symptoms as headache, pains in the body and limbs with fever, which when the temperature has been taken, has ranged from 102 to 104 degrees F. In most cases this has continued for three days. occasionally even to the fourth or fifth day. In the three-day class the fever has ended by crisis, in the others by lysis. In infants the disease is usually ushered in by a chill or convulsions, with vomiting, and in their case the symptoms approach more to those described in text books. Sore throat has in these been a very constant symptom, while in some I have seen severe and continued vomiting. In not a few instances patients state that they have suffered from a mere cold in the head and ridicule the idea of their having smallpox. It may, however, be noted that though during the two previous seasons these initial symptoms seldom approached the old normal type with a subsequent eruption often typical, yet during the present win-

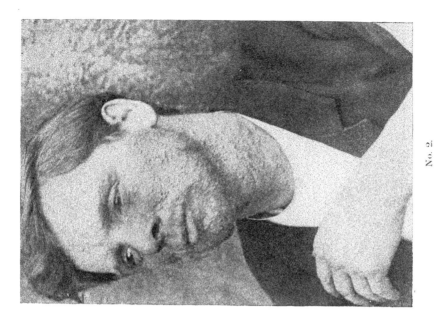

No. 2.

Photo supplied by Dr. C. A. Hodgetts.

Shantyman in Tent Hospital, Sudbury. Illustrating the vesicular stage of eruption.

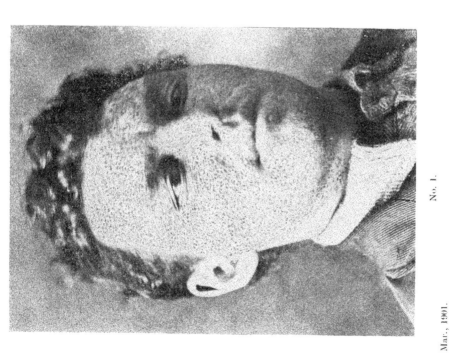

No. 1.

Mar., 1901.

Shantyman in Tent Hospital, Sudbury. Illustrating pitting after recovery.

[33]

No. 4.

Photo supplied through kindness of Dr. W. H. Tye, Chatham.

No. 3.

Jan., 1902.

Cases in Harwich Township. Father and son infected from same previous case in family. Both were unvaccinated, and boy had been diagnosed first as chickenpox.

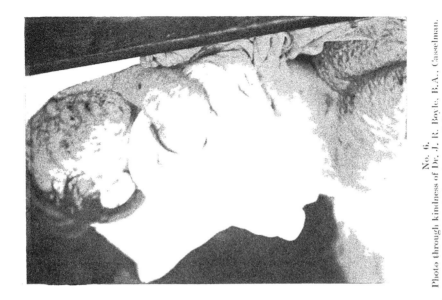

No. 6.

Photo through kindness of Dr. J. R. Boyle, B.A., Casselman.

Illustrating extreme variations in type of disease.

No. 5.

Feb., 1902.

Children in same family from same exposure, both unvaccinated.

[35]

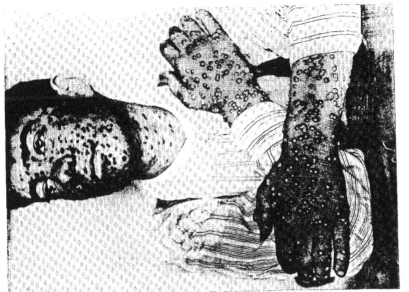

No. 7.

Feb., 1902.

No. 8.

Through kindness of Dr. J. R. Boyle, B.A., Casselman.

Illustrating in No. 7 inflammatory condition of subtaneous tissues, and in No. 8 a discrete case in which pustules of face have collapsed and are crusting, while pustules are still on hands.

ter the premonitory symptoms as well as the eruption have become more typical. The eruption has, however, undoubtedly caused the greatest difficulties as regards diagnosis. Even those who were familiar with smallpox in 1885 and in earlier epidemics, on being called to see a single case, have found great difficulty in arriving at a positive diagnosis, and it is not to be wondered at that those whose only knowledge of the disease has been obtained from text books, passed by such cases often without suspecting their character. The macule, papule, vesicle and pustule may each in turn have been modified, while the distribution, date of appearance of the rash and progress of its stages have presented great variety. On its appearance on the third day it has often been taken for measles. Its appearance successively on the face around the nose, mouth, along the line of the hair, then down the neck, over the chest, abdomen, back and extremities, has often been looked upon as successive crops of vesicles; but this I believe is due to the fact that the inflammatory patches on those portions of the body where the integument is thicker do not show the macule so marked as on the parts where the skin is delicate. I have found on close inspection the macule present when both medical attendants and patient have said nothing was to be seen or felt. Noticeably has this been the case on the hands, legs and feet, and in the hair. In these situations it takes the papule and vesicle longer to form, and hence it is said to have appeared in successive crops."

"In several cases of discrete or confluent smallpox these several signs are all better marked and appear generally well over the whole body; but in very mild cases faint macules will disappear, never becoming papules. Again some papules will abort, forming little dark crusts or scabs about the size of a pin's head, falling off within a week or ten days. Such cases as this occurred during the past July in children, infected directly from a well-marked case of the discrete disease, mild in its course but presenting all the typical appearances as to rash. Where I have been able to make close successive observations I have never seen the macule, papule and vesicle completing the stages within twenty-four hours as is the case in chickenpox; but still the macule may not present the distinct shotty feel, the papules may not be uniform in size, vesiculation is delayed, and the pustules may not all be full and tense on the fifth day. As regards umbilication some or all may become flabby and the disease may abort at this stage in a somewhat similar manner to modified smallpox. The vesicles form crusts and these are soon shed with the exception of those on the palms of the hands and the soles of the feet, often by the fourteenth day. These show brownish patches beneath the thickened epidermis, which require a knife or needle for their removal. (They are like a blood blister beneath the skin and exfoliate in a similar maner). "As regards pustulation the varieties are perhaps greater at this stage than in any other. It is often hastened or completed by the twelfth or fourteenth day; the flattened and superficial crust has scaled off in a manner similar to that in the vesicular stage. In other cases the pustules are larger and well rounded with or without a black centre. In some of these the pus shows evidence of admixture with blood and they appear dark in color. When the pustules are round and full I have noticed at times little evidence of umbilication; although in the same patient some pocks not so large and full have the umbilication well marked."

"The pustules in the milder cases remain discrete with but slight inflammation. while in others they coalesce, and present all degrees till they become semi-confluent or confluent, this again being accompanied or succeeded by others of a benign character. The amount of inflammation is always proportionate to the extent of the eruption; and the same may be said of the secondary fever While in the larger proportion of cases the secondary fever was absent, yet when present it has at times risen to 103 degrees F. and 104 degrees F., with accompanying rapid pulse and general weakness. As regards exfoliation, this may occur at any stage, and has often been observed to take place on the face, neck and chest, about the tenth day; while pustules on the body and extremities may take several weeks longer—especially on the palms of the hands and soles of the feet. That exfoliation is often succeeded by pitting we have ample evidence. The removal of crusts leaves a reddened and congested mark like an aborted secondary vaccination."

I have given quite fully quotations having a description of the salient points observed by one whose special duties were to diagnose all doubtful cases for purely prophylactic purposes. The typical cases have not been referred to, but it is of essen-tial interest to observe how closely associated these clinical features are with the various pathological variations described by Prof. Jaccoud. Other anomalies have been personally observed in cases where a recent vaccination with a lymph of insuffi-cient virulence to leave a true cicatrix had been performed. Here the rash appeared earlier than is normal; shallow, irregular vesicles were filled with a milky, grumous fluid, and the vesicle broke down and scabbed within two or three days in some cases. Except the history of exposure there was practically nothing to indicate the nature of the disease, the vesicles on the face being extremely few and transitory. Other occasional cases in fair-skinned, healthy children have presented in the few pocks present early development; but while the vesicles were in some cases little larger than a pin's-head, yet they presented as typical umbilication as do the vesicles appearing about the scarifications of a successful vaccination by the fourth day. It is remarkable that these in several particulars have a course markedly like vaccination in persons bearing evidence of a previous successful vaccination at no very long distance of years. The question has arisen as to whether such mild cases are protected permanently in practice against a severer type of smallpox. Fortunately probably for many, but unfortunately for scientific proof, the severe type has not yet been encountered by them. Certain it is that vaccination has occasionally been partially successful after such attacks, illustrating the axiom that theoretically there is no such thing as absolute immunity.

CHAPTER III.

SMALLPOX OUTBREAKS IN THE LUMBERING DISTRICTS OF ONTARIO.

The materials of this Chapter have been collated by Dr. C. A. Hodgetts, Inspector.

The result of the progress of the work of supervision under the special regulations has, on the whole, been gratifying, and notwithstanding that the inspector has not been able to devote all his time in the district owing to the widespread character of smallpox, calling him to all parts of the Province, there has been an honest endeavor on the part of the lumber companies to carry out the spirit at least of the regulations, and seventy companies and firms have reported the employment of medical men, although at the time of my first visit to the district in November I could only learn of two firms who up to that time had taken this action.

At that time it seemed apparent that those coming under the provisions of the Act of 1901 had little intention of complying with the regulations. All were awaiting action on the part of the Provincial Board of Health; the new order of things to be instituted in the camps was so radical in character that it required uniform action on the part of the companies, otherwise the employees would leave those camps where the regulations were being enforced, seeking by preference those where the old order of things prevailed. Another difficulty presenting itslf was that none of the companies had notified their men when engaging them that they must be vaccinated and must contribute a stated amount monthly for medical attendance; and the employees, being perfectly ignorant of the Act or its requirements, resented the impost of fifty cents per month as an unjust and illegal act on the part of the employers. In addition to this fact employment was abundant, and the men were consequently independent. Considering all these facts it is very satisfactory to report that seventy companies have this year intimated they have complied with Regulation XII., and contracted with a medical man for the inspection of their camps. The operations carried on by these firms include the districts of Nipissing, Muskoka, Parry Sound, Algoma, Thunder Bay, Rainy River and Renfrew County.

The following thirty-three companies have furnished the Board with reports of the inspections made by their medical men, viz.:

Booth, J. R.
Barnett, A.
Booth & Gordon.
Cook, J. W. & G.
Cutler & Savidge Lumber Company .
Charlton, J. & T.
Carter, W. W. & Co.
Dyment, N. & A.
Douglas, T. A.
Eddy, Jordan & Company.
Eddy Bros.
Ferguson & McFadden.
Fisher & Company.
Glover & Cashin.
Gordon, George & Company.
Hull Lumber Company.

Holland & Graves.
Keeling & Company.
Lowe & Cameron.
Michigan Lumber Company.
Moore & McDonald.
Munro Lumber Company.
McGregor, W.
McCormick & McLeod.
McNeil, McLeod & McCormick.
McLaughlin Bros.
North Shore Timber Camp.
Ryan, John.
Sims, T. C. & Company.
Sebin, John.
Victoria Harbor Lumber Company.
Wallace, McCormick & Sheppard.

The reports deal with sixty-four camps, in which in all 4,028 men were employed. There is positive information given that every man in fourteen of the camps was successfully vaccinated, the total number being 1,094; whilst in seventeen camps 611 men were vaccinated and 466 unvaccinated. In the case of the remaining thirty-three camps, employing 1,857 men, the replies given in the reports are so vague that numbers cannot be given; but it is evident that a good percentage of this number had been vaccinated. To this indefinite and somewhat indifferent method of investigation on the part of the several medical men is due the fact that we cannot give figures regarding nearly half of those reported on.

The following infectious diseases have appeared in eight of these sixty-four camps during the period of recent inspection, viz.:

Smallpox in 3, with five cases; enteric fever in 1, with eight cases; scarlet fever in 1, with two cases; measles in 1, with two cases; mumps in 1, with a number of cases ; also acarus scabie, in 1, with five cases.

Treating of the camps generally they are reported by the physicians as being, on the whole, clean; but in some few instances the fact that latrines are wanting and that kitchen refuse is said to be deposited on the ground, would of themselves indicate that the standard of cleanliness was not of a high order. There seems to exist an almost complete absence of any provision whereby fresh air can gain entrance to the dwellings; while ventilators in the shape of perforated barrels serve as a means for the outlet of air in the roof. The amount of air space required by the regulation is 300 cubic feet per man ; and we find that 40 dwellings, or 62 per cent., have the required 300 feet or over. The lowest amount reported is 141 cubic feet, whilst the maximum is 880 cubic feet. The height of these dwellings ranges from seven to eleven feet, and we find the several classes into which they were classified represented here—there being two instances of the camboose.

It is interesting to note the fact that 46 or 72 per cent. of the camps show in the first report hospital accommodation, while in the remaining 28 per cent. hospitals have been since provided in nearly every case, but in only 10 camps has the necessary bathroom been provided.

There has been greater attention paid to providing the laundry, 22, or one-third of the camps, providing this hitherto almost unknown luxury. The work in the camps being performed by native and not imported laborers, this provision, with the consequent weekly change of clothes, makes a marked improvement very noticeable in the men, and less "dirty linen" is to be seen hanging around the dwellings. We have in this par-

ticular matter an illustration of the companies charging the men a monthly fee for
their laundry and the men paying the same and availing themselves of the benefit;
while too often these same companies have complained that they cannot charge the
men with or collect from them a legal amount, viz., that for the services of the medical
inspector. It is quite evident that they do collect a sum of which there may exist a
doubt as to its legality; but by reason of what may seem an unwillingness they object
to take the same means in respect to a legal claim. They are anxious about the linen
of the men, but are indifferent as regards their bodies, which are part of the industrial
machinery. I am convinced that when the companies contract with the medical men
for medical attendance in all cases of sickness and provide proper hospitals there will
be few objections raised on the part of the employees, provided the companies see that
the medical man gives all proper attention to the cases. It is to be feared that during
this season the companies have only been looking to the monthly inspection of their
camps and expecting the men to pay for that service. Little wonder then is it where
such has been the case that the men have been dissatisfied, and it is quite evident that
the remedy is in the hands of the companies.

The arrangement of the kitchen separate from the dining-room is a distinctly
new feature in camp construction. Hence we find that only in three camps has this
regulation been complied with. As a rule the cooking is done in one end of the dining-room and the cook and his assistant have their bunks in one corner of this kitchen
end. In the case of the old cambooses the men eat and sleep in the same building,
which is kitchen also.

The source of the water supply, ever a most important matter, has apparently
received attention from the companies in the construction of their camps, and the reports state that in sixty of the camps they have pure spring or lake water uncontam-
inated by camp or other drainage. In the remaining four camps the doctors report
that there was a possibility of this water being contaminated, and it was in one of these
that the eight cases of typhoid developed.

The remaining questions to be referred to are the stables and disposal of kitchen
refuse and human excreta.

The stables themselves are on the whole well kept, and in some camps an air
of tidiness is noticeable there more than in the men's apartments. As the old system was to crowd the buildings together it is little wonder that we find in twenty-nine
camps the stables within the 125-feet legal limit from the dwellings.

In the disposal of kitchen refuse there is a marked need for improvement, the
methods reported are as follows : Closed drain, 3; buckets, 12; drain to water, 10;
fed to hogs, 19; deposited in ground, 20.

Of these several methods the feeding to hogs is to be commended provided that
the hogs are kept penned at a proper distance, and the refuse taken away from the
kitchen in buckets twice daily. The closed drain leading to a body of water might
be all right if the box were tight and never became clogged or frozen, since when it
does the refuse oozes up to the surface. The depositing of refuse upon the ground too
often means the scattering of it a short distance from the kitchen door, and in such
case the practice must be strongly condemned. The last but very important provision
to be complied with in the camps is the erection of latrines.   It would hardly seem
possible at this date that there could be found five camps out of sixty-four of which the
reports would read as follows :   (1) "No attention ;" (2) deposited some distance away;"
(3) "left on snow or ground;" (4) "no provision, in woods;" (5) "in woods;" yet such
is regrettably the case.

As an example of the camp or camps showing the least provision under the
Regulations the following may be stated: There are three camps, in which 182 men
are employed, and where the average amount of air space in each of the camps is as
follows : 185, 288, 324 cubic feet. In one camp the men eat and sleep in the same
building, and in this the cooking is also carried on; the men are reported as not all
vaccinated; there is no hospital, no laundry, no bath house, no cook house in any of
the camps. Fortunately a doctor is employed, though whether for monthly inspection
only or for medical attendance on the men is not stated. The doctor reports the camps

clean, and as a redeeming and attractive feature of camp life the firm offers a latrine in each camp. Certainly such conditions could hardly be worse.

In conclusion it may be stated that the companies have with but two or three exceptions expressed their willingness to comply with the Regulations, but without uniform action on their part enforcement has been somewhat difficult. Now, however, that they have once realized the fact that a general oversight of the work will be maintained there will, I am sure, be a great and rapid improvement in camp life. The employment of men from many parts of the Province often wholly ignorant of the Regulations, makes it desirable for the Board to make them as public as possible, especially throughout the northern and eastern portions of the Province, in which the shantymen principally reside. The chief points imperatively required at once are vaccination, the provision of a camp doctor and the erection of camp hospitals. With the shantymen informed as to the Regulations in these important points, the difficulties of the companies will be materially reduced and I am confident that the companies will soon possess camps fulfilling the requirements of the Regulations.

Cases of Smallpox in Lumber Camps in Unorganized Townships during the Winter Season 1901-2.

Algoma Commercial Co		4
J. R. Booth, Markstay	1 camp	20
J. R. Booth, Sturgeon Falls	1 camp	12
J. R. Booth (Conway)	1 camp	33
J. R. Booth (McAdams)	1 camp	44
" " (Reynolds)	1 camp	8
Bucknam Bros		14
Cleveland & Sarnia Lumber Co	2 camps	11
Conger Co	1 camp	2
Eddy, Jordan & Co	1 camp	4
Ferguson & McFadden	1 camp	22
Glover & Cashin	1 camp	5
G. Gordon & Co	2 camps	6
Gladman	1 camp	17
Hawkesbury Lumber Co	1 camp	45
Holland & Graves	1 camp	8
McBurney & Co	1 camp	2
J. J. McFadden	1 camp	2
Morgan Lumber Co	1 camp	23
Michigan L. & L. Co	2 camps	13
Mississaga Lumber Co	1 camp	5
Nipissing Lumber Co	1 camp	3
M. Quigge	1 camp	4
St. Anthony Lumber Co		8
Saginaw Salt & Lumber Co	1 camp	8
Sims Bros	2 camps	11
J. B. Smith & Sons	1 camp	18
Quarantine Hospital Sudbury		15
Mackeys	1 camp	13
McArthur Lumber Co	2 camps	40
Wallace, McCormick & Sheppard	1 camp	4
Anderson & Doolittle	1 camp	7

CHAPTER IV.

MUNICIPAL SANITATION IN ONTARIO DURING THE PAST TWENTY YEARS.

In all countries where free municipal institutions exist the degree of social advancement is accurately guaged by the stage which has been reached in the evolution of the varied machinery which is required to supply the needs of any community. Climate, character of the soil, nature of the occupations, their numbers and population density, are all factors which definitely affect the composition of any community, and which, combined, go to determine if not the actual needs, from a sanitary standpoint, at least the seeming requirements of the individuals which compose such community. The history of a hundred years in Ontario has afforded abundant illustrations of the principles just enunciated. The emigres coming from the United States upon the termination of the Revolutionary war were given tracts of land in several extended areas, notably along the St. Lawrence, in the Niagara Peninsula and along the Detroit River. Of different social grades from officers to privates, some with money and many dependent upon the bounty of the Government, these settlers established homes on contiguous farms or at isolated points, as the quality of the soil and convenience to places for obtaining supplies dictated, while the incoming settlers of subsequent decades often found that, owing to large tracts in the most eligible localities having been granted to soldiers, to the church or to favorites of the Executive, they were forced to points to which the roads were mere tracks through the forest, where supplies were difficult to obtain, and where with the most limited means the struggle for existence became acute and life in the log hut was of the most primitive character. The statistics of population in the successive decades of the century in our different counties tell with faithful accuracy how these conditions were repeated in one section of the Province after the other, until old Ontario had been very generally settled by the year 1860. The story of the early emigrant, leaving his native land, on the old-time sailing ship, the tedious ocean voyage, the outbreaks of typhus and cholera on shipboard, the journey inland by canal boats, the immigrant sheds and the rough trip along colonization roads, until at last the future scene of their labors in cutting out for themselves a home in the forest is reached, has been told again and again; but it has often been when the lapse of years has cast a glamor over the hardships of those years when hope in the young immigrant's heart was high and the promise of a competence for their declining years stimulated those pioneers to strenuous endeavor and manly effort. The scene which during the years between the union of the Canadas in 1840 and Confederation was presented in Ontario, when more than one million settlers found homes upon her virgin soils, was one which has had few parallels from whatever standpoint viewed, and the communities then established supply the basis, upon which the social fabric of Ontario as it exists to-day has been constructed, and with which our municipal institutions as now existing are to be compared. The log cabin and its surroundings of that period may be seen reproduced in New Ontario to-day; but with railroads and steamboats supplying food and the necessaries of life at convenient points, and with lumber companies, mining companies and other industries supplying steady wages and ready money, it is evident that those old-time primitive conditions are only imperfectly reproduced. The new town, making use of modern inventions, often is found advanced beyond old places with more population, while lumber villages and mining villages may here and there be found with sanitary surroundings superior to villages half a century old. Clearly everywhere may be seen the truth of the principle that elevation in the scale of social well-being becomes the measure of municipal evolution.

Municipal Dwellings. Reference has been made to the primitive log house of the pioneer, and in many of the newer parts of Ontario these are yet to be seen, set for the most part simply as logs on the earth with the floor on log joists a foot or more above the ground inside—often with no cellar, or at the most a small dark hole under the floor at one end. These abodes soon became, where the ground was damp, the occasion of malarial conditions owing to the collection and decay of organic matters beneath, which conditions were only antidoted by the small area of the house, its generally imperfect construction and the largely outdoor life of the settler. With curious and unthinking persistency the maintaining a tight, dark and often damp space beneath the house has been and still remains largely to-day ; the dangers of impure air and the possibility of light and dryness in cellars has been fully realized, and the dangers from opposite conditions fully recognized. Associated with foul air and dampness beneath the house have been and still remain largely to-day the dangers of impure air and the absence of means for systematic ventilation. Added to the absence of means for fresh air are the real dangers from gaseous products such as those of defective hot-air furnaces, with no or inadequate means for an interchange of fresh, warm air for house air. To be added to this too are the products of illuminating gas, which no municipality yet in Ontario has thought of systematically analyzing, to determine how far they are to be deemed actually inimical to health. The question of the air conditions of houses as regards moisture during the months of winter when houses are closed tightly, has been receiving some attention; but so far as the public go nothing has been done to give practical effect to a knowledge which has long existed, as to the beneficial effects upon health of house air having a relative humidity of 70 to 75 per cent. With regard to large buildings, as schools, churches and public halls, there seems to have been no recent development in the means for applying in a regular manner our knowledge of the laws of ventilation. There is nowhere in Ontario any municipal machinery for insisting upon buildings having a certain air space for schools, churches, public halls and factories; and while there are Provincial factory inspectors empowered to act directly or indirectly through Local Boards of Health in remedying evils, yet the absence of even any Provincial scientific facilities for aiding such in their work, has made progress in this direction practically impossible. With more complete equipment of the laboratory it will be possible for the Provincial Board to now institute such experimental work as will, it is hoped, produce directly practical results along these lines.

Municipal Management of Contagious Diseases. The past two years has brought into prominence both the virtues and defects of the existing municipal system in this particular. The wide-appearing outbreaks of smallpox have called into active service the train-bands of health, which in many instances have been found to exist on paper, like those members of the militia, which 40 years ago, were assembled on the Queen's Birthday to answer to their names, get a shilling and be marched up to the nearest tavern to be given an opportunity to spend it. Some 754 municipal Boards of Health have theoretically existed, of whom 600 actually were returned in 1901 by the municipal clerks. With 3,000 members and some 500 medical officers and more sanitary inspectors, it certainly does look like a good army of health; but if in peace there is little to do and in war such are found brave and often willing to do but badly prepared, then it is plain that work for a time will be done crudely and often ineffectually and at too great cost. Comparing such with the conditions of twenty years ago, and yet more those of 40 years ago, we see great differences. So far as Ontario is concerned it must not be lost sight of, however, that the conditions existing when many thousands of immigrants made their slow and difficult passage inland, dispersing to many parts of the Province every year, putting up at the inns *en route*, supplied the very best means for the dissemination of diseases of a contagious character. That they did so the epidemics of cholera in 1832-34, of typhus in 1845-47, of cholera in 1849 and again in 1854-5, amply attest. To-day the travellers are mostly by rail, are subject to the scrutiny of the public; are recognized very soon wherever they may be, should they develop disease, and in such instances there is everywhere machinery, somewhat a little out of gear temporarily at times, for dealing with suspects. Beneath all this is the supreme fact that the medical public and indeed everyone nowadays, knows the theory of the contagion and most are ready to bow to the application of its teachings within reasonable limits. The principle of old-time quarantines of the shot-gun order are practically eliminated from Ontario, and Boards of Health are taught and largely practice that houses and goods can really be cheaply and thoroughly disinfected without injury, and that expensive and clumsy contrivances give place to the rapid working with tents, which can be like any equipment rapidly transported from point to point. To such have we been led by the force of very obvious facts; and the last two years has seen camp after camp of smallpox tents established practically in a day, whether in the depth of a Canadian winter or in the heat of summer for dealing with patients, numbering at one point over one hundred. In a following article on smallpox this method of temporary tents has been described, and its practical utility demonstrated. (See Part II.)

When it is there stated that what cost the Provincial Board in different isolated cases $7.00 per diem per patient, when dealt with by some Local Board of Health, cost at the rate of 75 cents per day per patient in a camp completely equipped medically with cooking facilities and all camp conveniences, it is apparent that a lesson has been taught which if taken advantage of can be brought into operation in counties with even greater ease and equal efficiency. In the subsequent article it has been pointed out that during 1901 the outbreak of smallpox was an expensive item even when divided amongst our municipalities. If it cost $500,000, it means at least $1,000 for each, much of which would have been avoided had there been in existence a system of county health officers. Assume the existence of such a county officer (trained to know at once and deal with smallpox, which during these two years has had so frequently to be done by a highly paid expert) with a camp equipment such as now is owned by several town municipalities, and it must be plain that without friction, without loss of time, such a camp would have been promptly established at a convenient point and where a single case may have cost $1,000.00, it need not have cost $100.00. The functions of such an officer in similarly assisting through a properly equipped laboratory in diagnosing diphtheria and other contagious diseases, has before been pointed out; his assistance in establishing often on the very premises a tent where a sick child could be removed and nursed without danger to the household, or yet better to a municipal hospital of a simple character, and then follow up the work of preventing further cases is equally apparent. Passing into that larger sphere of prevention of disease, as where polluted water or milk supplies bec me the agents of the transmission of disease, and it is apparent that where the inquiry demands the continued application of scientific methods and equipment, the presence in a county of a properly-trained medical officer of health becomes the realization of the practical application of science to the routine concerns in the treatment and prevention of diseases.

The advances made during twenty years in the cities and towns are marked and notable. In the field of permanent contagious disease hospitals, erected, equipped and maintained either directly by the Local Board of Health or by the trustees of some general hospital, assisted by municipal grants, and managed by the hospital authorities. this period has seen great improvement. The hospitals receiving Government grants under the Charities Aids Act were in 1882 only fourteen in number, while in 1901 they were 56. Except in the larger centres where there may be several general and special hospitals, such institutions are usually in the larger county towns and cities, and for the towns where they exist frequently have added either an annex or separate building with wards for dealing with contagious diseases, notably diphtheria, while typhoid is still everywhere received into the general hospitals. Such serve many good purposes, and in some towns are so largely and favorably known that the great proportion of cases of diphtheria are taken to them. Where small hospitals, merely temporary in character, exist in some localities the most beneofficial results have been found in both the successful care of the sick and in the arrest of the spread of disease. The adequate use of contagious disease hospitals or wards in Ontario, of which in 1901 there were 28, has made very remarkable progress, and when it is seen that in the many outbreaks of smallpox in widely spread localities, temporary buildings or tents were used very largely, it becomes apparent that the law in this respect is very generally being put into operation. The position with regard to the treatment of tuberculosis in our municipalities is indeed an anomalous one. By both the law, the public and the profession it has become suddenly an almost unanimous conviction, owing to the chronic nature of the disease, the long-continued treatment that cases often receive in general hospital wards, their advanced stage when sent, the peculiar susceptibility of persons weakened in resistance by other disease to the infection which even in the most carefully disinfected cottages at sanatoria is found not wholly absent, that it is most undesirable from the standpoint of the general patients for the tuberculized to be in the wards of general hospitals. So far has this gone that the picture has been presented to the public of a disease the most fatal, the most prevalent, the most chronic and the most ruinous in its demands upon the individual and his family amongst 80 per cent. of the population, who are wage-earners in our cities, being practically refused admittance to the only institutions at present existing in our municipalities for their reception. To recogn.ze that everywhere in England and in the United States and in Canada there is with the medical profession a common conviction that such hospitals are not the place for consumptives makes the question in Ontario an essentially difficult one to solve. What can we do to relieve the present anomalous situation, brought about by public health demands, and in a Province that has done more in its legislation to assist towards the treatment of disease than any other State or Province on the continent ?

It must be remembered that the initiative in any local action must come from the people of the municipalities; but the whole health machinery, Provincial and municipal, is in such close relationship that in this as in many other matters this Board may do much to stimulate local action. The amount of money raised locally and supplemented by Provincial grants to hospitals, may well raise the question of whether by the closer association of local boards with the authorities of our general hospitals some common action may not be taken to provide for the reception of a definite number of patients suffering from consumption, to be treated in specially arranged hospital wards or in tent hospitals in locations favorably situated for the purpose. Such must be the first step, to which the supplement must be sanatoria for primary cases. The general dissemination of the disease will be the chief reason for the charitable citizens interesting themselves through their local hospital in such a movement. That the people when they are seized of the needs of the situation will act, the history of the last twenty years of charity work abundantly testifies. Your Board would then, through this Report, again call upon the people to protect their friends and our common citizens against the disease that more than any other defies ordinary measures of restriction, and adds annually to the long list of persons cut off in the prime of life, to the loss of the State and the community of which they are members.

Provincial Water Supplies. Progress in this field as has before been remarked, is one of the most delicate means for accurately measuring the evolution of municipal ideas especially as regards freedom from disease and, comparatively, is a work of common advantage both as regards household and business convenience and protection against fire. That the growth in 20 years should be from 12 public water supplies in 1882 to 110 in 1901 is very remarkable, and that so many towns should have undertaken such works with the initial financial burdens attached, must seem most creditable when in many old European towns and villages such works are still wanting.* It is further notable that proportionately it is the newer towns and cities which have been readiest to undertake such burdens. The energy of the settlers in new towns in the west and northwest in this respect is perhaps but one index of the existence of those qualities which have made them pioneers, and the needs and manifest advantages are not with such hampered by that precedent which tends to make old centres conservative in their methods. That such have been assisted by the supervision which your Board has exercised is but natural, and that these supplies all represent water of a first quality from the hygienic standpoint may be proved by a reference to the tables of deaths from typhoid fever already given. If the annual outlay has been great, the advantages reaped have been still more proportionate. This total cost has been so far as such can be gathered over $11,000,000.

The following table gives the towns with municipal waterworks in 1901 :

Table showing the places at the Municipal Waterworks and Sewerage Systems in Ontario.

Places.	Waterworks year constructed.	Sewerage system year constructed.	Places.	Waterworks year constructed.	Sewerage system year constructed.
Toronto	1849	1840	Lindsay	1892	1896
Hamilton	1857	1852	Listowell	1888	....
Kingston	1850	1886	*Lucknow	1885	....
London	1878	1896 (New)	Markham	1891	....
Ottawa	1874	1875	Meaford	1892	None.
Brantford	1889	1889	Merritton	1888	....
Belleville	1888	1864	Mitton	1888	...
Chatham	1890	1856	Morrisburg	1887	....
Windsor	1873	1876	Mount Forest	1898	....
Guelph	1880	None.	Mitchell	1873	....
St. Thomas	1891	1893	Midland	1901	....
St. Catharines	1878	1870	Newmarket	1887	None.
Stratford	1883	1885	Niagara Falls (Town)	1884	1896
Woodstock	1886	1880	Niagara Falls (Village)	1892	....
			Niagara on Lake	1891	1895
Towns and Villages.			North Bay	1892	....
			North Toronto	1892	....
Arnprior	1900	1900	Napanee	1888	1889
Alexandria	1895	....	Orangeville	1895	....
Amherstburg	1891	1896	Owen Sound	'80 & '90	1886
Aylmer	'91 & '01	None.	Orillia	1892	....
Alliston	1892	1883	Paris	1884	1898
Aurora	1886	....	Parry Sound	1892	....
Alvinston	1895	None.	Penetanguishene	1891	1885
Ashburnham	....	....	Pembroke	1893	1897
Acton	....	....	Petrolea	'96 & '97	1887
Beamsville	1895	....	Picton	1889	....
Beeton	1892	None.	Port Colborne	1898	....
Bracebridge	1894	....	Port Hope	1894	1897
Brampton	1882	....	Perth	'95 & '97	....
Barrie	'91 & '98	1891	Peterborough	1882	1892
Berlin	'88 & '98	1890	Prescott	1900	1900
Brockville	'84 & '92	1888	Port Arthur	...	1887
Bothwell	....	....	Renfrew	1895	1897
Blenheim	....	....	Rat Portage	1898	1899
Campbellford	1890	None.	St. Marys	'99 & '00	....
Collingwood	1890	None.	Sandwich	1891	....
Cornwall	1887	1887	Shelburne	1890	....
Cobourg	1888	1893	Stouffville	1897	....
Cardinal	1900	1900	Sudbury	'91 & '96	1896
Deseronto	1896	1890	Seaforth	1879	....
Dunnville	1891	None.	Smith's Falls	1895	....
Dundas	1888	None.	Sault Ste. Marie	1895	1895
Dundalk	....	....	Sarnia	1876	1881
Essex	1891	None.	Stayner	1898	....
East Toronto	1888	None.	Tilsonburg	1886	....
Eglinton	1891	None.	Tilbury	1888	1888
Fort William	1898	Some in 1890	Toronto Junction	1889	1892
Galt	1891	1896	Trenton	1895	....
Gananoque	1892	No general system	Teeswater	1889	....
Goderich	1888	1886	Thessalon	1896	1893
Georgetown	1891	No general system	Uxbridge	....	....
Huntsville	1897	None.	Watford	1893	1893
Hintonburg	1899	1900	Welland	1888	....
Hanover	1901	....	Wiarton	1889	....
Hensall	....	....	Waterloo	1889	....
Ingersoll	1890	None.	Walkerton	1891	1895
Iroquois	1886	..	Walkerville	1877	1890
Kingsville	1894	None.	Wingham	....	....
Kincardine	'90 & '94	None.	Weston	....	....
Leamington	1891	None.			

* For fire only.

Municipal Sewerage Works. It is perhaps not surprising that such should be slower in development than public water supplies. Fire protection has often been the dominating idea in the establishment of water supplies, while in sewerage it is often the sanitary idea, which plays the larger part. The evolution of the idea that sewerage is not necessarily or properly a part of drainage has been slow; since the old-tim˃ ideas, represented. in the great sewers of Paris, were that sewers were street drains and not necessarily carriers of house sewage. The separate system of sewerage which has been the type introduced in almost every new system for 14 years fully illustrates that the sanitary idea has prevailed. That the systems more or less fully completed should be 50 as compared with 7 in 1882 equally with public water supplies indicates ,the growing public sense of good health, as the measure of all municipal prosperity and the happiness of the citizens.

In this brief summary of the more salient features of municipal work there may have been seen something of what progress is pos⁻ sible under favoring conditions of country, climate, soil and freedom under those constitutional forms of government which Canada inherits through her Anglo⁻ Saxon origin. While the beginnings were small, the outcome in the history of Ontario's progress and present status, viewed whether from a material or social standpoint, is ,quite a remarkable one. That a paltry 10,000 a little more than one hundred years ago should have become 2,191,000, and that Ontario should not only have sent as many more of her children to neighboring States and Canadian Provinces, carry⁻ ing with them their laws and customs, and should have been the essential factor in the making of that newer and larger Canada of the west, a territory not vaster in its areas than great in future possibilities, must surely be as truly a source of pride ;and satisfaction to us as the high place which British colonies in every part of the world hold in the eyes of the mother who founded them. If, however, in this satisfac⁻ tion there is a tendency to natural vanity, it may properly be tempered by an acute appre⁻ ciation of the fact that that which has nevertheless been left undone ought to have been done and that which has been accomplished might have been better and ought still to be improved. Our municipal system, with its democratic principles, is not perfect, nor yet ap⁻ proaching it; while it inherits the virtues, it illustrates the vices of an elective system bor rowed not directly from England, but indirectly through Massachusetts. That its annual elections and its too numerous representatives have created a weariness of the electorate which has resulted in the frequent appearance on municipal boards of per⁻ sons wholly unsuited through education, experience or moral worth for the duties devolving upon them is apparent, and that, as our villages become towns, and our ǀtowns great cities, with their complicated machinery, the professional municipal pol⁻ ǀitician should under the system continue to grow and flourish increasingly must be ;manifest not only from general observation, but from the very nature of the case. During the past twenty years it has been the lot of your Secretary to see the working of the system in all its parts and in all sections of the country, and what is abundantly apparent is that until the political age in municipal affairs is superseded by the scien⁻ tific age manifest evils are not likely to be remedied. The scientific methods which railroads, steamship companies and indeed every great industry introduce and upon which they depend for success, are usually the last thing thought of in the ordinary municipal machine. Cheapness, pliability and other similar qualities are too often what are wanted in its officers, and common observation makes it plain that the public pay dearly for such. With the scientific method, which in studying phenomena cultivates the habit of first investigating, analyzing and understanding them and there⁻ after drawing correct inferences, there of necessity grows a love for truth which should be the dominating idea in all municipal as in personal ideals. Surveying the field of municipal activities, there are manifest evidences of a growing consciousness that what has served us in the past ought no longer continue to do so.

The Laureate's words :

       "Ourselves are full of social wrong"

are supplemented by the prayer :

> "Ring out false pride in place and blood,
> The civic slander and the strife;
> Ring in the love of truth and right,
> Ring in the common love of good."

and it is exactly in the sense of these words that all seem to be demanding that not alone the scientific knowledge to-day so available, but the common love of good shall be the end toward which our civic energies shall be directed. Daily we are made conscious of how seemingly slight influences may become great in their effects, and it would appear that much might easily and simply be done by which the evils which are patent could be minimized through legislation tending to greater concentration and permanency in the several divisions of the municipal machinery. In Brownings words,—

> "Earth's rose is a bud that's checked or grows
> As beams may encourage or blasts oppose."

Remembering the history of what we have done during one hundred years in Ontario and looking forward, conscious of our defects with confidence and hope, we shall enter upon the work of another century recalling the words of the poet of optimism in his Rabbi Ben Ezra :

> "Grow old along with me !
> The best is yet to be,
> The last of life, for which the first was made:
> Our times are in his hand
> Who saith, 'A whole I planned,
> Youth shows but half; trust God; see all nor be afraid !"

Respectfully submitted,

P. H. BRYCE,

Secretary.

PART II.

ANNUAL REPORT BOARD OF HEALTH.

THE CHAIRMAN'S ANNUAL ADDRESS.

By H. E. Vaux, M.D., Toronto.

January 8th, 1902

To the Members of the Provincial Board of Health :

Gentlemen,—Another year has rolled by and with profound thankfulness we can note that death has not invaded our circle.   We enter on this new year, the 25th of our existence as a Board, with more than usual interest, because the census returns will doubtless add to our information many facts relating to morbility and mortality, or at least group them together in such a way as to make them of greater utility.

On looking backward I think we can conscientiously say that the year has not been barren of results; especially may we note the greatly increasd facility which we now possess in dealing with contagious diseases in unorganized districts   The Government, by prompt recognition of the great danger arising from the migratory habits of the lumbermen in the large camps, which was brought to its attention by our Board, approved the Regulations, adopted by us and appointed Dr. C. A. Hodgetts as Provincial Inspector, an appointment which has already proved to be an eminently judicious one, satisfactory both to this Board and also to the large number of lumbermen, whose best interests are now suitably safeguarded.

The intense interest which a year ago was manifested in devising plans to prevent and cure tuberculosis has naturally during the last few months been overshadowed by the invasion of our country by smallpox.   Not that we have grown careless about the former disease, but because the latter has suddenly assumed proportions which have forced themselves on our attention and because the public are aroused to the danger confronting them.   Were they as alive to the far greater danger which, though more insidious, is also more fatal, viz., the spread of tuberculosis, our mission in this regard would be far more simple. · Last August we fondly hoped that we had successfully repelled the invasion of smallpox, for not a single case was to be found throughout the length and breadth of Ontario; but it proved to be only a truce. With the autumn months the enemy reappeared with increased force, until at the present time we have between 400 and 500 cases in our Province and a total aggregate during the year, 1901 of 1,838.

True, up to the present the type mercifully has been a mild one, with a mortality of not more than 1 per cent. This fact should not cause us for one moment to abate our vigilance.   We should rather be more on the alert, for we know not the day when the type which is now prevalent in New York and London may   reach our homes. Which shall we do ?   Attend to those rules of sanitation and hygiene which are antagonistic to all forms of contagious diseases and vaccinate.   It should in the light of past experience be unnecessary to urge the latter point; but it would seem that the lesson requires to be taught over and over by bitter experience, and even then how quickly is it forgotten !   If any one doubts the value of vaccination in preventing smallpox let him read the last reports from English hospital ships as given by our Secretary, Dr. Bryce, in his valuable quarterly report on smallpox, and he can doubt no longer.

·   Dr. Bryce says "in 233 vaccinated persons (and this includes all grades of vaccination) there were 47 deaths, or 20 per cent. In 97 unvaccinated there were 58 deaths, or 60 per cent." .

An analysis of deaths by ages is most instructive, proving clearly that the protective power of vaccine is not to be depended wholly upon after ten years.

Gentlemen, we enter upon this year's duties impressed with a sense of the high responsibility which rests upon us.   To us the people of our fair Province look for advice in those matters which are truly matters of life and death.   It is to me a great satisfaction to know that we have as our Executive officer a man of such wide experience and great executive ability, and that this Board is also assisted in the carrying out of its work by medical men in every town and district, who are the guardians of every household where epidemic disease makes its appearance.

[51]

SECOND QUARTERLY REPORT ON SMALLPOX.

By the Secretary, Dr. P. H. Bryce.

April 25th, 1901.

Mr. Chairman and Gentlemen,—The report presented to your Board on February 6th at the first quarterly meeting briefly indicated the presence of smallpox as having existed in the Province at Sault Ste. Marie, in a lumber camp at Batchewana near by and in a tie camp west of Fort William, some 60 miles, to which a case had come therefrom, and another case at London. But what then seemed practically the end of the outbreak, has in fact, proved but the beginning of the most extended outbreak experienced in the Province during 20 years, regard being had rather to the number of municipalities attacked rather than to the number of cases or their fatality. In fact, the cases have not been very numerous, as will be gathered from the accompanying table, while the mortality has been very slight. It is to the latter characteristic of the disease, and to the accident of the location of first cases in lumber camps, hidden far in the northern forests, away from physicians and the outside world, that we owe the unusually sudden and wide-spread character of the epidemic. The prompt action of the medical health officer of the "Soo," when the first case was brought there from Batchewana lumber camp, and the equally prompt action of the medical health officer of Fort William, enabled the Provincial Board to take such action with regard to the cases in the unorganized territories as to promptly stamp out these outbreaks.

At the very hour of the last session of the Board, on Feb. 16, events were occurring which have completely altered the serenity of the public health situation as regards smallpox. A case occurred from no known source at Penetang, which, fortunately diagnosed early, went no further. On the succeeding day a case occurred at Bracebridge, diagnosed and dealt with there with equal promptness, and became the means of tracing, with the detection of a suspected case four days later on the C.P.R. train to Ottawa, the presence of smallpox in a hitherto unsuspected place, Sudbury—a town supplied with physicians, and a Local Board of Health, to the extent of some eight cases actually then existing, either in hotels, the hospitals or in private houses. On February 11th a telegram sent to the Police Magistrate by your secretary brought the answer on the 13th that two cases of mild chickenpox were present in the American Hotel, but on the 12th the Local Board of Health had suddenly received information, for a telegram was received by your secretary from the Mayor, stating "he was handed doctor's certificate of several cases of smallpox in town, and to come at once." On the 13th Dr. Hodgetts was instructed to proceed to Sudbury, and on the 14th found eight cases in the pest house, having been placed there by Dr. Bromley, who had been brought from the "Soo" to diagnose cases which hitherto had been called chickenpox, grippe, etc. Within a week outbreaks were reported from Nairn Centre, Massey, Sturgeon Falls, Wahnipitae and Chelmsford, all between the "Soo" and North Bay, and within another week cases in Thessalon, Renfrew Town and several townships of Renfrew and in Toronto were reported.

The subsequent history of events in the territory between the "Soo" and Sudbury is found recorded in the report of Dr. Hodgetts, hereto attached. and in his weekly reports, all fyled for perusal.

The outbreaks in the organized municipalities have had with a few exceptions the usual history of prompt diagnosis and equally prompt action by the medical health officers and Local Boards of Health. while it must be mentioned with regret that there have been a few exceptions where licensed practitioners, usually men who have seen smallpox in former years, have persistently refused to accept the history of infection and depending upon some pre-conceived clinical picture of smallpox have declared the disease to be chickenpox. In every instance that I am aware of, where this mistaken view has existed, the hands of the Local Boards of Health have been tied, and the disease has spread to other cases or to other houses. It may be excusable in any physician to make a mistake in diagnosis, but to persist in such to the detriment of the public is enough to properly characterize him as an enemy of the State, and when such take an active part in stirring up opposition to the duly constituted officers of health and the law. it would seem that they deserve the strongest reprobation and that the dignity of the profession and the privileges the profession have had acceded them, as well as the medical act, demand that the Ontario Medical Council should summon before it such offenders and punish for unprofessional conduct men, much more dangerous to the public than self-confessed quacks. Equally to be reprobated are those medical men who, forgetful of their vows taken at graduation, have issued certificates and received money for the same, stating that the holders of certificates have been successfully vaccinated, when on subsequent examination by the train inspectors of the Provincial Board of Health or other medical health officers, they have again and again been found to have no vaccination whatever.

Leaving these unpleasant references, your Secretary desires to draw your attention to a matter of the greatest practical import to the welfare of the Province and the protection of its people, an importance which has been accentuated by the events of the past year, which have occurred in what is now popularly spoken of as New Ontario. For years past the difficulty of dealing with this great area of new settlements has been increasing, and several years ago your Board urged that special regulations should be passed giving the Provincial Board of Health more decided control of the health interests of the people scattered over this wide territory.

It is natural that to the greater number of our people and even of our legislators, who are unacquainted with New Ontario, its extent and importance should hitherto not have been appreciated. To illustrate the work which your Board must undertake there it may be stated that from the Mattawa on the Ottawa in Eastern Nipissing, to Ingólf, three miles west of Rat Portage, on the Manitoba boundary, is 1,000 miles along the line of the C. P. Railway; that south of the height of land there is an average of 100 miles north and south of many and growing settlements ; that in this area are over 400 townships surveyed, some settled and organized into municipalities, while many others have good settlements, but still unorganized, while over them in every direction are scattered lumbering camps, sawmill villages, mining camps and prospectors' camps, and during the winter timber rangers and hunters are in the woods and during the summer thousands of men people the streams with their drives and rafts of logs. What the extent of these operations means will be understood when it is estimated that the results of the work of 25.000 woodsmen during each winter must be brought to the mills on the lakes, and that 3.000 miles on the larger streams alone are traversed during their operations. But we have but imperfectly stated the conditions as they have long existed. A new condition of affairs has within five years been rapidly springing up. Mills and mines had been created, villages on Lake Huron and Lake Superior, whose shores give us 600 miles of territory, where populations exist demanding sanitary supervision; while to this we have in addition to the settlements along the 1,000 miles of the C.P.R. proper 180 miles on the "Soo" branch, 260 miles on the Ontario & Rainy River, 65 miles on the Port Arthur and Duluth and 50 miles already on the Algoma Central. Add to this the other projected railway lines, and the lakes and rivers of the Lake of the Woods and Rainy River region, with its 400 miles of shore line and mining and lumber camps and 200 more miles of the maze of river and lake shores of the Rainy Lake District. and we have of railway, lake and river lines, along all which settlement is rapidly taking place, a line of communications, and therefore of settlements and necessary sanitary supervision, the enormous total of 5,755 miles.

It is hoped that before the year has passed we shall have obtained from the census an accurate idea of the population of this district. But estimating roughly as we may the population from the imperfect death returns, I find that the deaths were in 1900:

Deaths.

Algoma.. 261
Muskoka (partly unorganized).. 145
Rainy River.... 288
Thunder Bay.. 98
Nipissing.. 205
Parry Sound.. 147

1,144

Assuming that 10 per cent. may be added for imperfect returns, and that as low a death rate as 10 in the 1,000 occurred in 1900, and we have as the population of the six territorial districts of the Province at least 125,000, which I believe will be found closely agreeing with the census and is about 1-20th of the total population of Ontario. To illustrate the distribution of the population in a district, the area included in the district lying in the angle formed by Lake Nipissing and North Bay to the south and east and Lake Huron and the Algoma Central R.R. and C.P.R. to the west, north and east, may be taken. In the area some 50 lumber companies operate, and several large mines are located, while during the open season several thousand men will be employed on the railway construction work. Since the shantymen began going home early in March some 5,000 men have been inspected on trains and vaccinated, while others have stayed in the camps or have gone in since to drive the logs on the streams. Since smallpox appeared in the camps many of them have been visited, but yet a staff of a chief inspector with seven assistants has hardly sufficed, though, to inspect all the trains on three lines of railway, to visit suspected camps, vaccinate at points where there are no physicians and bring out patients to the hospital camp. While in the territorial districts we have referred to probably 40,000 of the population is in organized towns and while quite a number of municipalities are organized, yet the major part of the large population already referred to has no municipal abode ; and while there are many small villages or settlements along railway lines on the shores of the great lakes and around mining camps, most of them are without any municipal organization, the people being largely a floating population. It is further apparent that this state of affairs not only exists, but must continue to increase.

The dangers due to diphtheria breaking out in lumber and mining camps, and other small villages has again and again been experienced in past winters, but the present outbreak of smallpox and that yet more fatal one of last spring at Port Arthur and other places, has caused the utterly unprotected condition of this great territory to be very widely felt. It must be said to the credit of the towns and even poor townships, that they have shown an activity, putting to shame often the work of old-settled and wealthy municipalities, but it is plain that in proportion as these do good work and equip themselves for dealing with disease, they become the Meccas to which all persons suffering from disease in the camps and outlying settlements tend towards.

With a view to dealing with the growing problem the Minister of the Department introduced a bill, now become law, providing for the better sanitary supervision of the unorganized territory. The following is a copy of the bill and suggested regulations which your Secretary brings before you for consideration.

All of which is respectfully submitted. P. H. BRYCE.

*Note : The B. Act, with Regulations, based upon it, has been issued as a separate pamphlet.

QUARTERLY REPORT ON SMALLPOX.

By the Secretary, Dr. P. H. Bryce.

Toronto, June 24, 1901.

To the Chairman and Members of the Provincial Board of Health :

Gentlemen,—Your Secretary begs leave to present the following statement regarding the smallpox situation as it at present exists in Ontario.

No new cases were reported except in Chelmsford in May, and ten during the past week. Convalescent cases exist at Beaver Mills and Emo, on Rainy River; Chelmsford and Renfrew, Nipissing District; and Sault Ste. Marie, in Algoma. The outbreak there is practically at an end. The quarantine camp at Sudbury has been disbanded, having treated 161 cases and 350 suspects. In the older counties cases exist in Brantford and Burford, in Brant; in Oso, Kaladar and S. Shefford, in Frontenac; in N. Cayuga, in Haldimand County; in Campbellford, and Percy, in Northumberland County; in Havelock and Lakefield, Peterborough County; in East and West Oxford Townships, Oxford County; in Pembroke Township and Renfrew Township, Renfrew County; in Euphrasia, in Grey; Medonte and Tay, in Simcoe County; in Carden and Eldon Townships, Victoria; in Hamilton, Wentworth County; in St. Catharines, Welland County; in Toronto, York County ; or in 22 municipalities and 5 centres in unorganized territory.

As in most of these there are but isolated cases growing from several original centres, and as most of these had occurred a fortnight ago, and are now convalescent, it may be said that most of the outbreaks are seemingly at an end. Probably not more than 50 cases in all are in quarantine, and should no further cases occur, our Province within another month will be declared free of the disease.

That the results concerning the many centres two months ago are satisfactory will be seen when it is remembered that in unorganized territories, with 4 territories and 38 municipalities (surveyed), and with 500 cases since January 1st, there have been of older counties, in all 24 counties, with in all some 250 cases. The problem which faced the Board in March of dealing with the 5,000 or more men returning from the lumber camps has been successfully solved, and while the remainder of the outbreaks have, in a large measure, been due to the northern centre, yet there are many evidences which show that undiagnosed cases from other directions have occurred, even to become centres in the counties of the western part of the Province.

That it has cost much energy and considerable expense will appear later, when the accounts have all been paid, but that the fight has resulted in preserving the business of all parts of the Province from anything like panic must be apparent. A very large number of persons have been vaccinated; but the work cannot be said to have been complete or hardly general. That, however, a more serious attitude on the part of the people to their duty in this respect is being shown, has recently been apparent to your Secretary; but the problem is yet one which demands much attention.

There have been no other outbreaks of communicable disease at any part of so serious a nature as to demand remark.

The Regulations approved by the Board have been approved by Order-in-Council, and an edition will shortly be distributed to lumbermen and others interested. It is hoped that machinery for enforcing the law will be shortly in operation.

All of which is respectfully submitted,

P. H. BRYCE.

REPORT OF COMMITTEE ON EPIDEMICS FOR THIRD QUARTER.

Presented by the Secretary.

Toronto, Sept. 30th, 1901.

Mr. Chairman and Gentlemen of the Provincial Board of Health:

Your Secretary begs leave to report on the epidemic of smallpox during the nine months of the year 1901, ending September 30th.

In addition to the reports received from time to time from medical officers of Local Boards of Health, answers were received to a circular sent out to the 777 Division Registrars representing the registration divisions of Ontario. In all 522 made returns. Of these 101 reported cases of smallpox as having occurred in 38 counties and districts, 760 being returned. In addition to these, 166 from various municipalities, mostly unorganized, were treated in the Sudbury Smallpox Camp, under the direct supervision of your Board. In all, therefore, 926 are known to have occurred, while doubtless some few may not have been returned. Six deaths in all were reported. It will thus be seen that the outbreak attained the proportions of an epidemic, many more cases having occurred than during any year within the history of the Board. The remarkable fact that there was less than 1 per cent. of deaths, is in keeping with the facts in the great number of outbreaks in other Provinces and in the neighboring States. This type of the disease has not been known in temperate climates for more than a century, although a similar epidemic is spoken of in the treatise of Sydenham in the eighteenth century.

One of the most interesting illustrations of the true character of the disease. is reported by Dr. J. Patterson, Dominion officer, placed in charge of the outbreak in the Northwest Territories. He writes that, 1,500 cases is a conservative estimate of the cases in that district and in which the total cases were not reported. The cases were most numerous amongst the unvaccinated French half-breeds, much fewer amongst the Indians, who are fairly well vaccinated, and none whatever amongst the recent Galician and Doukhoborsti immigrants, who, in addition to vaccination in childhood, had all been vaccinated on board ship or in quarantine. The same facts, the same medical opinion, and the same conclusions have come to us from every Province and State, from every Medical Congress, and from every Health Board. as to the nature of the disease, although as Dr. Patterson. who was for months in the Northwest districts, says (and Dr. Hodgetts, who has seen hundreds of cases in Ontario, repeats) "I am not at all surprised at medical men, who have only had an opportunity of seeing a few of the mild cases, contending that the disease was chickenpox." As will have been noticed during the past fortnight a number of new centres have appeared in the Province, some 20 cases in Ottawa, one family at Massey, several families in Howland Township, Manitoulin; two cases in Brantford, two in East Zorra, and one near Tavistock, and one near New Hamburg, mostly from undiscovered sources. but probably from some mild, undiagnosed case.

Such was to be expected, and once more creates the uncomfortable impression that unless physicians are fully alive to the mild and often abnormal appearances of the disease it will again obtain a foothold, becoming under winter conditions a type of much greater severity, as seen in New York City and district, where some 165 deaths occurred in July. That the disease had centres where a high virulence existed is seen in the Census returns of the United States for 1900, which stated that 3,484 deaths occurred during the year.

It becomes apparent, with our population not by any means well protected by vaccination, that our boards will have to keep on the alert, not only to deal with first cases, but to again insist on the compulsory vaccination of school children.

Glasgow has had her epidemic, London is now pushing with the greatest activity and success vaccination in infected districts. New York has hundreds of cases all cf normal virulence, and as your Board has pointed out again and again, and as Dr. Patterson experienced in stamping out the disease in the West, in vaccination only have we a sure preventative. The problem of active and pure vaccine has been the topic of discussion at our Medical Congresses, and the unsatisfactory character of much that has been on the market, once more raises the problem of a supply. In the judgment of your Secretary, Canada, with a population of 6,000,000, with a yearly influx cf immigrants, all resulting in a yearly birth rate of nearly 180,000, has arrived at a period of development when the Dominion Government should undertake the establishment of an Institute of Scientific Research, in which, amongst many other undertakings, the preparation of vaccines and anti-toxines against the diseases of both man and animals is urgently demanded. Millions are being spent for agriculture and commerce, while public health still lingers in the pre-scientific age. Surely, if we do not rapidly increase as a nation through immigration we ought to take every step to conserve the lives of our own people, more valuable than any immigrants.

It would seem a proper thing that work of this character, which to be done well should be done on an adequate scale, might well be urged by the Board on the Dominion Minister of Agriculture, who has charge of the public health work, whether of man or animals.

All of which is respectfully submitted.

PETER H. BRYCE.

REPORT OF THE COMMITTEE ON EPIDEMICS FOR THE FOURTH QUARTER.

Toronto, January 7th. 1902.

To the Chairman and Members of the Provincial Board of Health :

Gentlemen,—Your Secretary begs to report concerning the smallpox outbreak, which has prevailed almost continuously during the past year; occurring in, however, two outbreaks, that of the winter and spring, and that of the autumn months. For two or three weeks in August not a case was known to exist in the Province.

It will thus be seen that there were two distinct epidemics. the first being introduced from the west by way of Sault Ste. Marie. and the second from the east by way of Hull and Ottawa. The history of the first outbreak was presented to the Board in the report of the Committee on Epidemics, at the May meeting, and its particular characters as regards New Ontario are to be found in the paper by Dr. C. A. Hodgetts, Medical Inspector of this Board, printed in the report of the Executive Health Officers' Association for 1901.

The herewith submitted table gives as accurately as possible the distribution of cases by counties and municipalities during the year, and presents a very accurate statement of the total cases and deaths. It is probable that here and there a mild case, not seen by a physician, may have occurred, but with few exceptions. it is believed. the figures are complete.

What, of course, strikes one at once is that with a very considerable total of cases there should have been only 12 deaths in 1,838 cases. a rate of mortality exceeded perhaps by several other contagious diseases which have been present in Ontario during the year.

It must be remembered, however. that in Ontario we have not arrived at the stage where an accurate estimate is kept of the cases of whooping cough, measles, mumps. and chickenpox, and, indeed, in many cases of scarlatina and typhoid.

Were such figures accurately known it would probably be found that except the two latter the several diseases have been at least as low in mortality as the recent epidemic of mild smallpox.

The clinical features of the disease itself have been so well set forth in different papers and circulars that there is no need for referring to them here, but your Secretary begs to refer to one or two points.

1. The first point referred to is the large number of cases (1,838) which have occurred during the year.

While it may be of little satisfaction to those persons who have suffered in person, or to those municipalities where cases have occurred, it nevertheless by comparison is satisfactory to know that the cases were not more numerous.

Thus, the Weekly Public Health Report of the Marine Hospital Service in Washington gives the following very partial returns for different States :

	Cases.
Colorado, May 1st to November 30th..	673
Illinois, June 1st to December 7th..	241
Indiana, June 1st to November 30th	513
Kansas, June 1st to December 6th..	839
Massachusetts, July to December 14th..	458
Michigan (does not report numbers)..	
Minnesota, June to December 1st..	2,494
Minnesota, December 1st to 31st*	261
North Carolina, May to November..	587
Ohio, January to July (in most cases)..	3,478
Tennessee, April to September..	2,155
New York City, from June to December..	587
Pennsylvania..	1,614

2. A second point of interest is that of the low mortality in northern as well as southern climates, and the evidence here and there of another type of the disease, as in Boston, New York and Philadelphia and New Orleans, all international seaports.

Thus in Minnesota in the period referred to, with 2,494 cases, there were but 14 deaths, while in Ontario there were during the year but 12 deaths. Ohio with 3,478 cases, had 42 deaths; up to October Pennsylvania, with 1,614 cases, reported 76 deaths. The outbreak at Philadelphia had till then been apparently mostly of the benign type, but in Philadelphia the cases and mortality since then have altered greatly in number and virulence. Again Boston had from July to December 14th 400 cases with 47 deaths, New Orleans for the same period 70 cases and 6 deaths, while New York City had from June 23rd to December 7th 587 cases and 164 deaths.

It would appear, therefore, from these figures that two more or less distinct types of smallpox have been prevailing. The figures are pregnant with meaning, since in three of these cities the mild type of the disease had as elsewhere appeared and disappeared, with very few deaths, while New York is to-day suffering from a disease almost as virulent as in any previous epidemic, and quite as virulent as the type of disease prevailing in London, England.

3. Another point of interest attaching directly to the number of cases in Ontario is in a notable degree dependent upon the mild type of the disease. In the table showing the number of cases by counties and districts it becomes at once apparent that five centres account for over half the number of cases, and that in every one of these there is the direct history of neglect to deal with the outbreak promptly, owing to apparent or real doubt as to the character of the disease to be dealt with.

It will be remembered that it was only after the continued presence of the Medical Inspector of this Board in the Sudbury district with a staff of assistants, an hospital camp, a train inspection and vaccination of all going out from lumber camps, and a refusal of the railway to accept passengers without certificates of vaccination and non-exposure, that that district learned the character of the disease, and went to work with such assistance to stamp it out. Fortunately, the lesson was learned, and during the past three months every physician and local board has seemed anxious to stamp out any cases which have occurred. In the first half year there were in New

Ontario 510 cases with but six deaths. Again the case is illustrated by the special report presented to the board by Dr. Hodgetts in the Burford Township outbreak in Brant County occurring before the Provincial Board had been made cognizant of the presence of the disease. Then again the local physician who had himself seen the cases, many of them very serious confluent cases, could only reply that he knew it was not chickenpox, but could hardly, believe it was smallpox.

As a result there were locally 120 cases. It also was cleared up after direct interference by the Medical Inspector of the Board.

The third outbreak, and that which has been most serious of all owing to its location in a large city, is that in Ottawa.

As already stated, August saw the Province for a few days free of the disease. But just as the Board was congratulating itself, the cloud began to gather there, not certainly larger than the proverbial "man's hand."

On the 27th of August the Secretary of the Local Board of Ottawa wrote, stating there were at that moment six cases of smallpox in Ottawa three quarantined in Porter's Island Hospital and three isolated in their own dwellings. The letter goes on to say, "at a meeting of the Board of Health last night, it was stated that there is a feeling widely felt and expressed amongst our citizens, of doubt as to whether the patients were really suffering from the above disease." "The local board was unanimous in the opinion that under these circumstances and in order to satisfy popular feeling on the subject, it would be desirable to have a diagnosis by some medical gentleman, whose decision would carry weight, and accordingly asked me to write you and ask if you would yourself come down for that purpose." A telegram sent by your Secretary, expressing readiness to go or send an expert, which was replied to by telegram, recalling the request on the ground that most of the cases were nearly well, and that it was thought unnecessary. In October, within five weeks, the disease was in 40 houses, resulting in a total of cases to the end of the year of 174. Incidentally it may be remarked that Ottawa and its neighbor, Hull, in Quebec, which with even greater assiduity, hugged the idea that the disease was nothing at all, have been the immediate cause of nearly all the outbreaks in the northern lumber woods, since from both of them go very large numbers of shantymen every year, as well as from Carleton, Prescott. Russell and Glengarry, and nearly all of these occurred at a time when these cities were hoping that it was not smallpox. The action of Ottawa since October, when it was realized that an epidemic was upon them, has been on the whole satisfactory.

The fourth outbreak, illustrative of how fatal is doubt, or in this case cocksureness, occurred in Dover Township, in Kent. As early as October, a mother from Dover Township with a child had visited friends in Detroit, and after arriving home the child sickened within a few days. The Medical Officer of Chatham sent the child and the mother home to the neighboring township, telling her and the Dover medical officer by phone that he believed the child had smallpox, and urged isolation and vaccination. The parents, however, wanted further advice, and went to another physician, who has always plumed himself upon knowing smallpox, and who stated that there was no doubt that the case was only chickenpox. On the strength of this everyone, even the local health officer seemed satisfied. As a direct result there have been more than 150 cases directly traceable to this outbreak.

The fifth outbreak, small relatively, but practically as great, except that it occurred in a remote place, was the outbreak in Stephen Township. It appears that in July a person returned to his friends from Dakota and sickened; that a number of friends of the similar religious persuasion, who do not believe in medicine or physicians, suffered from the disease, and that in November there was a recurrence of the disease, it having appeared in five families in all. Considering all these outbreaks in their practical bearings it becomes apparent that upon the individual physician or citizen rests a most serious responsibility, in view of all that depends upon inaction based upon doubt, resistance to the action of those who are endeavoring to take positive steps, the assumption owing to professional standing of an attitude of infallibility, inimical to the public interests as judged by the results, or based upon a religious belief so irrational that, did it become general, would mean a country plagued with smallpox, and every other communicable disease, cut off from commercial communication with neighboring countries of the world, and would wither and paralyze the hand of that progress in science and medicine which during the past century has made fatal epidemics so largely impossible, owing to the elucidation of the natural laws which connect cause so clearly with effect in disease.

Only to-day has another illustration of this danger developed. where a woman from Dashwood, an exhorter of the Dowieite sect, has appeared in the Jordan district in the Niagara peninsula, carrying the disease apparently to another family of that community, and going about amongst the people, endangering the health and welfare of a whole township.

It is hardly necessary to say anything further in connection with this point, that if outbreaks have been associated with doubt in the mind of the physicians as to the nature of the disease those other outbreaks which have been allowed to spread where families have not reported disease, owing to a belief that it was chickenpox, may to some extent be relieved of moral responsibility in the matter.

4. The next point demanding reference is the much discussed one of vaccination. It is the *bete noir* of the family physician and the health board.   The family physician, if he suggests it, finds on short experience that he is looked upon as either soliciting for an extra fee, that he is viewed with suspicion as wishing to commit some scientific experiment aginst the peace and well-being of the household, or that he is conjuring up unnecessary fears against a disease, which kills very few, and besides is not likely to come their way.

Local Boards of Health and councils, in addition to the fear of being looked upon as in league with the health officers, are further fearful of being held wasteful of public funds if they supply vaccine and pay public vaccinators.

The mildness of the disease and prompt stamping out of it in the past are principally, I believe, responsible for these difficulties, since it has been the experience of your Secretary that the great body of the people in the presence of general exposure to smallpox of a severe type, are ready to be protected by vaccination, and indeed are believers in its efficiency as proved for a hundred years.

Medical Health Officers, as from Ottawa. and many other cities where numerous cases have occurred, have once more repeated the oft-told tale of the protective virtues of vaccination, but the latest London statistics from the hospital ships may be quoted as amply illustrative.

Thus in 233 vaccinated cases there were 47 deaths or 20 per cent. of deaths.

In 97 unvaccinated there were 58 deaths, or 60 per cent. of deaths.

In 19 doubtful cases there were 11 deaths. or 57 per cent. of deaths.

In the 349 cases we have a table by ages, the 19 being added to the vaccinated :

Age.	Cases.		Deaths.	
Under 5 years	23	vaccinated...... 0	19	vaccinated...... 0
		un- " 23		un- " 19
" 5-10 years	19	vaccinated..... 1	10	vaccinated...... 0
		un- " 18		un- " 10
" 10-15 "	39	vaccinated.. ..23	9	vaccinated...... 1
		un- " 16		un- " 8
" 15-20 "	55	vaccinated 41	8	vaccinated...... 1
		un- " 14		un. " 7
" 20-30 "	99	vaccinated ... 81	21	vaccinated..... 11
		un- " .... .18		un- " 10
" 30-40 "	59	vaccinated ... 53	20	vaccinated····· 16
		un- " 6		un- " 4
Over 40-55	55	vaccinated......41	29	vaccinated 16
		un- " 14		un. " 13

Familiar as the tale told by these figures is to us, yet for the public a general comment on them may be made. It must first be remembered that until quite recent years the proportion of all persons vaccinated in England was nearly 90 per cent. of the children born.   Hence so far as the native born are concerned the chances of exposure of vaccinated persons was 9 to 1.

Remembering this, we find that not one vaccinated child under five years took smallpox.   Of 23 unvaccinated under five years, 19 died or 80 per cent., and of 18 under 10 years 55 per cent. died.

The wearing out of the complete protection of vaccination after 10 years begins to be seen, for the vaccinated cases to unvaccinated is greater, or as 23 to 16, under 10 to 15 years, but the death rate is as 1 to 8.

The story is repeated for successive years with the same results. Remembering that the class of population in which most cases have occurred has been that in the poorer districts, it is surprising that the protective qualities of vaccination are so apparent since so many patients would tend to fall victims to pneumonia, etc., in all these ages, if attacked with any disease.

As to how far the Provincial Board of Health in this Province should go in calling upon health boards everywhere to insist upon a general compulsory vaccination has been a matter of serious consideration.   Remembering that school boards everywhere are empowered, and when called upon, the boards of health are required to demand certificates of successful vaccination, and recalling   that   under   the   Smallpox Regulations, vaccination is compulsory in every municipality where smallpox exists, it does not seem that more could be done at present than to press on all boards in such places where the outbreak seems to be in any great danger of spreading, to see that such compulsory powers are being carried into effect.   The thoroughness with which local work has been done has been exemplified in very many outbreaks, but the particulars as far as they are known will be found in the table, also given.   From this it appears that at least 200 distinct introductions of the disease have occurred, and that, including the three large outbreaks, there has been but 8 cases to an outbreak. At least 30 outbreaks occurred where there was but the first case, 15 where there were but two cases, so that it is apparent that very prompt action has been taken in a very notable proportion of outbreaks.   Remembering the fact that the Medical Health Officers are with the exception of four cities all in regular practice, that very few of them receive anything more than nominal remuneration, and recollecting that the office is, so far as dealing with smallpox, and indeed any other contagion is concerned, a direct injury to practice, it may be asserted without any question that there is no class of citizens who at the present moment is rendering either the same amount or quality of service to the community with the same certainty of abuse, whether he succeeds well or ill, as are our local Medical Health Officers.

To the gentlemen in question the people owe debts of gratitude which it is feared will not be repaid in honoraria; but there will be some satisfaction in having assisted in stamping out a disease which a century ago was the scourge of the world.

All of which is respectfully submitted.

P. H. BRYCE,

REPORT ON THE OUTBREAK OF SMALLPOX IN THE TOWNSHIPS OF BURFORD, OAKLAND AND WINDHAM.

By C. H. Hodgetts, M.D., Medical Inspector.

To the Secretary of the Provincial Board of Health :

Sir,—After a most careful investigation of all the cases in the above named townships in the vicinity of the Village of Scotland, I beg to report as follows :

The total number of houses inspected was thirty-four (34), which includes one in the City of Brantford, and one in the Village of Princeton, in which were living one hundred and fifty four (154) persons, male and female, of whom 92 were unvaccinated and 62 vaccinated.   Of the latter number only two within the last seven years, the vaccinations having recently been performed by Dr. Anderson.

There had been in all since the beginning of the outbreak 98 cases, 81 being variola and 17 varioloid, of the latter 9 were "varioloid sine eruptione," while the remaining 8 had the disease in an extremely mild form.   It will here be noticed the great difference between the vaccinated and unvaccinated who contracted the disease—13 of the former having the eruption as against 88 per cent. of the latter, and of the vaccinated affected none had been vaccinated within the last seven years, while a number were over twenty years ago, and a few over 40 years.   Of the total population 36 per cent. had smallpox since its first appearance in Scotland.

Attention is directed to a few important facts relative to the spread of the disease amongst the unvaccinated as well as to the immunity shown by the vaccinated, although the operation had been performed at periods more remote than 7 years, in some instances over 40 years ago.   In nine houses the total number of inmates was 46, none of whom had been successfully vaccinated, and all these persons had variola. In seventeen houses the only persons who did not contract the disease were the 36 persons who had at some previous date been successfully vaccinated, whilst only eleven who had never been vaccinated had at the time of my inspection, July 6th, been free from the infection and of eight of this number it is yet too early to speak, as the period of quarantine had not expired and in the case of the remaining three the exposure had been very slight indeed.

A number of persons claimed to have been vaccinated, but careful examination in every case failed to find even a trace of the typical scar.   So common has it become for the public to say they have been vaccinated, although on close questioning they own "it was not successful" or "has left no scar," that I discriminated, distinguishing between "vaccination and "successful vaccination."   Too often do medical men perform the operation and immediately issue a certificate, thus certifying to what they do not know is a fact, for judgment cannot be passed thereon until about the 9th day, and it cannot be claimed that the patient has been vaccinated until we have had all the typical reaction due to the vaccine virus.

It is a regrettable fact that in this district, which is one of the oldest settled portions of the Province, in a community numbering 154, that 60 per cent. were unvaccinated.   My investigations lead me to the conclusion that this is but a fair sample of the condition of the population at the present time—it is only in parts where a smallpox scare has recently existed that a more satisfactory state is to be found—here we find sixty (60) of the 98 cases were 20 years old and under, and all were unvaccinated.   Certainly a more rigid enforcement of the law by the local authorities, as applied to school children is greatly to be desired ; indeed, the spread of the disease in rural and perhaps other districts is largely due to the increasing unvaccinated element.   The general complaint I meet with on this subject from M.H.O.'s is the growing indifference   of   both   the   public   and   medical   men   to   this   most   essential operation.   The   mildness   of   the   present   outbreak   is   a   large   factor   in   producing this lamentable condition, and the public have yet to learn that the person who has been successfully vaccinated and revaccinated is far better protected against the more severe form of the disease than I believe is the unfortunate who has suffered from it in its present form.

Of the thirty-four houses inspected the sanitary surroundings were in all respects better than any I have ever inspected ; in only two the sanitation was somewhat inferior to the rest, and in each house the only immune was the vaccinated person. A striking instance of the protective power of vaccination was that of the Rev. ——'s family.   Here the father and mother, whose parents were wiser than themselves, in having them successfully vaccinated, slept with one or other of their children during their illness, but proved immune, whilst others unvaccinated   contracted   smallpox from the baby during its illness.

The measures recommended to and adopted by the Local Boards of Health were briefly as follows :

(a) The immediate quarantining of the houses at present infected by the pre-sence of cases of variola.   Ten in all.

(b) The enforcement of compulsory vaccination.

(c) The cleaning with perchloride solution 1-1000 of bedding, linen, etc., also the houses themselves with their subsequent fumigation with formaldehyde by the Medical Health Officer.

(d) The closing of the churches within a given radius for an indefinite period.

(e) In no case was permission given the quarantined to collect milk or berries.

(f) The retention of a medical man to attend all cases, Dr. Anderson of Scotland being appointed.

The first case happened in the Johnson family, the daughter had visited for a portion of a day at a house of Mrs. E. —— in Brantford, at a date early in April, where "chickenpox" existed; she returned the same day to Scotland and in two weeks time was taken ill and the disease ran its course; she returned to school, spreading the disease to the children, it reaching the adults at a later date.

In tracing up the Brantford case it was found that the E —— family contracted the disease from the D —— family, who were neighbors, and the father of this latter family brought it from London, Ont. We were thus able to trace 12 cases in three households in this city; the only person escaping was the mother, who had been vaccinated. Some of these cases had been seen by medical men, who had failed in coming to a correct diagnosis. Just how far the disease spread in Brantford I am unable to say; but the example of Scotland is a fair sample, and it may not be far from the facts to infer that the cases on the Indian Reserve found their origin closer at home than Sudbury.

Before closing I would refer to a most important fact, viz., the lack of knowl-edge on the part of many medical men of what constitutes a successful vaccination. This is in the main to be attributed, I believe, to the use during the past few years of "vaccine" inferior in quality and producing no constitutional disturbance and but little local inconvenience—producing what the manufacturers of the product as well as some American authorities claim and teach is a "successful vaccination"—due to the virus being "aseptic." So simple and mild is the operation that it has grown in favor among the ignorant and indifferent of the profession, who through the re-presentation made by the manufacturers have been taught to regard as "ex cathedra" all they print. The result to-day is that thousands in the Province as well as many thousands more in the States and Canada are living in a fool's paradise, innocently believing that they are really vaccinated and are protected against smallpox. For the protection of the public, for the education of the profession as well as for the sake of vaccination itself, the Board should at once issue bulletins on the subject, along with a description of smallpox as it is seen to-day.

Respectfully submitted,

Respectfully submitted,   C. A. HODGETTS.

REPORT ON SMALLPOX.

BURFORD DISTRICT.

Report No. 2, by C. A. Hodgetts, on the Same District.

Revisiting the above district some two weeks later I found as follows :

At Burford, about one mile from the village, a fresh case, who contracted the disease at Niagara Camp, sleeping in the same tent as the patient Eddy of Scotland. The patient had been placed in a tent which was situated in a well isolated spot.

Dr. Johnson, M.H.O., reported that nearly all the houses had been carefully cleaned under the supervision of himself or Dr. Anderson.

Dr. Anderson reported that of the previously quarantined houses only two now remained infected, but there were two new houses in quarantine—one a case from

Niagara Camp through infection from Eddy, and the second house where a man Eadie contracted it at his brother's previous to quarantine being placed thereon.

It would appear that the complaints reaching the department are made without good reason. The officers and the public of the district are fully alive to the necessity for the stamping out of the disease and the results in .Burford speak for themselves.

I am pleased to report that the quarantine officer of Oakland Township reports no fresh cases and that he is cleaning up the last house.

In company with Dr. Bell, M.H.O., Windham, six houses were visited in the township, five of these being new houses since my last inspection, but clearly places where the disease had been present for some weeks unknown to the local authorities; now that they have been quarantined there is little fear of further spread.

The Medical Health Officer, Townsend, was interviewed regarding some mild cases in his district, which he considered chickenpox, but of which there is every reason to believe the infection came from a case in Burford Township.

The Carpenter family in Walpole were visited, but the Medical Health Officer had visited the house that day and begun the cleaning up process.

I am pleased to report that the Medical Health Officer, Brantford, has cleaned up the three houses referred to in my former report.

In addition to the cases previously examined I saw twenty others in seven houses. with a total population of 37, all of the 20 had never been vaccinated; in three families all the unvaccinated had been ill, and in the remaining four houses were eight unvaccinated, leaving only nine vaccinated out of the thirty-seven.

Respectfully. submitted,   CHAS. A. HODGETTS, M.D., Inspector.

THE QUALITY OF VACCINE LYMPH AND OF VACCINATION.

By the Secretary.

(Abstract from Quarterly Report Ontario Provincial Board of Health, April 26, 1900.)

The importance of this subject would be an excuse for again referring to what has been written about so often. The Vaccination Act demands that a child shall. within three months of birth, be taken to the medical practitioner for the purpose of being vaccinated, and the practitioner is required to vaccinate the child. Upon the eighth day following the vaccination the child shall again be taken to the practitioner by whom the operation was performed, in order that he may by inspection ascertain the result of the operation.   If successful, upon inspection the practitioner shall give a certificate to that effect.

Fortunately in this matter modern science has developed nothing leading us to the belief that the law of thirty years ago calls for a practice no longer tenable. Bovine vaccine and glycerinized lymph are capable of producing the old typical clinical phenomena caused by the use of humanized lymph, and we have a right to claim the following as representing our beliefs in the matter of vaccination and the part it plays as a prophylactic against smallpox.

It is hardly necessary to say that the whole value of vaccination depends upon its ability to protect either against infection with smallpox or to modify the virulence of an attack, should it occur.   That such results have followed vaccination, the history of a hundred years has proved.   These two points in the experience of twenty years having been absolutely demonstrated in hundreds of outbreaks and thousands of cases, the question to be determined is,—upon what factors in vaccination such satisfactory results depend.   Briefly, these are :

1. A normal vaccine, that is one where the assumed microbe of the disease is actively present.
2. The use of a vaccine when fresh and active.
3. The absence of extraneous microbes in the vaccine.
4. The careful inoculation of patients and subsequent treatment of the wound.

The question arises at once, what is normal vaccine ? In our experience it is a lymph which produces a history of evolution of the vesicle exactly as set forth by Prof. T. A. Ackland, one of the officers of the English Royal Commission of 1893 to 1896 to enquire into alleged injuries due to abnormal vaccinations, and which is found in Allbutt's System of Medicine, Vol. II. Its stages are: (1) Scarification and immediate inflammatory reaction, subsiding within a few hours; (2) on third or fourth day, pale red papules appearing, which, during the next five days, develop into compound vescicles, becoming pustules by the ninth day; (3) vesicles distended with lymph, and plump at first, and as the lymph thickens, the centre becomes depressed, forming a scab and surrounded with distinctly raised marbled border ; (4) an area of redness and inflammatory thickening of tissue around the pustule of an inch or more in diameter; (5) a decrease from tenth day of the inflammatory area and a drying of the scab, which falls by the twentieth day; (6) a cicatrix, usually with a hard scar centre, with rays more or less distinct.

The same article gives a table showing variations in the development of the pock, most of which, it states, however, are slight, such as abnormal rapidity or delay in the evolution of the vesicle. In the same work, in another monograph by Dr. M. Copeman, dealing more especially with the morphology, chemistry and preparation of vaccine, he here points out how bovine lymph has in England taken the place of humanized, and then proceeds to speak of glycerinized lymph. He speaks of the practically constant presence of extraneous microbes in lymph, and notes his experiments as early as 1891, which proved that a 50 per cent. solution in water of chemically pure glycerine to one part of vaccine pulp, set aside from light for a few weeks removes all saprophytes as well as tubercle bacillus and streptococcus. Thereafter, follows the satisfactory statement that in vaccine thus properly produced, "We have then a preparation, which, while even more efficient as vaccine than the original lymph, can be produced entirely free from extraneous organisms," and he points out how scientific workers in France and Germany have borne out these statements. Referring to the operation on the calf, Monkman points out that on the fourth day the pustule is mature, and that the lymph is then taken and treated, thereby showing that with glycerinized lymph the evolution of the vesicle is the same as with the lymph unglycerinized. It may be further remarked that in the experimental work of Chambon and Menard, of the Animal Vaccine Institute of Paris, the history of normal vaccination is the same as that given above. The immunity of bovines and of children and of monkeys thus vaccinated to revaccination is not only relative, but for several years practically absolute. Of the protective qualities against exposure to smallpox of vaccination in the persons of physicians and nurses, it is unnecessary to dilate, as we have personal knowledge of the facts in the case of hundreds during the past twenty years, as well as the protection up to the fourth day after exposure by immediate vaccination of exposed persons. Copeman gives many illustrative examples of the same fact. That in a whole series of cases with relatively inert vaccine, such immunity does not exist against even mild smallpox has been brought to our knowledge in different outbreaks within the last few years; and, further, that those with no cicatrices from a previous vaccination, within periods from a month to a year, have been revaccinated with perfect success.

Copeman, speaking of the necessity for efficient vaccination, points out in a study of recent statistics, compared with those of former years, "that we are taught a variety of lessons, of which the most important is that while infant vaccination affords an almost absolute immunity from smallpox up to ten years, to do so it must be efficient." Absolute immunity, he further states, is practically obtained with a revaccination after ten years. He points out that the more closely the vaccination of patients in recent epidemics has been studied, the more obvious has it become that a deplorably large proportion of the nominally vaccinated have been most inefficiently vaccinated, and are consequently almost unprotected against smallpox, and says : "So long as medical men, in their mistaken good nature, are found ready to yield to the ignorance or vanity of applicants for vaccination, and to make only one, or perhaps two, insignificant insertions of lymph in a child's arm, and to certify cases of that kind as successfully vaccinated, so long shall we have to struggle against the fallacies and sophistries of anti-vaccinationists." Asking, further, how efficient vaccination is to be secured, he states : "That the Local Government Board prescribe that public vaccination shall in all ordinary primary cases produce at least four good-sized separate vesicles not less than half an inch from one another. The total area of vesiculation of any one part at the end of a week should not be less than half a square inch.

In a statistical study by Dr. Thorne Thorne, of 13,775 cases in the London Small-pox Hospital, in two series, the following results for the second series, from 1852 to 1867, or in 10,661 cases are given :

Stated to have been vaccinated—

	Percentage of Deaths.
With no cicatrix	39.4
With one cicatrix	13.8
With two cicatrices	7.7
With three cicatrices	3.01
With four cicatrices	0.9

He further points out that of 13,775 admitted, vaccination was very defective in 11,172, of whom 1,072 died. Of 1,079 reasonably good, 21 died; and of 1,505 with good normal marks, only 13 died. Such statistics can be duplicated from many sources.

In conclusion, it may be stated that we have yet to learn of any facts which can alter the biological, clinical, and statistical evidence upon which the Royal Commission of England, after seven years of investigations, based its conclusions, which are essentially those set forth in the preceding references, and which in every detail, whether biological, clinical or statistical, are supported by our own experience.

The urgency of the situation demands that this Board make public its views on a subject which the public have been ignorant or careless of, and that it impress its views in the most positive manner upon local health authorities in all parts of the Province.

REPORT ON TUBERCULOSIS BY THE COMMITTEE ON EPIDEMICS.

October 6th, 1901.

Mr. Chairman and Gentlemen :

Your Committee, in view of the renewed interest taken in the causes of the prevalence of tuberculosis in man and animals, and in the enormous mortality due to it, more than 100,000 deaths having occurred from it in the United States in the census year of 1900, believes it to be the duty of this Board to indicate, as briefly as possible, its views as to the most practical direction in which the public, physicians and public health authorities in Ontario can take action towards lessening the prevalence of a disease the cause of so great suffering, mortality and family and economic loss to the community.

*In the recent address by Prof. Robert Koch, the eminent bacteriologist, who will ever remain illustrious as the discoverer of the bacillus or germ of the disease, he refers, in the first paragraph to tuberculosis as a preventable disease : and it is pointed out by the writer that this fact became self-evident by the fact that its cause had been discovered. Referring to the fight for its prevention, Dr. Koch says: "Such a conflict requires the co-operation of many, if possible of all, medical men, shoulder to shoulder with the State and the whole population."

In the paragraph on "Special preventive Measures needed for Various Diseases," he points out how these may vary for different diseases, and cites plague, cholera, hydro-

*Address at International Congress on Tuberculosis, in London, 1901.

phobia, leprosy and tuberculosis, and states what this Board has expressed and referred to in its circular issued in 1900, that "Sputum is the main source of infection," and that the lungs are the chief source of this disease. In the next paragraph he refers to the "Differences between human and bovine Tuberculosis."

This difference was noted by Prof. Cruickshank in 1889, and more recently by other writers, notably Prof. Theobald Smith of the Bureau of Animal Industry of Washington. Prof. Koch's conclusions have gone further, however, than some others in seeming to assert that the difference is not only in morphology or appearance, but that the two diseases are different in essence, and that the bovine disease is not communicable to man. The view so subversive of what for over ten years has been a general belief, has not been accepted by many, who are, however, ready to admit with him that infection of the human from the bovine, is not as frequent as from the prevalence of bovine disease, and the common use of the meat and milk from cattle might be expected.

Some of the reasons why some refuse to accept his conclusions are :

1. That the human germ, accustomed to a temperature in man of 98.4 degrees has its optimum or best growing temperature at this point, while, the normal temperature of the cow being 101 degrees, the bovine germ finds its optimum at the latter point; and that, in keeping with the well-known fact of the great variability of these simple forms of vegetable life under different environments and the multitude of generations of any germ within a short period, it is reasonable to suppose that the bovine germ, taken into the human body with milk, may live for days and weeks on the mucous surface, undergoing variation in successive generations, and may, as other germs do, even the human germ itself, find an entrance into the tissues whenever through a congestion or abrasion of the mucous surface, an opportunity arises.

2. That this assumption is probable, is seen in the fact that of the thousands of people dying of other diseases, a percentage of post-mortems up to even 90 per cent. shows that such have been attacked at points of the mucous membranes, by germs, which have not succeeded in causing any general disease of the system.

3. That in consumptives who constantly swallow their own sputum, only a few relatively have tuberculosis of the intestine ; and it is the same fact illustrated by Prof. Koch's experiments, that hogs fed with bovine tuberculosis become infected in the neck, glands, etc., but not necessarily in the intestines.

4. That, as argued by Lord Lister, very few tuberculized persons, even children, who of necessity must swallow with food in infected rooms, and in the mucus from the mouth and nose, the germs of the human disease, are attacked in the mucous membrane of the stomach and intestines.

5. That some diseases, as for instance anthrax, the most sudden and fatal of all diseases, do not attack human beings with the same readiness or near the same fatality as it does cattle ; while smallpox, a disease so readily communicable and so fatal in man, is not taken at all directly by cattle, but yet has been shown by various experimenters to be, through a series of transmissions from calf to calf, at length capable of producing mild smallpox or cowpox in cattle.

6. That the bacillus tuberculosis, like all other micro-organisms, varies greatly in the virulence of the germ from different patients in animal inoculations, and in the degeneration of the germ in laboratory cultures. This fact is supported most strongly by Prof. F. Hueppe and Weleminsky of Berlin, who both combat strongly Koch's position, since, though differing still more from bovine tuberculosis, they have succeeded by making successive cultures in grafting avian or bird tuberculosis on animals.

7. It is a recognized law that the anti-toxin or serum produced in the blood of animals by the presence of the germs of one disease is a specific only against germs of that disease; but it is found that the anti-toxin (tuberculin) produced by the bacillus tuberculosis, (even from a mild germ propagated in the laboratory for years through successive cultures), is equally delicate in diagnosing the presence of tuberculous nodules in man and in cattle.

8. Experiments made in Berlin (on smaller animals), under the direction of the Commission of 1901, have not established any difference between human and bovine tuberculosis.

9. Prof. Virchow, the great German pathologist, refers to occasional cases of peritoneal tuberculosis of such enormous extent as to lead to the suspicion that they may have been due to bovine germs, though holding that the transmission of bovine to man is probably not very common.

10. Many seemingly authenticated cases of infection of veterinarians and others through wounds of the hands and by use of known tuberculous milk are reported.

Prof. Koch dealt fully with the subject of bovine tuberculosis, quite incidentally, in his most practical paper, in which he desired to press home that it is the human sputum which is the great source of human infection, and points out how, though the well-to-do classes may by large houses and careful nursing protect against the dangers of infecting inmates, yet it is quite different amongst the poor, who may live in two small ill-ventilated rooms.

He asks, "How can the necessary cleanliness be secured under such circumstances? How is such a helpless patient to remove his sputum, so that it may do no harm?" Thus, while families are infected and die out, and, as he says, the people say the disease is hereditary, "So it is the over-crowded dwellings of the poor that we have to regard as the real breeding places of tuberculosis," and says it is gratifying to see how in all countries efforts are being made to improve the dwellings of the poor.

The statistics of tabulated deaths for Toronto in 1898 too sadly confirm this statement, as do those from all sources.

The advice given in the circular issued in 1900 by your Board very fully recognizes this fact, when it refers :

1. To the need of supplying isolated wards for consumptives in public institutions.

2. That in private families there should be as much isolation as possible, and special care taken to destroy expectorations.

3. That vacated rooms should be thoroughly disinfected.

4. That Local Boards should make rules for the notification of cases of consumption; while at the same time it points out that this is not an order that houses should be placarded, but that Boards may assist householders especially the poor. by supplying printed rules and directions for limiting the dangers of infection.

5. To the need for municipalities establishing sanatoria for giving aid to persons. especially the poor, affected with tuberculosis.

Prof. Koch's arguments in his address all lead up to this latter point. which is referred to in the paragraph on "The need for Hospitals for Consumptives." He says : "I know very well that the execution of this project will have great difficulties to contend with, owing to the considerable expense it entails," and points out that "its execution opens a wide field of activity to the State, to municipalities, and to private benevolence."

As, however, this cannot be done at once, Prof. Koch argues that notification be made the law in order that such aid already referred to may be given to householders.

His concluding section deals with the special subject of Sanatoria, or Cure-Homes for Consumptives, since, as he points out, the disease is curable in its early stages.

Quoting from the report of the German Central Committee for the establishment of sanatoria for the cure of consumption, he states that 5.500 beds will be at the disposal of those institutions at the end of 1901, making it possible to treat 20,000 patients every year. And then, referring to statistics of cure, points out that 4,000 persons would leave these cured, and the balance having their lives greatly prolonged with profit to their family and the State.

Your Committee is constrained to ask: How in this Province. where on every hand trade, commerce and agriculture are prosperous, and where our population has increased slowly, can we afford to neglect so potent a means of not only saving life, and increasing population; and, furthermore, preventing the loss of time, labor and expenditure, incidental to the sickness and death caused by the annual occurrence of 3,000 deaths from this disease.

Your Committee would present as a part its report the resolutions adopted unanimously at the recent meeting in Buffalo of the American Public Health Association, representing the advanced scientific opinion on this subject, of the sanitarians of the United States, Canada, and Mexico, and would desire to draw particular attention to the practical recommendations contained in them.

Thus, of 2,264 deaths, in which the occupations of 691 men were given and of 337 females, with 1,237 under 15 years or with no occupation given, it was found that excluding 172 business men, which includes 81 clerks, etc., 26 professional men, 14 gentlemen and 8 public officials, 837, or the balance, includes those earning a daily wage or wholly unable to individually maintain a long struggle against disease.

In concluding its report, your Committee would quote the concluding words of Prof. Koch :

"If we allow ourselves to be continually guided' in this enterprise by the spirit of genuine preventive medical science, if we utilize the experience gained in conflict with other pestilences, and aim, with clear recognition of the purpose and resolute avoidance of wrong roads, at striking the evil at its root, then the battle against tuberculosis, which has been so energetically begun, cannot fail to have a victorious issue.

Resolutions of American Public Health Associations.

Resolved, That notwithstanding the advances of sanitary science, the mortality from tuberculosis continues to be appalling. It has been demonstrated that by the application of proper measures this mortality may be diminished rapidly, and to a great degree. Therefore, every effort should be made by sanitarians to carry into effect all reasonable methods which have been shown by experience and research to be efficacious towards this end ;

Resolved, That the increase of tuberculosis in cattle and swine, as shown by investigations of recent years, and by meat inspection statistics, is a serious matter from a commercial as well as sanitary point of view, and calls for more systematic attention from those responsible for the integrity of the food supply, and for the protection of the public health ;

Resolved, That this Association is of the opinion that sufficient facts have not been offered by Prof. Koch or other investigators to prove that human and bovine tuberculosis are different diseases ; it is further of the opinion that the variability under different environment common to micro-organisms may, on further investigation, be found sufficient to account for the differences that have been noted, and that the germs of these diseases may yet be proved to be closely allied or identical. Irrespective of the question of the communicability of bovine tuberculosis to man, the inspection of animals and premises is absolutely necessary in order,

1. That the meat and milk of animals suffering from this and other constitutional diseases be not used as human food.

2. That the sanitary condition of dairies, stables, etc., as regards cleanliness, water supply and ventilation may be maintained.

3. That the health of dairymen and other handlers be closely supervised to prevent the spread of diphtheria, scarlet fever, human tuberculosis, etc., through the milk supply.

Resolved, That this Association, while desiring to express its positive opinion as to the importance of dealing with animals and their products, as indicated in the preceding resolutions, does at the same time insist upon the necessity for dealing with the still greater dangers now universally recognized of the transmission of tuberculosis from one person to another by continued personal association through inhalation of the air of infected living rooms. the contamination of clothing, handkerchiefs, and similar objects with sputum and other secretions, and would therefore urgently recommend that municipalities adopt regulations. as follows :—

1. Against expectoration on pavements and in other public places.

2. For the compulsory notification by physicians of cases of tuberculosis, in order that literature may be supplied to householders and municipal aid given where necessary to lessen the dangers to the families of infected persons.

3. For the establishment of municipal sanatoria for the benefit of persons and families of limited means.

4. For the regular inspection of tenements, factories, workshops, schools and other public institutions to promote cleanliness, ventilation and other sanitary conditions. (Adopted.)

The proper course for Executive health authorities to assume seems to your Committee to be this: That, whilst ready to listen to all that Prof. Koch and others have to say, and whilst waiting for the further developments which we may expect from the investigations of the Commissioners which have been appointed, and of other scientific bodies, we should not relax any of the vigorous inspection that has been recommended for meat and milk. And our Board unites with Prof. Koch and others in the continuance of efforts to prevent the spread of tuberculosis from tuberculous patients by dealing properly with sputa and by providing for the proper care and comfort of those suffering from consumption and forms of tuberculosis, especially amongst the poor.

All of which is respectfully submitted.

REPORT ON BERLIN SEWAGE FARM.

October 6th, 1901.

By the Committee on Sewerage.

Mr. Chairman and Gentlemen :

In consequence of a notice by the solicitor of the town of Berlin, that the township of Waterloo has issued a writ against the town for polluting the creek flowing to German Mills, with a request that your Board would interest itself to prevent a suit if possible, your Secretary wrote to the solicitor to state that if appealed to, your Committee would visit the town and try to obtain such facts from the two parties to the suit, as might possibly be of assistance in aiding it in making suggestions, with a view to at once improve the working of the Farm and to prevent litigation.

Having therefore been requested, your Committee visited Berlin on September 26th and took informal evidence of the chief facts in relation to the working of the sewage farm, which are herewith appended.

From the facts set forth, several conclusions may be drawn.

1st. That for the amount and character of the sewage, the area of the sewage beds, constituted as they are largely of gravelly clay, is insufficient for dealing with the sewage without much greater labor being given them than has been the case up to the present.

2nd. That with the addition of the septic tank of the size indicated, and the two artificial sand-bed filters, the area of the beds is insufficient, certainly in winter and in wet weather.

3rd. That with nearly eight acres devoted to cultivation, and receiving but little sewage, there has been a difficulty, even in dry weather, in filtering the 325,000 gallons daily, of sewage supplied.

4th. That in consequence there has been, from time to time, a direct pollution of the stream, with night sewage of a relatively pure character.

5th. That so far as the flooded areas of the beds giving off effluvia of a noxious character are concerned, such may become a nuisance to the persons living within little or greater distances from the sewer farm.

6th. That, while speaking generally, the best managed sewage farms are seldom free from certain odors, yet the Berlin Town Council must show that it has been taking every reasonable means to limit the effluvia from such farm before it can fairly claim protection against actions brought against the town, for causing pollution of the stream and effluvium nuisances.

Your Committee desires, therefore, to indicate some of the chief reasons for the unsatisfactory operation of the sewage farm, and at the request of the two parties referred to, would make suggestions with a view to improving the working of the farm, which will, it is hoped, not only be satisfactory to the Board, but also productive of improved results in the operation of the farm.

It will be remembered that the Town of Berlin has an unusually large number of manufactories, all of which pour wastes into the sewers, and that as the system of sewerage is separate, the sewage arrives at the farm in a highly concentrated form. The following is an analysis of average samples of sewage submitted.

	Parts per 100,000.			Total solids.
---	Chlorine.	Free amon.	Albumens. (organic.)	Mineral.
Lawrence, Mass..........	4.8	1.2	0.4	Total in suspension $\begin{cases} 43.0 \\ 8.2 \end{cases}$
Worcester, Mass	4.2	0.55	0.17	Total in suspension $\begin{cases} 43.4 \\ 9.9 \end{cases}$
Exeter, Eng..............	5.0	3.7	0.212	(04.7 n. 2) Total suspended .. $\begin{cases} 5 .4 \\ 1 .5 \end{cases}$ 24.5 m-16.0

Such are fairly typical sewages, without anything unusual, such as excessive chlorine, etc., but Berlin varies from some in certain particulars, especially in the reception of waste tarry products from gas works, in the exceptionally large relative amounts of organic refuse, both animal and vegetable, from tanneries, and in the effluent from one rubber factory.

Now, it happens that in all these establishments, wastes are given off which have elsewhere, and seemingly here, been found to be germicidal in action, and which very notably affect the nitrification of sewage which goes on in what is called domestic sewage.

Thus, there may be seen every day at certain hours. the tan-colored washings from hides, which have been taken from the vats for further finishing. In one tannery foreign hides are largely used, which, in the experiments of Massachusetts. are shown to have had arsenic used in the curing process. A third tannery, using the lime process, probably does no harm, and any lime solution going down is likely to be beneficial rather than otherwise.

The tarry products of the Gas Works may also be seen floating on the surface and giving their peculiar odor to the sewage in every part of the field ; while, as in the Rubber Works, it is understood that carbon bisulphid is used, sulphuretted products are given off, which in oxidation become an active germicide.

What has been done. The original farm comprised some 10 acres, laid off in beds, levelled and surrounded with embankments, each of about one acre in extent. These were all underdrained at a depth of about three feet, and the beds were flooded with sewage in rotation. Those having preserved the natural loam on top supplied a fairly good effluent, and filtered at a fairly rapid rate. Other beds which had to be graded as the farm was enlarged, had left a surface of clayish soil without organic matter and, though underdrained. did not have any upper humus to either absorb or assist in nitrification. Such beds were usually utilized for the tannery sewage, and always presented ponds filtering away slowly and losing much by evaporation.

Some of the better beds years ago grew good cabbage, but this was given up as the area required for simple filtration increased. Any such beds, in which the trenches over the tiles were filled with tanbark, have been rendered largely useless as filters, the waters passing downwards very slowly. As there has usually been but one ploughing of the surface of these beds annually, and no systematic record kept of the amount of water applied to each bed, or of the frequency of application of sewage, no data are available for really estimating the amount of work done, either as a whole, or comparatively by the several beds.

The growing needs of the town induced the Council in 1900 to accept the Provincial Board's approval of the Engineer's plan, of a 75,000-gallon septic tank, and two artificial filter beds of gravel and sand.

These have been in continual use for some nine months, and the great bulk of the sewage has passed, day by day, through the septic tank, and thence been distributed to the older beds, or to the artificial beds. It was noted at first that the septic tank seemed, not only to be of great service for holding back suspended matter, but, also, that the effluent from it was almost wholly soluble, and passed downward through the filters much more rapidly than the raw sewage. It was further found, that the artificial beds not only handled a very large amount of sewage proportionately, but that they also, after some time, gave a clear and better effluent than did any other beds.

Observation seems to have shown that from some cause, whether the notably increased flow of sewage during the past year, nearly 100,000 gallons, or some substances present in the sewage, the scum or mass of decomposed sewage which floats on the septic tank, supported by the gases of fermentation, has not lately formed, as at first, and as such especially indicates the decomposition of nitrogenous products going on through the microbes present, the conclusion is arrived at that the tank is not performing the amount of work it should.

The following table of analysis shows the amount of decomposition of sewage in samples taken on October 2nd.

Parts per 1,000,000 parts of water.

—	Color.	Odor.	Number of microbes per c.c.	Free ammonia.	Alb'mnoid ammonia.	Nitrogen as nitrates in water.	Oxygen consumed.	Chlorine
Tank sewage..	Redish grey	Sulp. hydrogen	1,200,000	6.375	28 5	44.156	12C0.1	810.0
First filter ...	Greyish	"	139,050	5.10	1.35	31.626	27.0	900.
Second filter..	"	"	202,950	0.5625	1.95	1.9572	38.25	885.

Assuming that any properly filtered sewage should have an average reduction of organic matter, to the extent of from 70 to 80 per cent., it will be noticed that the effluent in this case should show an equal reduction, had the tank sewage been the same as that flowing directly from the town. The raw sewage from the sewer was not, however, sent at the time.

An illustrative case of disposal of practically the same amount of sewage, at Stratford-on-Avon, is given by Dr. L. Barwise, M.H.O., of Derbyshire, England, in his recent work on "Sewage Disposal."

The population of the town is 9,000 ; volume of sewage, 270,000 gallons. The sewage was run into a tank with precipitant added, over night, removing roughly, as usual, about 50 per cent. of the organic matter. Thence it is pumped, during ten hours, over nine acres of sand and gravel, levelled and underdrained (six to twelve yards apart) and is laid out half for irrigation and half in ridges three feet wide and furrows one foot wide and nine inches deep.

Five acres of clay land is occasionally irrigated, being sown with rye-grass. Another ridged ground is planted with mangolds and cabbage. Sewage is supplied intermittently.

The effluent contains 0.056 parts of albumenoid ammonia per 100,000, well within the provisional standard of 0.100 per 100,000. The author quotes, after reviewing reports, that a standard of 0.15 parts per 100,000 of albumenoid ammonia, and 1.5 of oxygen, absorbed at 80 degrees F. in four hours, is one which may fairly be demanded as the quality of effluent from sewage farms, the nitrification to be shown by the effluent containing at least 0.25 parts per 100,000 of nitrogen as nitrates. We may fairly, then, enquire what measures may be applied to improve the Berlin Sewage Farm? In reply your Committee would suggest the following as likely to maintain the Sewage Farm in a sanitary condition, if carefully carried out:

1st. The Town Council should, by resolution, place the management of the farm under a regular engineer, and, while accepting his suggestions, make him responsible for the conduct of the farm.

2nd. Require of the tannery-owners, the construction of a roughing filter of coke on their own premises, whereby tanbark extract would be filtered out, and any arsenic present removed by combination with the small amounts of iron salts usually present in coke. The upper layer of the coke can, with the organic deposit left, be from time to time removed, and burnt in the furnaces. The soluble organic materials remaining in the effluent therefrom can then be allowed into the sewage and treated with the domestic sewage.

3rd. Require a similar coke filter to be used for removal of the tarry products of the Gas Works; these being hydro-carbons, may also be removed with the upper layer of coke and burnt in the furnace. The effluent therefrom may be then received in the domestic sewage.

4th. Require the sewage from the rubber works to be passed over a filter of powdered haematite, or over sand with lime added to the sewage, whereby the sulphur compounds will be deposited as sulphites.

By these measures, which, it will be seen, can only with difficulty. and then imperfectly, be applied after these have become mixed in the common sewage, we have a sewage similar to domestic sewage to be treated, and in which microbic decomposition can be set up readily. The results of these processes would have to be watched carefully, analyses of different effluents being carried on frequently.

5th. Extend the septic tanks to at least twice their present capacity; it being remembered that the Exeter, England, tanks, for instance, are large enough to hold a whole day's sewage. By this means not only will the work of decomposition be very greatly increased, but the expense of removing sludge from them will be lessened.

6th. Multiply the artificial sand-bed filters to the extent necessary to give an effluent from them, as well as the several other beds which may receive occasionally charges of sewage of a standard equal to that already set forth as practical.

7th. Cultivate flat beds frequently, so as to promote the nitrification of deposits by the thorough aerating of the upper layers of the beds, and frequently pass the cultivator through the rows of cultivated crops, which may be grown in summer with profit.

8th. Until such additions to the works as are here indicated. have been made, secure the temporary use of such neighboring land upon which sewage may be pumped, and thus be prevented from flowing into the creek.

While the town has held the distinction of being the first in Ontario to have established sewage disposal works, it has, through the yearly changes of management, under the different chairmen of committee, suffered necessarily from the want of continuity of plan in the development of the sewage farm; much too small amounts of money have been set apart for it, while the amount of sewage has greatly grown and its character has increased in complexity. The fortunate accident of no pumping at the sewage outfall, makes it an easy matter for the town to add to the expense of development such an amount as the several suggested extensions may require; while the fact must not be overlooked, that like town waterworks, extension and development is always inevitable in a rapidly growing town like Berlin.

All of which is respectfully submitted.

E. E. KITCHEN.

PETER H. BRYCE

W. J. DOUGLASS.
per P. H. B.

BERLIN, Sept. 25, 1901.
Enquiry into conduct of Berlin Sewage Farm at a meeting of Dr. Bryce, Provincial Health Officer, and D·. Kitchen, Chairman of Committee on Sewers of Provincial Board of Health, with the authorities of the Town of Berlin, and there being present Mr Schafer, Reeve of Waterloo Township, Dr. Roberts, Medical Health Officer, Mr. Cressman of the Board of Health, Mr. Lehmon Shirk, Mr. Daniel Weber and Mr. Peter Shirk from the township.

(Dr. Kitchen in Chair.)

Dr. Kitchen stated the object of the enquiry, it being made at the instance of the Town of Berlin, in consequence of a writ to restrain being served by the Council and Board of Health and a private complainant, Mr. Lehmon Shirk of German Mills.

The following is a statement of the main facts relating to the operation of the Sewage Farm, got from the Mayor, members of the Sewer Committee, and Mr. Baetz, foreman of the Farm :

Dr. Herbert Bowlby, Mayor : Am Mayor of Berlin and have been in Council for several years and was Chairman of Sewer Committee in 1900 ; knew the method of working the farm, which was then and is now as follows : (1) Farm consists of twenty acres of land, laid out in beds of 3-4 and 1-2 acres in area, all with subsoil drains, grad ed. and with dykes around each bed; carriers from main sewer are arranged to discharge sewage on to beds in succession, under the charge of Mr. B. Baetz, foreman of the Farm.

(2) These beds consist of a gravelly clay and covered in some beds with a loam composed of fertile humus.

(3) There is also a septic tank, constructed in 1900, under the supervision of Mr. M. Davis, Engineer ,of 75,000 gallons capacity.

(4) In addition there were two filtering beds, constructed in 1900, of coarse stone and gravel, with field tiles in bottom to extent of three feet in depth, and of a superficial area of 50 x 75 feet ; the working of the farm and tank and filtering beds is as follows : As the sewage reaches the end of the main sewer it enters a manhole some seven feet in diameter and of about nine feet in depth, from which it empties into the first part of septic tank, called the grit chamber, which, as chamber is filled, flows into compartment No. 2 of tank, which has several divisions therein; then over a weir, flowing into carrier to beds, sometimes to the new gravel filter beds and at others to the ordinary beds; this tank contains some 75,000 gallons, or about six hours flow of sewage, there being about 328,000 gallons of sewage per day, an increase of 12,000 gallons over 1900; the septic tank is covered and is not a source of effluvium nuisance; the septic tank is cleaned regularly the grit chamber, by an elevated pump, worked by horse-power, every two weeks, and the compartment No. 2 by allowing sewage therefrom to flow to No. 1, being cleaned when necessary; this has been done three times during 1901, January 30th, March 14th and August 1st. The contents of tank is hauled away to farm and used as fertilizer. The sewage as it leaves the septic tank flows as dirty water, at times brownish from tannery water, and carrying but little suspended matters; when turned on to gravel filter the effluent appears clear, much like swamp water, of a roily tint, except when tannery water comes through it is not so good and smells a little; this water empties in creek; these two beds hold a charge of sewage for about two hours each, each bed holding about 15,000 gallons each, each being about 50 feet square by 75 square; after two hours water is drawn off and bed rested 24 hours; when these two beds are filled we turn sewage on beds as mentioned in plan in succession; each bed would receive a dose of sewage once in four or five days, those beds being flooded which are not used for cultivation; those which are used have been in 1901 four in number, viz., No. 3, No. 4, No. 10, No. 11; on No. 3 Swede turnips, No. 4 sugar beets, No. 10 sugar beets, No. 11 mangolds, No. 5 carrots were tried not successfully; the beds Nos. 3, 4 and 5, under cultivation, are useless for filtration, the underdrains being clogged; Nos. 10 and 11 filter fairly well; the beds of sugar beets of 3.75 acres will probably yield 2,500 bushels of beets; turnips are poor; mangolds, to extent of one acre, are good; the cultivated beds are scuffled occasionally; each has been done four times since planted this spring, and they are hoed; the other beds were ploughed in order, each bed since spring, No. 1 three times, No. 2 once, No. 6 three times, No. 7 once, No. 8 twice, No. 9 twice; these were not scuffled or harrowed; Mr. Baetz has a horse which is used for cultivation and working of pumps; ploughing

is paid for by day work, when required; the ploughing is about six inches deep, to gravel over tiles; after ploughing the filtration is, I suppose, twice as fast, but effluent is not so clean, sewage will appear in tiles some two hours after a ploughed bed is flooded, but is better and does not appear as quickly if bed is not ploughed; Nos. 10 and 11 give cleanest effluent except gravel beds; the water which flows from tiles sometimes smells strong of gas liquor and of tanbark smell at times; there are no fish in creek that I am aware of; the smell from beds is noticeable at times quite far away, but I do not mind it; generally at 9.30 to 12 in forenoon the tannery water comes down, as I can tell by its red color; it goes through the tank, but I separate it by putting it in Nos. 10 and 11, if I have room, if not, in 9 and 8; this comes down every day when they work; the gas liquor comes down at any time, as I can tell by the smell and oil on top; I do not do anything with that (different); the solution from Erbs' Glove Tanery is whitish, lime being used; this occurs every day about an hour; in forenoon about twelve some blue dye water comes down, not every day, two or three times a week; the new beds will take the color out best.

Dr. Roberts asked Mr. Baetz how many times the septic tank was cleaned? He stated three times. Would the sediment be above the partitions? No. Is the smell so bad that it makes you sick? No. It must have been, if at all, the first year, when I had to take a smoke.

Mr. Cressman asked : Why is it if water comes out so clear that it comes so bad down the stream? I do not know. Mr. Cressman says this is most of summer.

(Mr. Baetz is employed all the year at the Sewer Farm ; the sewage sometimes runs directly from the beds into the creek in winter.) "I have allowed this at night when the sewage is clear, and only when the beds are full; when the rains come the beds get too full and we may not have room enough, and we may then let in night water."

Would the cultivated beds, if in proper shape, and not cultivated, use all the sewage? They would use some more, but not so very much more. .

Statement of Claim—Describing statements of complainants.

(1) Pollution of Snyder's Creek. Claim to clear stream.

(2) Town of Berlin, by construction of sewers, has polluted and has allowed firms and persons to connect with drain.

(3) Flushing drains to creek.

(4) Town buildings pollute said creek.

(5) Filth deposited on land of riparian owners.

(6) Shirk says, "land and mill depreciated and family health endangered."

(7) Board of Health and plaintiffs have long protested.

(8) State that in 1891 farm for disposal established causing accumulation on farm and makes effluvia endangering health; they have demanded some efficient means of purifying; defendants have been appealed to in vain; located in Waterloo Township and Local Board have right to abate nuisance.

(9) Establishment of works caused and causes a nuisance and plaintiffs claim relief, and Mr. Shirk damages.

The following statements were made :

Dr. Roberts : There is one question this gentleman, Mr. Baetz said, the farm is composed of twenty acres, eight acres is for cultivation. Does he mean that the balance is in use for sewage? Yes, by examination of the plan you will see.

I have been connected with the Board of Health eight or nine years, and it has been a bugbear to the township ever since. My impression is this : In the first place it was a mistake to put the farm where it was put, it is not a gravelly soil; in the second place there was a faulty construction; in the third place it has not been cultivated as well as it should have been; and, in the fourth place, I think the construction of the septic tank was a failure, it should not have been called a septic tank at all, but a catch basin. As long as you have the chemicals from the tannery and gas factory, it is absurd to expect bacteria to break up your solids. I may say that the Board of Health of the Township of Waterloo have been patient and long-suffering with the Town of

Berlin ; every year since I have been connected with the Board of Health, the people down the creek have been complaining very much of the state of the water, and have urged us to do something in the matter. We have met and seen a committee of the Council a number of times ; we have also had the Provincial Board of Health here before and we always got an abundance of fair promises ; they would say, "Give us time"; we gave them time, but things have been going from bad to worse. I have taken the evidence of the people down the creek, and they are still in this state of affairs and worse than ever. We knew that the construction of sewer farms in Canada at least was experimental, that is why we were patient with the people. We expected, after waiting som time, that things would be better after the septic tank was constructed, but I am sorry to say it is no better. If we do not act, the Board of Health would be a laughing stock to the Township of Waterloo.

Dr. Kitchen asks : Do you find any difference regarding the health down the stream ? No, but two cattle died this year; the people are compelled to go from the doors on account of the odor, and the water is not fit for the cattle to drink.

Dr. Roberts continues : One fault I think in regard to the management of the farm in my estimation is that a certain man is appointed Chairman of the Sewer Committee, and after getting into the working of the farm thoroughly, election comes on and another man is appointed, and the whole thing has to be gone over again ; that is detrimental to the working of the farm.

Mr. Clement asks : In what respect do you think the farm has not been thoroughly worked this year ? It has been better worked this year than before, but result no better, rather worse.

Mr. Abram Cressman stated : I live on the second farm below the sewer farm, about a quarter of a mile from it, and my house is about fifty rods from the creek.

Dr. Bryce asks : Do you notice any odor from the farm at times ? Yes.

When ? When wind is blowing from the west.

At all times of the day ? Generally when the wind comes from that way, a little all the time.

When is there most? In close, foul weather the odor is worse.

I supose you regard it as very disagreeable ? Yes ; sometimes in the night when we have the windows open and screens on, we wake up and notice the smell, and it has caused me to wake up.

Supposing you go down to the creek in the day, do you notice it particularly at that time ? Not any time unless you stir up water and then a little.

Do cattle drink water? Yes, ours do.

Without any noticeable result? Cattle do not seem to do as well as in Wilmot where we had a fresh water creek. Now tell us if you noticed that this smell has been as bad as other smells? Much worse.

In respect to the odors? The state of the creek, color of the water; sometimes it would look like soap-suds, other times a darker color again, always some color.

Is the water very clear ? Sometimes; sometimes cannot see down in water; where we cross the bridge the water is clear, but below sewer farm is not clear.

Before the sewer farm was established I understand the tannery poured their refuse into the creek, was water colored then ? Not like it is now.

Dr. Bryce asks : How long have you been on your farm? I have been there twelve years.

Mr. Clement would like to know whether thickness of water is due to tanbark or to refuse material or filth? Do not think the color wholly due to tannery matter, but due to other substances. This, however, is mostly in winter time that I have seen solids.

Mr. Lehmon Shirk stated : I live about two miles down below Sewer Farm.

Do you notice that the water there is discolored or dirty or filthy more than it should be ? I think it is.

Does the water there have any odor ? Yes.

What kind of a smell; is it like carbolic acid or creasote or like tannery smell or like a smell from a barnyard or what is it like? It smells like sewage.

Have you noticed any particular sickness there? No, not especially

Does the pond rise and fall in season? It is sometimes higher and sometimes lower.

Are there any fish in the creek? Last year there were lots of fish and many came to the surface dead, but there are no signs of fish now.

Is there a deposit on the land that is exposed on the shores of the pond ? Yes, there is; it is of a slimy substance.

When you start the mill in the summer time, is the smell almost unbearable? Yes, it scents the whole mill; it is worst when we start it.

Is the smell same as sewage? Yes. It is far worse in winter time, as there is no escape for the odors. (He never noticed any odor in the flour or wheat.)

Mr. Daniel Weber called : When did you lose cattle ? This summer.

Where do you live ? In German Mills.

You live down stream ? Yes; two miles.

How many cattle did you lose ? Two.

Were they on flats ? Yes.

Drinking creek water ? Yes.

When did they die? One died in July and one in September.

What was the matter with them ? Doctor says anthrax ; comes from sewage, he says.

Was it the spleen of your cow that was sent to Dr. Minchin ? Yes.

Which one died of anthrax ? Last one. They were dead within twenty-four hours after they took sick. Did not see the veterinary after the post-mortem. I had eleven cattle in the field at different times, but have not turned cattle in since two animals died in September. I am afraid to. This is first summer that cattle have died.

To Dr. Bryce I think the first cow was a case of anthrax; the veterinary said so. The spleen was examined by Board of Health, but did not get report from Dr. Bryce ; the second was also sent to Toronto, but no report. I have been bothered with bad color in other years ; this year it is worse; odor is bad when weather is damp, and when wind blows from pond; do not use water for other purposes except for cattle.

Peter Shirk stated : I do not live in neighborhood of creek, but have noticed bad odors from creek in passing along the railway and highway.

SEWAGE PURIFICATION.

By the Committee on Sewerage.

Mr. Chairman and Gentlemen,—Your Committee on Sewerage desires to present a brief report on the present status of the work of sewage disposal as it exists in the Province.

During the last twenty years many special reports on this subject have been prepared, dealing with either the general principles of purification or some special method which has been adopted in some particular instance.

These have ranged from the broad irrigation of lands for growing Italian rye grass to chemical methods for precipitating sewage or electrolytic processes of sterilization with subsequent deposition of sewage.

With the progress of modern ideas relating to the decomposition of organic matter through the agency of nitrifying microbes, the attention of Government and municipal health authorities everywhere has been turned to the study of these biological processes, with the result that on every hand experiments are being carried out or experimental purification plants installed to test the practicability of this natural process for dealing with sewage under all or any conditions which may occur in any town or city.

It will be evident that in this as in any other matter there may be so many varying conditions and climates as regards soils, meteorological conditions, character of the manufacturing processes in the different places, that no hard and fast method can be made suitable to every case.

Probably the greatest immediate difficulty in dealing with the sewage of many of the larger cities lies in the fact that in all of them the sewers first built have been with a view to dealing with storm water as well as with house sewage. However good an end may thus have been served in rapidly removing the water from the streets, it has not wholly served the intended purpose, since in almost every city the main sewers, however large, have at times proved unable to carry away the water in the heaviest rainfalls, thereby causing the flooding of cellars and other damage, but they have created several other objections.

1st. That the cost has greatly delayed the adoption of general sewerage systems.

2nd. That the sewers which during the greater number of days are dry weather sewers, have but a small portion of their area filled with water, and hence are filled with foul air, largely the result of a microbic decomposition.

3rd. That these gases being kept from passing upward through the soil pipes, since few towns have adopted the outside vent to the house sewers, are forced out of the manholes, creating ill-smelling and dangerous nuisances at the street level.

4th. They have enormously increased the difficulty of the problem of dealing with the sewage at the outfalls. In order that the problem of sewage disposal, apart from forcing the sewage into lakes and streams, may be dealt with economically and effectually, it is apparent that it will be necessary to consider how some of these difficulties incident to combined systems may be lessened; while it is apparent that the very necessity for dealing with the sewage in any new plants, will inevitably prevent new towns adopting any but the separate system.

Taking the City of Toronto as our largest city, in which the evils of the combined system exist, it will be apparent that if the traps were taken off the house drains and each allowed to be a ventilator to the sewer, that the removal in this way of sewer air would result in the sewer air being largely replaced by fresh air passing in at the manholes, and at once removing the ill-smelling gases discharged at the feet of the passer-by.

The second, and by far the most immediate necessity, is for checking at once the enormous waste of water by placing a meter on each water service. If by this means the waste of water could be reduced by 50 gallons per head daily, still leaving 50 gallons, or 20 more than is allowed the citizens of most English cities, and a few American ones, it is quite clear that the economy in the cost of pumping would leave an amount which would go far to pay the interest on the expenditure necessary for disposing by some proper system of the sewage at one or more sewage outfalls.

To make the case plain, it is found that the coal consumed in Toronto in 1900 amounted to 12,000 tons at a cost of $38,668.54, or reducing this amount by one-half, there would be enough to pay interest on nearly $750,000 at 3 per cent.

It is simply amazing that year after year such primary principles are neglected. keeping the tax rate high and making it more difficult for the people to proceed to the second point of adopting some adequate scheme of sewage disposal. If in addition in the case of Toronto the amount yearly wasted in dredging the slips were added it is probable that sewage disposal works could be carried on without any outlay greater than that wasted to-day in unnecessary pumping. But this is only the beginning of the economy, for if the amount of sewage passing into the sewers were reduced by 50 per cent. the amount of liquids to be dealt with as sewage would be reduced by one-half.

Proceeding, however, to the problem of sewage disposal, it may at once be said that to-day there are but two methods of sewage disposal being considered anywhere, viz., that of disposal on sewage farms of wide enough extent to enable purification to take place without any local nuisance, and the cultivation of crops to repay in whole or in part the outlay, and that of tanks where the sewage is allowed to decompose, thereby becoming largely liquefied, the liquid containing the organic matter in solution, being subsequently carried to areas of land for purification, cultivation of crops being carried on at the same time; or to make filters of sand, gravel, cinders or coke, there to be purified by aerobes, completing the nitrifying or purifying process during filtra- tion, a series of beds being flooded at regular intervals.

That these methods are practicable may be seen at the experimental station of Lawrence, Mass., where the work has gone on without interruption for 10 years; and in several towns of that State, while in Ontario we have examples of what may be accomplished in the Sewage Farm at the London Asylum for the Insane; at Berlin, at Stratford, and in the works just completed at London.

An illustration of the best which may be expected from chemical filtration can be seen in the costly plant at Hamilton.

Now, what has been said might lead the ordinary reader to conclude that the whole matter is a simple one, and given the necessary preliminary conditions it is com- paratively so. But like any other work the success will depend upon intelligent, sys- tematic and continuous attention to details. For instance, in the Sewage Farm at Berlin neither of two necessary conditions has up to the present time existed. First the soil utilized for the sewage farm is a calcareous clay, although the location of the farm is such that all the sewage can be carried there by gravity, and, second, it can scarcely be said to have been managed at all the farm having for ten years passed from the supervision of one chairman of committee to another, with the result that each usually managed to undo much that his predecessor had learned to do from ex- perience. No records have been systematically kept and no intelligible history of the farm is obtainable.

And yet much has been learned of what ought not to be done and something of what must be done.

On the other hand, at the London Asylum there has been the same management under the superintendent, a gentleman of highest intelligence and unusual executive ability, with a farm foreman, the same for 12 years. As a result the sewage farm, irrigated by the sewage from a population or village of 1,200, produced in 1900 a gross revenue of nearly $2,000.00, the amount of land used being about 6 acres. It is pro- bable that no where in the world can be found results greatly superior.

With these two illustrations it might be thought that everything depends on soil and management. These are undoubtedly large factors, but in practice it is found that the problem is by no means as simple as this. For instance, taking the town of Berlin as an example, it is found that the contents of the sewage of manufacturing towns vary notably from that of house sewage alone.

In that case tarry products from the gasworks escape into the sewers with their germicidal qualities, the lime and tannin, and the arsenic, etc., used as preservatives, from tanneries, being also allowed to go directly to the sewers; the sulphur compounds from the rubber works being further added to these other constituents, while the dyes from several kinds of manufactories complete the germicidal materials which go to the septic tanks.

In other towns, as for instance, Worcester, Mass., the sewage at certain hours is so distinctly acid that a trained attendant is required to add from time to time such amounts of alkalies as are necessary to neutralize the acid sewage.

Clearly then the question of sewage disposal is one requiring (a) a thorough practical knowledge of the engineering, geological and agricultural conditions likely to be most suitable to any given conditions; (b) an equally intelligent knowledge of the chemical and biological conditions necessary to keep the sewage in any given case in a condition most favorable for a rapid and natural decomposition by biological pro- cesses, and (c) a consecutiveness of thought and purpose in the oversight and manage- ment, so that the trained operator will learn thoroughly at least one particular plant, so that economy in management with a maximum of good results may legitimately be expected.

The municipal council, however, which by law is required to adopt such means as will prevent the pollution of the adjacent stream by its sewage, may very naturally ask, How are they to be expected to be equal to such things ? The answer of the law is that the means of abatement must be found by the person who creates the nuisance. It might further be said that a town should not erect industries until they know that they can prevent them from becoming nuisances.

All these answers might equally be given with regard to methods for dealing with contagious diseases, and perhaps with more reason since there are some 2,500 trained physicians in the Province supposed to know all about how to deal with smallpox and other diseases. But as a matter of fact the Government, through this Board, gives constant and great service to municipalities through its officers and laboratory, and there can surely be no logical reason why, if it can be found practicable, in the more difficult and complex biological and chemical problem we are considering, some assistance should not be given, both to improve works already established and to advise in the operation of new works, which with our rapidly growing industries must from year to year be instituted.

The coming year is likely to see the work taken up in three or four cities, smaller towns will be introducing sewerage, and your committee feels that a great step forward in the Board's work would be gained if the Board were placed in a position, first, to gain for itself all the available knowledge as to the methods being adopted elsewhere in working out these problems to a successful issue, and thereafter to give our cities the benefit of our knowledge.

All of which is respectfully submitted,

P. H. BRYCE.

E. E. KITCHEN.

W. J. DOUGLAS.

REPORT ON THE EXTENSION OF THE SEWERAGE SYSTEM OF AMHERSTBURG.

By the Committee on Sewerage.

To the Chairman and Members of the Provincial Board of Health :

. Gentlemen,—Your Committee on Sewerage begs leave to report as follows on the proposed extension of the sewerage system of Amherstburg.

It will be remembered that in the report of 1900 the sanitary condition of Amherstburg was reported upon and the evils associated with undrained cellars were then pointed out. It was further indicated how, by a proper intercepting sewer being carried down Main street to a point well below the waterworks. the sewage might with safety be allowed to discharge into the river.

The proposed sewers then referred to were approved. and are found very satisfactory. It is now proposed to extend the system by constructing a lateral sewer along Rankin street to discharge into the main sewer.

The town is flat, and it is desirable that sewers be utilized directly, or with tiles laid in the same trenches for subsoil and cellar drainage.

The report of last year approved of the sewerage extension on condition that a plumbing by-law be adopted, and put in operation by the Town Council

Your Committee now recommend approval of the present proposed extension of the sewer along Rankin street. under the same conditions as attached to the approval of the plans in the matter of the Dalhousie street sewer.

All of which is respectfully submitted.

(Signed)   PETER H. BRYCE, M.D.

E. E. KITCHEN. M.D.

REPORT OF COMMITTEE ON SEWER EXTENSIONS IN PARIS.

By Dr. E. E. Kitchen, for Committee.

To the Chairman and Members of the Provincial Board of Health :

Gentlemen,—Your Committee visited the Town of Paris on August 2nd to examine into the proposed new sewer, which is to be built on Main stret, and will be used largely for the new buildings on this street, which have been erected during the past few months to take the place of those destroyed by the great fire of last year. The representative of your committee was met by Dr. Dunton, the very efficient Medical Health Officer, and Messrs. Brown & Patterson, members of the Local Board, and Mr. John Kay, the contractor.

The following facts have been learned and are now tabulated the better to enable you to understand the case :

1st. Paris is a town of about 3,000 inhabitants, divided into upper, lower and station districts, but under one municipal council.

2nd. The town has already a private sewer, from the Arlington Hotel, running down William street into the Grand River. Also the sewage of the public school back of the hotel runs into this sewer.

3rd. The proposed sewer is 365 feet long and extends down the centre of Main street, intercepting the Arlington Hotel sewer, and terminates in the centre of the Mill Race. It will be built 12 feet deep, and consist of 15-inch salt glazed pipe.

This main sewer will not only receive the sewage from the Arlington 9-inch-pipe sewer, but also from 15 stores along on either side. Perhaps by the time the sewer is laid down this number may be increased to 20.

Of these 15 connections 8 will be made of 6 and 8 inch pipe and will enter the main sewer at an acute angle, while the remaining 7 will be of 6-inch pipe, and will enter the lateral sewers before they reach the main sewer.

5. The Race (Mill) is a covered archway, reaching across the street, and through its walls the main sewer will be carried about 8 feet to its middle. This race is supplied by Smith's Creek, a branch of the Grand River, which supplies power for the electric lighting, etc., owned by the town, after its discharge at the wheel. On the day of visit it was running swiftly and about 1 1-2 feet deep. When the wheel is in operation I was told it would be 2 feet deep.

6th. The storm water on William street is discharged into the Grand River by a sub-sewer and a surface sewer, while Main street is discharged into 'the Mill Race by a surface sewer. .

7th. The sewer will be flushed by the fire hose, the town having a large and splendid water supply, with great force.

8th. This change of Arlington sewer into Main sewer will largely reduce the great nuisance at present caused by the discharge into the river at the bridge.

9th. Calculating that 100 people on Main sewer and 50 at hotel and 150 pupils at school, in all 300 people will be making use of this sewer, and that each person will use 100 gallons daily, the maximum amount and 3-10ths of a pound of organic matter, it will be seen that the amount of sewage going into the fast-running Mill Race (covered) and passing into the river will not be such as to create a local nuisance.

In view of the above facts your committee would recommend the approval of the plan of the proposed sewer and extension. They would likewise recommend that the approval of the Board be made conditional upon the adoption by the Town of Paris of the model plumbing by-law, such as that set forth in the pamphlet published by the Provincial Board of Health in 1897. It must also be understood that so soon as dangers from pollution of the river are evident the Town Council as a condition of this approval must take such steps to prevent such pollution by filtration or otherwise of the sewage as will meet the views of the Board.

All of which is respectfully submitted.   E. E. KITCHEN.

6 H.

REPORT ON THE SEWERAGE SYSTEM OF THE TOWN OF COBOURG.

By the Committee on Sewerage.

To the Chairman and Members of the Provincial Board of Health :

Gentlemen,—Your committee on sewerage begs to report on the proposed sewerage system of the Town of Cobourg. It will be perceived from the plans that a number of old sewers have, from time to time, been constructed dealing with a limited amount of sewage. The council now propose to complete the sewerage of the town by constructing a general system of separate sewers to discharge by a common outfall into the harbor.

The problem to be considered by your committee is whether such an amount of sewage can be safely discharged into the harbor, first, so as to create no local nuisance or serious filling of the harbor; and, second, whether the deposit of such sewage into a harbor such as that shown on the map is likely to be dangerous through contamination of the town water supply.

Your committee assumes that the sewage from a town of 10,000 must ultimately be dealt with, which, assuming that 7,000 population is sewering to the main outlet would mean that about 1,200 pounds of organic matter would be discharged daily into the harbor, and about as much more inorganic matter. While in practice it is found that the organic matter rapidly decomposes and comparatively little of such deposit tends to accumulate, yet the mineral matter might after some years require that the harbor be dredged.

This does not become a serious matter from the standpoint of health. The real question at issue is what dangers to the public will result from pouring such an amount of sewage into the end of a harbor protected by a breakwater for 1,000 feet, from carrying the sewage toward the intake of the waterpipe. Your committee is of the opinion that, owing to the position of the outlet of the harbor, as regards the intake pipe of the waterworks, that in the nature of things the element of danger from the direct current of sewage being carried direct to the waterpipe is largely obviated, since a southwest wind will hold the water in the basin and a northwest wind will carry the sewage out into the lake. But the danger would to some extent be present if a northwest wind, blowing for a time thereby carrying the water from the basin out into the lake, veered to the southwest, thereby carrying sewage, possibly to the waterpipe. Of course, its diffusion and dilution would probably in such case be very great, but this, as proven by experience, cannot always be depended on.

Your committee, therefore, while not convinced that any practical danger will for the present, not perhaps for years, arise from the drinking water being polluted with sewage, would approve of the disposal of the town sewage in the basin or harbor, through a pipe carried into deep water with the express provisos :

1st. That at any time when the Provincial Board of Health is convinced, through evidence gained from the outbreak of typhoid or other water-borne disease or from, analysis, of the pollution of the town water supply the town will be prepared to adopt such measures as will purify the sewage or take the water supply from such point as will be free from the danger of pollution.

2nd. That a model plumbing by-law be adopted by the town as a condition of approval of the sewerage system.

All of which is respectfully submitted.

P. H. BRYCE.

E. E. KITCHEN.

THE SEWAGE DISPOSAL OF SUBURBAN HOUSES AND PUBLIC INSTITUTIONS.

By Dr. P. H. Bryce, M.A., M.D., Secretary.*

To the President and Members of the Ontario Architects' Association :

Gentlemen,—It gives me pleasure in complying with your invitation to prepare a paper on some sanitary problem connected with your work, to present a paper on the title indicated, as being of extreme importance, connected as it is directly with the problem of "Pure Air in Houses," which I discussed before you last year.

As we are well aware, there is a more or less marked difference in the air of country places and of towns and cities, indicated by a small excess of carbonic acid (Co2) in the latter and the absence of ozone, or oxygen in a nascent condition, due to the excessive presence in towns and cities of organic matters on the surface, in houses, lanes, manure heaps, drains and so on, constantly undergoing decay or reduction to simple compounds by the action of various living organisms, especially bacteria, which utilize oxygen in their biological processes. Sometimes they find this oxygen in the organic compound itself, especially in the azotic or nitrogenous compounds, but also in the carbon compounds of a starchy character; in other and under ordinary circumstances, they utilize the oxygen free in the air. As will be supposed, there are different species or classes of this minute form of largely vegetable life, some of which do not thrive in free oxygen and air and some forms which live within the bodies of animals and external to them in free air as well.

To the first class Pasteur long ago gave the name an-aerobes or microbes living apart from air, and the second he called aerobes or those which require free oxygen for their development.

The two classes have properties differing more or less from one another, one especially peculiar to an-aerobes being the liquefying of organic compounds by growing into these and really dissociating their solids, as, for instance, gelatine, forming, of course, by-products during the process both of gaseous and liquid character. The constitution of these chemical compounds varies; that of the gases being principally Co2, H2O, H2S, and many highly organized volatile compounds, such as those given off by the breath of man and animals, those from the many foods and fruits, which develop during their mellowing and decay, and especially the extremely unpleasant emanations given off from putrefying meat, fish and the solid wastes, which pass off to the sewers as excreta, and kitchen and house wastes of every sort. It is a fortunate fact that the products of aerobic decomposition are less disagreeable and injurious than those from an-aerobic decay, since such are those which are most constantly exposed to air from surface decomposition of outside matter everywhere. With these preliminary remarks it will be easy to see something of the nature of the problem to be dealt with in disposing, safely and conveniently of the house wastes which go by the name of sewage, or those matters which are conveyed by water into underground pipes or sewers.

It is the experience of every local health officer, and a source of constant difficulty to the Provincial Board of Health,that in those towns where a sewerage system does not exist and in many houses in the suburbs of towns, even where such systems are, in rural districts and in the large temporary summer resorts, hotels and cottages, the problem of what to do with excretal matters, both animal and vegetable, has been everywhere, if not difficult, yet the most constant one which the local boards have to deal with in the matter of nuisances, and which in many cases proves the most constant danger to the household immediately interested, and where streams or lakes are polluted, not unfrequently has become the occasion of some sudden and serious outbreak of typhoid fever or diarrhoeal disease. The fact that 253 examinations of water were made during the past season by the Provincial Health laboratory shows that the causal relationship between polluted water and typhoid and diarrhoea

*Paper read at the Annual Convention of the Ontario Architects' Association.

Is well recognized, and general observation, as well as laboratory work is quite agreed as to the direct connection between such pollution and some accumulation of decomposits of animal or vegetable matter.   Privy vaults, deep pits, or cesspools, constant contamination of the area around the house pump with kitchen washings and slops of every kind, hotel stables and barnyards, soakage from slaughter houses, the wastes from cheese factories and creameries and the heaps of refuse from canning factories, and indeed every kind of manufactory in which organic products are used, may become direct means of pollution to wells and sources of public water, and many are moreover the cause of serious injury to health from their creating effluvium nuisances.

Now, perhaps, gentlemen, as it may be only occasionlly that as architects you are called upon to deal with more than one of these sources of ill-health, viz., this one of the disposal of house sewage, including excreta, kitchen and chamber wastes, in places where there are no public sewers, it is most essential than some general principles should be laid down and acted upon with a view to the safe, economical and aesthetic method of disposing of such organic wastes.

Probably every one here accepts the theory that in the economy of nature nothing can be lost, or that matter is indestructible, and perhaps all will, in a general way, agree that whatever is yielded by the soil, as, for instance, the potash, phosphates, ammonia and so on, which are contained in the grains and other fruits of the earth, should be given back to Mother Earth for her goodness to us.   So in spite of man's foolish waste and ignorance, they ultimately are returned to her, but at an enormous cost of time and energy.   Carried to the sea, sewage will form deposits ultimately forming new land, or in solution will become the food of microscopic vegetable forms of many species of the deeper ocean planton and of the larger plants of the ocean littoral, which in turn become the food of the microscopic infusoria and fiually the food of fishes, molluscs and other sea animals, and so is brought back finally as food to man.   Were we intelligent and careful we would see to it that not a single pound of organic waste matter is allowed to decompose out of its place, in other words, to so act as to return to the earth every ounce of C, H, O and N, which taken from the humus or upper layer of soil is year by year being used up by cultivation and must be returned there, if fertility of the soil is to be maintained.

As, however, it is found in practice in most parts of this country that there is a lack of appreciation of the manureal value of such materials, and that the adoption of what is known as the dry-earth system in houses and institutions has not proved free from objection, owing to neglect to supervise it carefully, owing to its cumbersomeness, and as, moreover, it does not do away with either the need for water pipes and a supply of water being laid on in the better houses, or of the need for disposing of the kitchen and chamber wastes, in any case it is evident that the growing appreciation of modern conveniences in houses is demanding some systematic method for dealing with all house wastes, whether for kitchen or closet by the water-carriage system.

I propose, therefore, to indicate how in practice such a system may be established, at once efficient and economical.   In the Annual Report of the 'Provincial Board of Health for 1898 a chapter is devoted to "The Biological Principles Involved in the Purification of Sewage," which to those interested will be found to contain a very full discussion of the scientific principles of this whole matter.   There will be found a table giving the average analysis of town sewage.   While probably less concentrated than the sewage of a single house, since it would contain water from factories, from sub-soil drainage and so on, yet it will very well serve as an illustration of the contents of sewage.   It is as follows :

(1) Solid matters in suspension—

     (a) Organic.. .. ..20 Grains per gallon.
     (b) Mineral.. 10   "   "

                                               —
       Total 30   "   "

(2) Solid matter in solution—
(a) Organic.. ... ...20 grains per gallon.
(b) Mineral.. ... ...50　　"　　"

　　　Total ......·..... ... .70　　"　　"

Or expressed in parts to 1,000,000 such a sewage would yield :

Total Solids.	Solids in Suspension.	Chloridne.	Free Ammonia.	Albumenoid Ammonia
1,428.0 parts	428.0 parts	120.0	50.0 parts	10.0 parts

Assuming what is in experience ample, 20 gallons per head per diem of sewage, it will appear that for an ordinary dwelling with 10 inmates, with a water supply laid on, there will have to be disposed of daily 200 gallons. By reference to the analysis it is clear that half the organic matter, or that in suspension, could easily be removed by any crude filtering method, as by a screen, a grit chamber or even by passage over coke or some readily destroyed material, should it become clogged.

Assuming, however, that all the materials are carried to a common receptacle or tank at the end of the house sewer, there will be deposited daily 8,000 grains of organic matter, whether suspended or in solution, and 12,000 grains of mineral matter or altogether some 3 pounds, of which two-fifths is organic, or is capable of undergoing decomposition, most of which will gradually be carried away when dissolved in the 200 gallons of water daily passing into the receptacle, the balance of carbon gradually being deposited in the tank. Of the mineral matter 50 parts are in solution, as potash, lime and other salts, which will likewise be carried away in the water. It thus appears that some 100 grains of insoluble mineral matter will deposit in the tank daily with small amounts of carbon, or in 365 days for such a household not more than 10 pounds of mineral matters will have accumulated. That such is true may readily be proved by anyone caring to make the experiment, as I have done, that such a tank at the end of a year has not had a total deposit of solid matter, greater than can be held in a half-bushel measure. If the balance, then, after decomposition, is capable of being carried along with the 200 gallons of water daily, it is clear that nearly all of it is capable, like any other soluble material, of soaking away into the soil with the water, if the conditions are favorable.

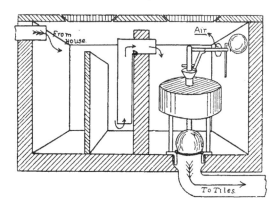

I have had drawn up for your inspection the diagram of a tank, which is intended to deal with such materials in a way to give the organic matter an opportunity to decompose, the water carrying the soluble materials, being gradually removed from the decomposing tank, which we may call the septic tank—the word septic meaning putrid or decomposing—to a second tank, whence it may be discharged by a simple apparatus, at such intervals as may be found practical to produce the best results. The question then arises: In what manner can we dispose of this organic matter in solution, conveniently and in such a way as will not create a surface nuisance, or a pollution of ground water ?   Let us assume that by a series of sub-surface tiles, laid in a proper manner, we can distribute the 200 gallons over an equal number of feet of surface.   It is plain that each square foot would receive 1 gallon of water daily.   As soils vary in their capacity for water, from a coarse sand which will hold in its inter-stices not more than 25 per cent. of its volume of water, to a tenacious clay which holds 75 per cent. of its own volume of water, it is apparent that if one gallon of water were poured on the surface of a cubic foot of dry soil, there would not be any water leaking away from the bottom of even a coarse sand, since a cubic foot of water equals 6.25 gallons; so that it requires 1 1-2 gallons to be poured on such foot of dry sand before it begins to drain away from the bottom.   A dry clay would hold three times as much before it began to leak.   In practice it will be seen that two four-inch tiles, laid side by side, would distribute such water fairly well over the surface of a cubic foot of earth; and also that the water contained in them soaking out of the open joints and pores of the tiles would rapidly dispose of the small amount of water received by each tile daily.   In practice it is found that in any ordinary porous sandy soil or sandy loam, tiles filled twice daily will rapidly dispose of the charge of soluble sew-age poured into them; and, lifting up tiles after several years' use I have found them lined only with a fine stain of black carbon, the volume of the tile not being mater-ially lessened.   I have further found that even heavy clay soils with an occasional underdrain have been quite adequate to dispose of the amount of sewage poured into them from an institution of 125 inmates.

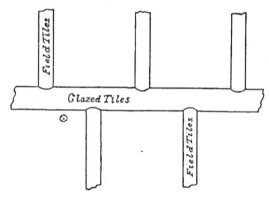

It may be proper now to briefly describe the method of construction of such a system of tanks and sub-surface tiles. As in any system of house sewerage it is con-venient to arrange all the fixtures so as to discharge into one soil pipe. These being brought out beneath the ground floor through the foundation, or, if the house be on a hillside, it may occasionally be possible to bring them out under the cellar floor so that the washtubs there may be discharged into them—if this unsanitary place for the laundry be adopted—the soil-pipe will be led to the top of a tank made of brick and cement in a manner similar to that shown in the diagram.   If most convenient, this tank can be built directly against the house to save iron pipe and to prevent its ap-pearance on the lawn, since, as will be seen in a moment, it is necessary that the dis-charge pipe of the tank on level ground be not more than a foot beneath the surface. The capacity of this tank in the case we are discussing will be such as to hold in each compartment 100 gallons, to be discharged twice daily.   It will be seen therefore that a compartment 2 x 3 x 3 feet will nicely hold 100 gallons, or a tank of interior measure-ment 4 feet long by 3 wide and 3 deep is adequate for two compartments each hold-ing 100 gallons.

The arrangement of the interior of the tank is shown in the diagram. As in all sewage tanks, the plan is adopted of having several divisions, the sewage becoming less dense as it passes from one to the other, thereby aiding to make that discharged from the valve chamber as thoroughly liquid as possible.

It will be seen that from compartment No. 1 to No. 2 the fluids are drawn off by an overflow pipe from about midway beneath the surface since at the bottom will be found sediment, while the whole surface is covered with the decomposing matter, which appears to the eye a solid mass, but is really the organic material kept floating by the contained gases of decomposition. The liquids, which pass over of course contain a large amount of organic matter in solution, being composed especially of ammonia (NH3) and carbonic acid (CO2) combined as ammonium carbonate with the sulphur compounds as ammonium sulphide. These are held in the second compartment until 100 gallons have accumulated, at which moment the flush valve operates automatically and discharges in a minute or two the contents of the tank into the sub-surface tiles. It is apparent that the size of the tanks may be made such as to deal with 1,000 gallons quite as readily as with a 100.

The sewage thus discharged must, it is evident, be carried to tiles so laid that each tile will get its own share of sewage and no more. It is apparent that with a rapid discharge the tiles laid on an exact level will each receive this amount, if together they hold exactly 100 gallons, provided the air which is in them be displaced. It is found in practice that in a loose soil the air from tiles laid near the surface readily gives place to the water, if discharged under the head in the tank. Where the soil is level, as of a lawn or garden, it is apparent that the matter is a simple one. If on a slope it is equally apparent that some careful detail work will be necessary in order that the tiles may, at the same time, be kept at the same depth beneath the surface and also receive each its own share of sewage. To complete the description of the tank it is apparent that as some gases, in excess of what are in solution, may be given off into the space over the sewage, it will be necessary to prevent them from accumulating and forcing themselves through the cover of the tank. This is obtained by making the cover of rough boards, and if thought proper they may again be covered with earth and sod. The gases, if any pass outward, will be absorbed by the soil. In addition to this, however, it is necessary to provide for the ventilation of the tank. This is done by a 4-inch goose-neck leading from the distal end of the tank, which admits cold fresh air and thus will displace the warm gases of decomposition which are carried up through the soil pipe to be discharged above the roof as in ordinary house plumbing in cities where the separate sewerage system is in operation. It may be asked, what ultimately becomes of the organic matter carried away in solution ? In reply I would say that through the action of the microbes of the soil the ammonia salts are rapidly nitrified—that is, are changed into nitrates or nitric acid, which at once combines with the lime and potash salts of the soil and thus has become a neutral salt in a condition to act as plant food for the grass or vegetables growing above it.

The following table by W. D. Scott Moncreiff, from the Ashstead, England, experiments, 1895, illustrates the change : —

. Effluent from cultivation tank.

Chlorine	Free N H 3	N. Oxygen.	Consumed	Nitric Nitrogen	Total Oxidized N	Total N of all 'kinds
9.0	12.5	10.3	9,843	0.12	0.12	12.46

From final filter tray after complete nitrification.

| 7.5 | 0.25 | 0.2 | 0.58 | 9.0 | 9.0 | 0.6 |

As the tank arrangement from which these experiments are taken was essentially a tank of this kind, except that, instead of the microbes of the earth to do the work Moncreiff had arranged a series of artificial filters holding pieces of coke over which the sewage from the septic tank flowed, by which means the liquids for anyalsis could be obtained, there is nothing different in principle to the system we are discussing.

Little more need be said, I think, to make it clear that in these results of the study of biological processes, which convert oxganic matter back to its original constituents, we have not only a practical lesson of how to apply science to our every day needs and convenience, but we may also see how economical is Nature and how wholly wise in her operations if she does not have man attempting in his ignorance to violate some of her primary laws. To me it daily seems more true, the more that I try to comprehend the meaning of the process of Nature in this fine old world of ours:

> "That nothing walks with aimless feet,   .
> That not one life shall be destroyed,
> Or cast as rubbish to the void
> When God hath made the pile complete."

REPORT OF COMMITTEE ON POISONS.

By J. J. Cassidy, M.D.

Toronto, January 9, 1902.

To the Chairman and Members of the Provincial Board of Health.

Gentlemen,—In the December, 1901, number of the Canadian Journal of Medicine and Surgery editorial notice was given of bulletin No. 76 from the Inland Revenue Department,Ottawa, which gives analyses of 100 specimens of canned salmon, collected in June, 1900, at different parts of the Dominion. The chemist of the Inland Revenue Department examined for evidences of mineral poisoning, and did not make any search for ptomains. It is satisfactory to learn from the bulletin that the proportions of lead or other metal found in the samples of fish analysed were so small that symptoms of poisoning could not have been caused by minerals.

Symptoms of poisoning from the dietetic use of canned salmon do, however, occur, and so accurate an observer as Professor Vaughan of Ann Arbor University, has reported a case in his book entitled Ptomains, Leucomains, Toxins and Antitoxins, 1896, p. 56, which shows that a healthy man after eating canned salmon was affected with gastro-enteritis, and that a subsequent examination of the incriminated fish revealed a micrococcus present in great numbers. This organism, grown for twenty days on a sterilized egg, produced a most potent poison. The white became thin, making markedly alkaline and ten drops sufficed to kill white rats.

According to Mr. MacFarlane, who prepared bulletin 76, the number of cases of disease apparently attributable to the use of tinned goods would average about 138 per annum in the whole of Canada. The total number of cases which terminated fatally amounted to fifteen in the above-mentioned average period. In conversation with Dr. J. J. Mackenzie, late bacteriologist of this Board, he expressed the opinion that if proper assistance were supplied to your present bacteriologist he could make examinations when required, of such samples of tinned fish as might be considered causative of illness, viz., gastro-enteritis. A medical health officer may not be consulted at all on such a case of illness ; the ordinary medical attendant may not order an analysis, and when the question comes under the notice of the legal authorities an examination is out of the question as the suspected fish has been thrown away. I think that in cases of this kind it is the duty of the medical attendant to secure a sample of the suspected fish. Owing to the wide area of territory affected, including the Province, we think such examinations should be made in the laboratory of the Provincial Board of Health.

Respectfully submitted.

J. J. CASSIDY.
E. E. KITCHEN.

PART III.

ANNUAL REPORTS OF MEDICAL HEALTH OFFICERS OF CITIES.

SUMMARIZED REPORTS OF COUNTIES BY MUNICIPALITIES.

BRANTFORD.

REPORT OF DR. F. G. E. PEARSON, MEDICAL HEALTH OFFICER, FOR YEAR 1901.

To the Chairman and Members of the Local Board of Health :

Gentlemen,—I herein submit to you a report of the sanitary conditon of the city for the year ending October 31, 1901.

MORTUARY STATISTICS.

As the death rate is the principal indication of the health of a community, I am pleased to note that as far as we are concerned the death rate for the past twelve months is the lowest for a number of years, viz., 219 deaths (exclusive of still births), which, in a population of 16,685, give a rate of 13.18 per thousand. Among the causes are found : Typhoid fever, 10, three of which are from last year's cases; scarlet fever. 1; diphtheria, 1; cholera infantum, 4; pneumonia, 12; tuberculosis, 24; menengitis, 2; all other causes, 165.

CONTAGIOUS DISEASES

Taking into consideration the total number of this class of diseases for the sanitary year. viz., 136 cases, with 12 deaths, 3 of which deaths were, as above stated, from cases included in last year's report, it is my pleasant duty to state that it is the lowest record for the past eight years, and, compared with last year. when 216 cases and 15 deaths occurred, I think the showing very satisfactory.

SMALLPOX.

During the past summer it became the onerous duty of this Board to deal with an outbreak of smallpox, which at first threatened to be of a serious character, but from which we escaped with 17 cases and no fatalities, although a number of them were of a rather serious type. In this limited number I think we have been fortunate, when it is considered that infection was first launched in one of the large manufacturing concerns of the city, where between five and six hundred fellow employees became exposed, and again. infection was not confined to a single source, for no less than nine distinct centres had to be controlled. while at the same time certain cases supposed to be convalescing from chicken-pox, had freely mingled with the public before detected. These cases, as with all the others, were promptly isolated, premises disinfected, and as far as possible those exposed vaccinated and quarantined, but not before possible danger had occurred. Among other difficulties that we met with was the fact that lapse of time had bred a feeling of security from smallpox. Vaccination, the most potent preventive against it, had been neglected, and scepticism had grown up, so that even with the disease in our midst it was with great difficulty, unaided by compulsory vaccination, that we accomplished as much as we did, and there yet remains a large number unvaccinated. who, as far as smallpox is concerned, are not a protected community, therefore it is inevitable so long as this state of affairs remains that we cannot rest secure from possible re-occurrences of the disease.

Before leaving the subject I wish merely to give a couple of observations from our late outbreak, viz., Among all the cases occurring there was but one who could show a typical vaccination scar, and this was over fifteen years old. Again, the virtues of vaccination were demonstrated where, in a family of seven persons, three unvaccinated all developed the disease, after which the other four, who were vaccinated. were allowed to mingle freely with those infected, even eating and sleeping together, yet not one of them contracted the disease.

Typhoid Fever.

During the last year the total number of cases of typhoid reported was 67, with seven deaths, the lowest record for the past four years, and as compared with last year, when 112 cases and nine deaths were reported, is, I am sure, a very satisfactory decrease. Thus, without going into the causative factors of this disease more than to state that impure drinking water and defective sewerage are the most important. I will note the proportion of cases from the various water supplies, viz., city 17, wells 29, city and wells 21, while, as in preceding years, we found that repeated tests demonstrate the purity of the city supply and the impurity of the wells. Therefore, I would urge this Board to follow up the action already begun, and section by section abolish all wells; at the same time a general extension of the sewerage system should be gone on with, all of which has been outlined in previous reports.

Scarlet Fever.

With this disease it is gratifying to report that we have had but 22 cases, with one death, as compared with 59 cases in the year preceding.

Diphtheria.

As with the other contagious disease of the past year, diphtheria has been kept down to a very low record, but four cases, with one death, occurring.

Of measles, chickenpox, etc., we have had but 36 cases, with no fatalities.

Milk Supply.

Among other things, the milk supply has received special attention, and it is gratifying to know that the purity and butterfat are maintained at a good standard, while the stables, etc., for the most part, are well kept and ventilated.

Garbage System.

Before concluding his report I wish to call your attention again to the absolute need of a practical garbage system, and which I hope will be in operation before another year. Another matter which should receive your attention is the need of having the Isolation Hospital finished and made habitable for patients.

Laboratory.

For the past two or three years I have called your attention to the necessity of having in connection with the office a well equipped bacteriological laboratory, upon the needs of which I think you will all agree, and hope that some effort will be made towards its establishment at once.

All of which I submit for your consideration. I am, your obedient servant,

F. G. E. PEARSON, M.H.O.

BELLEVILLE.

REPORT OF DR. R. TRACY MEDICAL HEALTH OFFICER, FOR YEAR 1901.

To the Chairman and Members of the Local Board of Health :

Gentlemen,—The sanitary state of the city for the past year has been fairly good. In all there have been 165 cases of scarlet fever, of a mild type, no deaths; diphtheria, no cases; whooping cough, 13, 1 death; croop, 1 case, 1 death; typhoid fever, 7, all cases contracted outside city limits, with 2 deaths; measles, almost an epidemic, with no deaths; tuberculosis, not reported, but 12 deaths reported; smallpox, no cases, but we had a suspected case in March, which was at once quarantined, and the whole family at once vaccinated; all danger having passed in a fortnight, the quarantine removed, and no further danger; the man, I may say, had been working in a shanty north, which made the case look more suspicious. The son was the party affected, but all appearance of rash disappeared in five (5) days, leaving no marks, and he took from vaccination, so I considered all danger passed and removed quarantine. Improvements are gradually being made in our sewerage system and water supply, which will have a good effect on the health of the city. Milk vendors have been carefully looked after, and tests as to quality made during the season. The quality of the milk has much improved since, and milk of the very best quality is being sold to our citizens. The inspectors have carefully looked after the privy pit, yards, byres and cellars, inspection at various times during the summer having been made. I am keeping a careful lookout for any suspected case of smallpox now that cold weather has set in, and the Board has a house that can be got on short notice for any such case, but I trust we will not require one. I have tried to get the School Board to compel each child to produce a certificate of successful vaccination before being admitted to school, but so far have not succeeded, but I shall continue to press the point.

R. TRACY, M.D., M.H.O.

KINGSTON.

CHAIRMAN'S ANNUAL REPORT FOR YEAR 1901.

Gentlemen,—In accordance with the provisions of the Board of Health Act, I beg to report as follows :

1. I acknowledge the compliment paid me in including me as a member of the Board of Health for the year 1901.

2. Associated with His Worship the Mayor and Medical Health Officer, I attended the conference held at Ottawa in February last, under the Presidency of His Excellency the Governor-General on the subject of tuberculosis.

3. The conference was attended by medical practitioners and members of Provincial and Local Boards of Health from all parts of Canada, and undoubted benefits will result in time from the deliberations and discussions which took place.

4. Three points were distinctly and forcibly made : 1. That consumption or tuberculosis is communicable; 2. that it is not hereditary; 3, that in early stages it is curable.

5. The ravages of this plague will be understood when it is known that in Canada alone one-fifth of the mortality is attributable to consumption. During the last year between 7,000 and 8,000 of the deaths which occurred were traceable to this dire disease, and in the United States for the same period, 170,000.

6. In some parts of Canada, and very near us, smallpox broke out. Your Board of Health most anxiously strove in the performance of their duties to accomplish two definite objects : (1) To adopt the statutory and prescribed remedies, namely, vaccination and isolation; and (2) to guard against any unnecessary alarm.

7. When it is reflected upon that the presence of one patient in our city tainted with smallpox would entail a necessary expenditure of about $1,000, the economic portion of our citizens especially must feel grateful that we have been spared this visitation.

8. Your Board, in their anxiety to prove equal to any emergency, which might unfortunately arise, made energetic efforts to procure the disused Military Hospital, in the adjoining Township of Pittsburgh, to be fitted up for patients. The Council of the Township of Pittsburgh were visited by myself, and humanely gave permission to the Board of Health to use it for the purpose.

The Government, however, through the Military Department, refused to grant permission.

I would strongly recommend that renewed efforts be made to procure that building.

It is the most suitable that can possibly be obtained, and it is so situated as to preclude all possibility of contagion.

9. I append copies of the reports furnished by our Health Officer during the present year, from which it will be observed that the health of our city is in a satisfactory condition.

(Signed) JOHN McINTYRE.

Dated 30th November, 1901.

Summary of contagious fever cases reported to November 14, 1901.

Months.	Typhoid fever.	Diphtheria.	Scarlet fever.	Memb. croup.	Measles.	Total.
January	2	3	14			17
February	1	6	17			24
March	1	1	19			21
April			17	1		18
May			7			7
June			4		1	5
July	2					2
August	6	1	2			9
September	12	2	1	1		16
October	4	5	6			15
November		1	3			4
Aggregate	28	19	88	2	1	138

HAMILTON.

REPORT OF DR. W. F. LANGRILL, MEDICAL HEALTH OFFICER, FOR YEAR 1901.

To the Chairman and Members of the Local Board of Health :

Gentlemen,—I have the honor to herewith submit to you the annual report of the Health Department for the year ending October 31st, 1901.

There were reported 428 cases of infectious disease of all classes. Of these 93 were diphtheria, with 25 deaths, a mortality of 26 4-5 per cent.; 58 were typhoid fever, with ten deaths, a mortality of 17 1-4 ; 88 were scarlet fever, with four deaths, a mortality of 4 1-2 per cent. These percentages of deaths are unduly high, as mild cases are not always reported. There have been more cases of typhoid fever in the city than the register shows as 71 have been treated at the City Hospital alone. Hitherto some physicians have not known that the law required them to report cases of typhoid. I have endeavored to remedy this. It is not necessary to placard where typhoid exists, but a thorough inspection of the premises should be made to discover if possible if there be a pre-disposing cause in unsanitary environment, and have it removed. It is also desirable that all cases of true typhoid fever should be reported as a test of the purity of water supplied the city. A familiar quotation has been paraphrased thus: "Show me a city's statistics of typhoid fever and I will tell you the character of its water supply." Pure water and a high typhoid rate are quite incompatible. In a work by Mr. John W. Hill on "The Purification of Public Water Supplies," a list of 68 cities in Europe and America is given, stating the source of supply and death rate in 1896 from typhoid per 100,000 population. They range from Amsterdam and Munich, with a rate of three deaths per 100,000 to St. Petersburg, with a rate of 142 . The rate for Hamilton this year per 100,000 is 18.5, so we occupy a comparatively good position, but by no means the best. Some other cites were as follows :—Berlin (Germany), 5; Vienna, 5; Paris 11; London, 14; Brooklyn, 15; Edinburgh, 16; New York 16; St. Louis, 19; Buffalo, 20; Detroit, 20; Toronto, 28.5; Boston, 32; Cleveland, 43. From the report of the Provincial Board of Health for last year I find that our rate is lower than that of other cities of Ontario, but when the excellent geographical position Hamilton occupies is considered, drawing its water supply at such a long distance from any point of contamination by sewerage, it seems to me that our death rate from typhoid fever should be lower than it is. There is an evil somewhere in the water system, either in the source of supply or the mode of filtration and storage.

Ninety-eight cases of diphtheria, with 25 deaths, is not large, compared with other cities, but it is a sad loss of life from a preventible disease. While unsanitary surroundings predispose to it, it is almost always communicated from one person to another. Rigid quarantine is the most effectual means to stamp out the disease, and such is carried on as far as possible by this department, but the difficulty is that there are many cases of diphtheria so mild that it is impossible for any physician to diagnose the case from the clinical signs. Owing to the mildness of the attack the patient said to be ill with ulcerated sore throat or tonsilitis is not isolated, and thus the infection is spread until in a delicate subject it assumes a malignant form. Such a history has repeatedly been traced out by every sanitarian. Just recently a child died from what the attending physician called laryngitis. When the death report came into my hands to be examined I thought it looked suspicious, and summoned the physician for an interview. He claimed that the disease was not diphtheria, but admitted that two children in the same family had just previously had "a sore throat with some traces of membranes, which disappeared in a couple of days." In the meantime a public funeral had been held, small boys acting as pall-bearers. The sequel was that five neighboring children were infected with diphtheria from these cases, all in a severe form. There is no doubt but that these first cases were diphtheria, but the physician's defence was from the clinical signs, he could not diagnose it as such. Just such excuses will be given, and such results happen, as long as our city is unprovided with a laboratory for the bacteriological examination of swabs from the throat of suspected diphtheria cases. By this method a positive diagnosis can be made within 24 hours. I hope during the ensuing year this Board will fall in line with other cities and establish a well-equipped laboratory for doing this work, as well as for the weekly bacteriological examination of our city water and for the microscopical examination of the sputum of suspected cases of tuberculosis.

The city is to be congratulated that through the philanthrophy of Mr. John Billings, a new wing has been added to the City Hospital, and that by means of the bequest of Mrs. Hunter a separate insolation building for diphtheria has been constructed and is now in operation. During the year 54 cases of diphtheria have been treated at the hospital, and 11 of scarlet fever. In houses of one story, of which there are so many in this city, it is impossible to satisfactorily isolate cases of diphtheria and scarlet fever. To take them to the Isolation Hospital solves the difficulty. For this reason I am of the opinion that every facility should be afforded for the entrance of such cases, and their treatment there by their own physician. Were this done, but few cases would be treated at home, and thus the great danger of contagion removed. A more comfortable ambulance should be provided than the one in use, and kept under the control of this Board. The other cases of infectious disease were: Chicken-pox, 113; measles, 10; mumps, 4; no deaths occurring from any of these. Forty-three cases of whooping cough, with four deaths. May 25th a case of smallpox came to the notice of this department, and within a a couple of weeks nineteen cases developed in seven houses in different sections of the city. The disease was of a mild form, similar to that prevalent in other parts of the Province and United States, and had been for a time in the city masquerading as chicken-pox, thus accounting for the number of cases. Owing to the prompt and efficient measures taken by this Board, and its officers the outbreak was quickly stamped out. Only one case spread from the houses under quarantine. The patients were successfully treated at the Isolation Tents, no deaths occurring. From the experience of the spring, this Board has had a good opportunity to feel the need of a proper permanent Isolation Hospital for smallpox, and it is to be hoped your earnest efforts to secure the best available site and erection of building will soon bear good fruit. It is satisfactory that the children attending the public and separate schools, and a large proportion of the employees of factories and shops have been during the year successfully vaccinated ; many thousands of vaccinations were performed, and I have yet to learn of a single injurious result. To keep the schools efficiently vaccinated I advised the School Board to require a certificate of vaccination from all new pupils. I regret this was not done. From the point of view of the Sanitarian it is a great mistake.

MORTUARY STATISTICS.

Excluding 51 still births, which are not counted in mortuary statistics as deaths or births, 760 deaths have been recorded at the Registrar's Office during the past twelve

months. The assessor's enumeration gives us a population of 53,781, thus showing a death rate of 14.5 per 1,000, which is low, and places Hamilton among the most healthful cities on the continent ; of these 780 deaths, 428 were males and 352 females, thus showing about 10 per cent. greater mortality in the male portion of the population. There were 197 deaths in children under five years, and of this number 146 were under one year, showing that nearly 20 per cent. of the deaths occurred under one year. The chief 'factors in the causation of this high infant mortality are premature births, heredity, intemperance, neglect, illegitimacy, unsanitary surroundings and improper food. Industrial conditions figure largely in the neglect of infants, since mothers in employment return as soon as possible after their confinement to their work, and entrust their offspring to the care of older children and others, by whom they are improperly fed and looked after.

There were ten deaths from cholera infantum and diarrhoea ; this is a low rate from this cause, and as these derangements of the digestive organs in infants are nearly always due to impure cow's milk it would help to show that the quality supplied the city this year has been generally good. One hundred and fourteen persons reached the three score and ten limit, the span allotted to man, only 14.5 per cent.; fifty lived to be 80 years of age, and four over ninety, the oldest being 99 at the time of death.

Thirteen deaths were recorded of the inmates of the House of Refuge; of these nine were over 70 years of age; six at the Infants' Home, three at the Aged Women's Home, and one each at Boys' Home, St. Mary's Orphanage, and the Home for the Friendless. The death at the Boys' Home was due to diphtheria, where thirteen cases developed; all were treated at the City Hospital. The cause of the outbreak was not discovered though careful enquiry and inspection was made. The disease is thought to have been brought under control and stamped out by immunizing the rest of the inmates with anti-toxin.

Twenty-five deaths occurred from accident, including burns, scalds and railway. Five were killed by the Street Railway.

Among the general causes of death were 40 from cancer, 7 from appendicitis, 75 from pneumonia and 97 from tuberculosis. I call your particular attention to this last-named disease. That rate shows that last year one person out of every eight who dies in this city was afflicted with this scourge of the human race. Perhaps of all subjects which to-day press themselves upon our attention as a Board of Health is that ever present one, the restriction of tuberculosis. It has been proven conclusively again and again that it is an infectious disease, being communicated from one person to another by means of micro-organisms which in advanced cases exist in great numbers in the sputum. A person in the third stage of consumption if no precaution be taken to disinfect his sputum will distribute abroad some millions of these germs every day. How are the ravages of this disease to be diminished ? It is generally admitted the seed must have a favorable soil. In this case the soil is prepared by the natural forces of resistance of the body becoming weakened and the great cause leading to consumption is vitiated air. Tuberculosis was unknown among the Indians when they roamed the forests and prairies of this country, but now shut up in small houses on reservations it carries off 50 per cent. of them. Sir F. Broadbent, President of the British Association for the Prevention of Tuberculosis, has said that if people could be induced to live with their sleeping rooms partly open the deaths from tuberculosis would be decreased one-half in a year.   All of us spend about a third of our life time in a bed room.   A French scientist has estimated that there are over the sea but six germs per cubic metre, in a new house (in Paris) 7,000, in an old house 37,000, and in a hospital 78,000.   I quote these to show the importance of fresh air.   Hence in the homes of our people, in their offices and work shops, in schools, in factories, indeed, everywhere, the problem of how to maintain the purity of the air precedes all others.   The need of better regulations for the inspection of plumbing is a point that comes to mind just here.   In conjunction with sanitary operations along this line isolation of consumptives as much as possible is required. Germany, a country in the van of medical progress, has demonstrated that the disease can be lessened by the erection of Sanatoria at various centres.   The Ontario Legislature has not been behind in this matter and passed an act whereby municipalities may erect Sanatoria for consumptives and receive Government aid in purchasing lands and in the erection of buildings to an extent not to exceed $4,000 and in maintenance granting $1.50 per week for each patient.   With 98 deaths from this disease last year facing this Board it is our duty to take earnest and determined action to lessen such a loss of life.   The city hospital is not a proper place for consumptives to be cared for and it is time some steps were taken that this municipality should, taking advantage of the liberality of the Government, erect and equip a proper institution for the treatment of consumption.   Nature has provided us with an excellent location on the mountain.   It is a matter of congratulation that our citizens are becoming alive to the importance of the subject and several public meetings were held during the year, but beyond forming an Anti-Tuberculosis League and passing resolutions nothing was done.   Many requests have been made to this office during the year to disinfect rooms and houses after death by consumption; this has been done in every case where asked.   Some method of notification should be adopted, so that it may be done in all cases.

The scavenger system gives fair satisfaction; the chief fault I find is that citizens do not provide suitable receptacles for garbage ; many think any old box, no matter how large, can be handled by the scavengers. The bi-weekly collection during the summer months was not taken advantage of by the citizens as it should. Mixed garbage continues to be dumped at various points within the city.   There is no question it would be a great improvement in the appearance and health of these localities to have ashes collected in one receptacle and used in making land, and vegetable and animal refuse in another, to be burned in a proper incinerator.

I append the Health Inspector's report, also forms showing how diseases and deaths are distributed by wards.

In conclusion, permit me to thank you for the generous and kind treatment I have received from your hands since my appointment as Medical Officer.   I also wish to commend the Sanitary Inspectors for their faithful and honest work in the discharge of their several duties, ever willing at all times to assist me. Respectfully submitted,

WALTER F. LANGRILL, Medical Health Officer.

Hamilton, 22nd November, 1901.

To Dr. W. F. Langrill, Medical Health Officer :

Sir,—Below please find synopsis of the work done by your three inspectors from the 1st day of November, 1900, to 31st day of October, 1901, inclusive. Yours respectfully,

No. of inspections made.. 5,270

No of Privy vaults notified to be cleaned   714

No. of Privy vault permits issued for new ones..   8

No. of Privy vault permits issued to contractors to clean...... 1,241

No. of Privy vaults abolished..   75

No. of cesspools notified and cleaned by contractors..   26

No. of cesspools, permits issued for new ones..   1

No. of cesspools abolished.. 11
No. of dry earth closets notified to clean 35
No. of sewer connections to make.. 27
No. of sewer connections found defective.. 82
No. of foul drains to abolish.. 5
No. of stagnant waters to abolish.. 21
No. of dirty premises to clean.. 13
No. of other nuisances to abate.. 616
No. of complaints unfounded.. 2
No. of houses placarded.. 131
No. of houses fumigated.... 188
No. of milk licenses issued.. 190
No. of milk samples collected and tested 570
No. of milk dairies found in clean condition.. 7
No. of dairies found in fairly clean condition.. 7
No. of shops found in clean condition.. 77
No. of cow byres found in clean condition.. 24
Now of cow byres found in fairly clean condition.. 42
No. of cows found in dirty condition.. 2

WORK DONE BY YOUR SCAVENGERS.

No. of team loads of garbage and refuse collected........10,124½
Burnt at Crematory—
No. of dogs.. 329
No. of cats.. 204
No. of fowl.. 55
No. of goats.. 2
No. of pigs.. 3
No. of rabbits...... 4
No. of barrels and boxes of fish.. 62
No. of loads of used rags. etc., from the city hospital.. 54
No. of bedding. etc., from infected houses.. 18

Infectious diseases by months.

Disease.	Nov.	Dec	Jan.	Feb.	Mar	April.	May.	June.	July.	Aug.	Sept.	Oct.	Total.
Scarlet Fever..	16	3	4	7	8	9	3	4	7	4	7	16	88
Diphtheria	9	13	5	2	12	2	5	6	8	6	13	12	93
Typhoid Fever.	12	5	1	0	0	0	0	2	1	13	13	11	58

Table showing number of Infectious Diseases during past six years.

Year.	Scarlet Fever.	Diphtheria.	Typhoid Fever.
1896.........	47	60	116
1897............................... ...	205	63	41
1898	214	162	36
1899	123	99	75
1900	144	86	61
1901 ,.....,......................	88	93	58

Infectious Diseases by Wards.

Ward.	Diphtheria.	Scarlet Fever.	Typhoid Fever.	Chicken Pox.	Measles.	Whooping Cough.	Small Pox.	Total.
1	20	14	7	12	1	0	6	60
2	4	5	8	20	3	7	1	48
3	9	6	5	49	0	20	2	91
4	10	15	11	8	4	9	8	65
5	23	13	5	4	1	2	1	49
6	18	22	9	4	0	0	0	53
7	9	13	13	16	1	5	1	58
Total.	93	88	58	113	10	43	19	424

Deaths from Infectious Diseases by Months.

Month.	Diphtheria.	Scarlet Fever.	Typhoid Fever.	Whooping Cough.	Tuberculosis	Pneumonia.	Total.
November.......	4	....	4	....	8	2	18
December	2	....	....	....	8	7	17
January	2	....	....	....	8	13	23
February........	....	....	....	1	8	13	22
March	4	1	1	....	12	10	28
April.	1	....	....	1	14	9	25
May	2	....	1	....	7	4	14
June	2	....	1	1	8	7	19
July	1	....	1	1	6	3	12
August.	2	....	....	....	5	....	7
September	3	1	1	....	6	5	16
October	2	2	1	....	7	2	14
Total	25	4	10	4	97	75	

Deaths from Infectious Diseases by Wards.

Ward.	Diphtheria.	Typhoid Fever.	Scarlet Fever.	Tuberculosis.	Total.
1...............	3	....	....	10	13
2...	....	... .	1	12	13
3	2	....	....	14	16
4...............	3	2	1	16	22
5...............	6	3	....	15	24
6...............	7	1	2	14	24
7...............	4	....	....	12	16
Total	25	4 in hospital. Total 10	4	4 in hospital, address not given. Total 97	

LONDON.

REPORT OF DR. T. V. HUTCHINSON, MEDICAL HEALTH OFFICER FOR YEAR 1901.

To the Chairman and Board of Health :

Gentlemen,—I have the honor to submit my annual report upon the sanitary condition of the city during the year ending Nov. 15, 1901, and other matters affecting the public health.

The number of deaths during the year was the same as last, viz., 510. It is also a singular fact that the number of stillborn and premature births was also the same as last year, i.e., 18 and 12 respectively.

The death rate for the city during the year was 12.5.

7 H⁻

There is a very satisfactory decrease in the number of deaths from preventible and infectious diseases.   There were 36 cases of typhoid fever, with only 5 deaths. Of diphtheria there were 70 cases reported and 8 deaths.   Scarlet fever 50 cases, with 4 deaths.   This is the lowest number of deaths from typhoid fever, scarlet fever and diphtheria the city has had for many years.

Cancer caused the death of 30 persons, as compared with 17 last year.   This disease is becoming more and more prevalent every year.

There were 13 deaths caused by violence, of which 5 were due to railway accidents and 1 to poison.

Four persons reached the ages of 92, 99, 102 and 104 respectively.

CONSUMPTION.

There is also a very satisfactory reduction in the number of deaths from consumption, namely, 48 as compared with 60 last year.   This is perhaps due to the better understanding by the people of its contagious character, and the adoption of more careful sanitary precautions and isolation.   The number of deaths from consumption in Ontario last year was 2,360.   This is about one person in every 9 dies of consumption.   The greater number of these die during the bread-winning period, or between the ages of 15 and 65.   Economists place the value to the State of each life at from $750 to $1,000.   Taking it at the lowest figure, this represents an annual loss to Ontario of $1,777,000.   Add to this the loss of wages and expenses by sickness and the total sum becomes enormous.   Consumption among the Jews is comparatively rare, they having about 1 death from this disease where we Gentiles have 5.   This has been ascribed to the fact that their dwellings are never dry-swept, but always cleaned by wet cloths.   Contrast this excellent sanitary practice with the unsightly trailing skirt, dragged through tuberculous sputa and all kinds of filth, then carefully hung up in closets or bedrooms to dry and the dust disseminated by means of brooms through the dwelling for the inhalation of the inmates.

UNSANITARY POLICE CELLS.

I have for the third time to call the attention of the Board of Health to the unsanitary and disgraceful condition of the police cells.   In rainy weather the surface water from the streets comes over the lower floors, the roof leaks, the building is dilapidated, rotten, has long survived its usefulness and is entirely unfit for further occupation.

The basement of the Covent Garden Market is in very bad condition. The floor being of brick, it is impossible to keep it clean.   Filth finds good holding ground in spite of all that can be done, and the stalls are badly lighted.   The floor should be of non-absorbent material, such as asphaltum, which could be readily washed.   If this cannot be done the basement should be closed, for in its present condition it is unfit for the storage of food.

SMALLPOX INVASION.

During the year the city had an invasion of smallpox, the first three cases appearing on January 4 in men who worked in a cigar factory.   The factory was promptly closed for three days, while being thoroughly disinfected with formaldehyde gas, and no more cases occurred in this place.   About the same time a young woman, also a cigar maker, returned to the city from a visit to the neighborhood of a Michigan lumber camp.   She escaped, but three persons where she boarded took the disease.   There were in all sixteen cases, fifteen of these occurred during the winter, three of the semi-confluent type, five of a less degree of severity and eight comparatively mild.   One of the severe cases was that of a farm laborer who came in from a neighboring township with the disease well developed, and sat himself down in a physician's residence. The doctor was out. He said he had plenty of time, and would wait—and he waited. On the 9th of November a young man, coming from west of Brandon, Manitoba, became so ill that on reaching this city he got off the train to consult a physician. The disease was smallpox. He was taken to the isolation hospital, and discharged in five weeks. Of the above sixteen cases not one had been successfully vaccinated; there were no deaths. Three cases were traced to cigar factories, 1 to Michigan, 1 to Cleveland, 1 to Chicago, the last one coming from Manitoba. In addition to the above sixteen cases fifteen more were discovered scattered through the city; these were of a very mild type, many not having any medical attendance. The source of infection in the majority of these could not be traced, neither could any marks or other evidence of vaccination be found. To these 31 cases the neglect of vaccination .brought its own punishment ; every unvaccinated person is a centre of danger to his neighbor, and emphasizes the necessity of a rigid enforcement of the act relating to public vaccination.

SEWER SYSTEM.

The new sewer system of the city is not yet completed; one filter bed is in operation, and does its work thoroughly, the effluent discharged into the river being clear, and, it is believed, a bacteriological examination would show it to be innocuous. The system is entirely successful, and will, as far as London is concerned, put an end to the unsanitary mediaeval practice of turning a sewage into the river. All of which I respectfully submit.

T. V. HUTCHINSON, Medical Health Officer.

REPORT OF DR. C. T. CAMPBELL, CHAIRMAN LONDON BOARD OF HEALTH.

The following report of Dr. Cl. T. Campbell, Chairman of the Board of Health, was received by the City Council on Monday night :

The terms of the city by-laws require that the Chairman of the Board of Health shall by the 1st of December of each year present to the council a report of the actions of the Board and of the sanitary condition of the city. The reports made to our board by its medical health officer and its sanitary inspector assure us that during the year 1901 the general health of the city has been good, that infectious diseases (with one exception) have been comparatively light, and that its death rate has been as low as usual.

EPIDEMIC OF SMALLPOX.

In December of 1900 a case of smallpox was discovered in the city. As it was located in the suburbs, your Board considered that it was doing all that was required by enforcing a strict isolation of the house until the patient's recovery. In the early part of the present year, however, other cases appeared, and we were forced in the interest of the public health to take the more comprehensive measures required by the Provincial laws, even though a large expenditure of public money was involved. A building was rented near the city limits, and a temporary smallpox hospital opened. The building had to be furnished and properly equipped; the commissariat department arranged for, and an ambulance service organized. Few people care to have any dealings with a pest house, and those who do insist on the highest prices. Fortunately, however, your Board has been able to do all that was required, with the aid of its efficient health officer, Dr. Hutchinson, at a cost far below that incurred by other cities. The entire outlay, up to December 1st, including expenses incurred for public vaccination, and for the isolation of suspected parties in private houses, has been $2,120.13.

During the winter and spring there were fifteen patients in the hospital, for several months in the summer there were none, but the Board deemed it safer to keep its establishment ready for any emergency. The wisdom of this course was apparent when a stranger from the Northwest appeared on our streets on the evening of the

9th November, with all the symptoms of smallpox. We would have been in a serious dilemma without the hospital, for he could not have gained admission into any hotel, and the law would not permit us to send him out of the city. There have been in the hospital altogether sixteen patients; many of them were light attacks; only three seriously ill, and no deaths. In addition, we have traced at least as many more cases in the city, which from their mildness were not recognized at the time. Some had no medical attendance at all; and it was only as we tried to investigate the history of recognized cases that we obtained evidence of the others. The first case in the city, so far as we can learn, received the disease on a visit to Michigan. Returning to the city, she went to work in a factory and thus spread the contagion. All of the cases, however, were not from this source. One we traced to Cleveland, another to Chicago; while the last one received it in Manitoba.

The Board of Health at the beginning of the year notified the council that it would require at least $5,000; half of that sum being estimated for the epidemic of smallpox. Our actual outlay for that purpose to date has been as follows : Public vaccination, $60; bonus to owners of property, $300; rent, $150; repairs and furnishing, $272.13; attendance, $614.40; maintenance, $613.60; ambulance service, $120; total, $2,130.13. Accounts unpaid, with the probable expenditure for December, will aggregate about $130. Per contra, we have obtained $80 for rent of pasturage during the summer. Omitting bonus for property and furnishings, the cost per patient has been about $100. In Toronto it was $200.

THE CITY SEWERAGE.

The new sewer system of the city being now so far completed as to be in partial operation, and the money appropriated for the purpose being exhausted, a brief review of our sewerage work seems necessary in order that the facts connected therewith may go on record.

Twenty years ago our system of sewerage consisted chiefly of three large brick sewers (3 feet by 4 feet 6 inches) on Richmond, King and Wellington streets, aggregating some 13,000 feet, with a number of tile drains connecting. With the adoption of our present system of water supply it was evident that more extensive sewer accommodation would be necessary. Not only were our sewers insufficient, but the discharge of the sewage into the river was a cause of unsanitary conditions that could not be allowed to continue. While this was apparent to many of the citizens, it was emphasized by the complaints made by the neighboring municipality of London West. These complaints, as well as petitions from some of the residents in the town of Westminster, were submitted to the Provincial Board of Health, and that body ordered an investigation, which was conducted on June 2 to 6, 1885, the result being that a decision was rendered practically forbidding the discharge of sewage into the river, and ordering the adoption of a more complete and satisfactory system by the city.

From that date until 1895 the local board of health and the council were engaged in spasmodic efforts in the direction of sewage disposal. In 1887 a report was obtained at a cost of $519.40 from Col. George E. Waring, one of the most prominent sanitary engineers in the United States, but his examination of the condition of affairs had been very brief, and his recommendations were not deemed satisfactory.

As Chairman of a committee of the Local Board of Health I recommended a partial system of chemical precipitation at the termini of the three principal sewers, which, at a small cost, would have so far remedied the evil as to remove all legal grounds of complaint from our neighbors. No action, however, was taken by the council.

In 1892 a very complete report was presented to the council by Mr. Willis Chipman of Toronto, recommending a system of sewage collection and disposal by filtration, at a cost (exclusive of lands and beds) of $90,000. Nothing was done with this report except to print it.

Meanwhile legal complications were arising. Suit was entered against the city by London West, and judgment given against us; but execution was deferred by the court on the promise of the city authorities to proceed as rapidly as possible with the adoption of remedial measures. Other suits were threatened; some entered, and one of these was also decided against us.

Matters culminated in 1895, when, after repeated warnings, it was plainly intimated to us by the sanitary officers of the Province that further delay would not be tolerated. Action being thus forced upon us, the Mayor, Mr. J. W. Little, and myself, as Chairman of the Board of Health, secured the services of several of the leading sanitary engineers to examine the situation and advise. Plans and reports were received from Mr. Horetsky, the Ontario Government's sanitary engineer; Mr. Chipman of Toronto and Mr. E. A. Goodenough of Boston. Subsequently Mr. Rust, sewerage engineer of Toronto, was consulted as to the size of some of the proposed sewers.

After comparing the several reports, the Board of Health prepared a scheme in harmony therewith, which I submitted for the approval of the council. This proposed two main sewers, draining the northern and southern portions of the city—uniting at King and Ridout streets in a trunk sewer to carry the sewage across the river to a place of disposal beyond the Cove; together with a London South branch sewer for that part of the city, connecting with the trunk sewer at its point of crossing the Wharncliffe road. At the terminus of the trunk sewer the sewage was to be treated by filtration. The estimated cost, including lands, was $207,000.

The council approved the plan and prepared a by-law for raising $150,000 of debentures. It was proposed to supplement this amount by appropriating $55,000, a sum which had accumulated in the working out of the city's consolidated fund. The necessary act was secured at the 1896 session of the Legislature, and the by-law was adopted on the 2nd of September by a vote of 1,716 to 663.

On the 12th of October the Board of Health, after a conference with Messrs. Chipman and Rust, prepared a report arranging the detail of the work, which was approved by the council, and on the 2nd of November the engineering department was ordered to proceed with the construction of the sewers, Mr. Willis Chipman being retained as consulting engineer. The work was divided into sections, and has been completed as follows :

A—From sewage beds to west end of syphon. B—Syphon across the lowlands of the Cove. C—Along Evergreen avenue and Becher street to west bank of river. D—Bridge across river. E—Steel pipe across river to corner of King and Ridout streets. F—Along King, Ridout, Bathurst, Talbot, Horton and Richmond streets to Grey street. G—Along Grey, Clarence and Hill streets to Wellington. H—Along Hill, Waterloo and South to William. J—From King street along Ridout to Lichfield. K—Lichfield, Talbot and Mill to Richmond. I—From Richmond along Pall Pall to Maitland. M—Along Maitland, Central avenue, William street and Princess avenue to Adelaide. N—Adelaide street and Lorne avenue to Ontario. O—Ontario, Queen's avenue, Quebec and Dundas to Egerton. P—Wharncliffe road, from Evergreen avenue to Bruce. Q—Along Bruce to Edward, Edward street, from Bruce to centre of Briscoe, River street, from Evergreen avenue to the river.

The work of sewer construction commenced at the east end of Becher street, December 17, 1896, and the last section was taken off the contractor's hands in March, 1900. The filtration bed was put into operation on Sept. 20, 1901. A regular plan for the sewering of the entire city has been adopted, and all new sewers are now laid down in accordance therewith.

The original plan of the Board of Health was to dispose of the sewage by intermittent filtration. The only change made has been to adopt what may be called rapid filtration, by which very much less land is required, though the cost of constructing the beds is proportionately greater. One filter bed has been completed, but as the money appropriated has been exhausted, the work has stopped. A second bed has been partially finished. This should be completed, and at least one other bed constructed, the amount required being about $6,000. A table of receipts and expenditures of the sewer debenture fund is herewith given, prepared by the city auditor, Mr. Jewell, from which it will be seen that, had the City Council of 1898 not taken a sum of $7,000 from this fund and applied it on street repairs the work would have been fully completed within the limit of the amount originally voted:

Receipts.

Proceeds debenture issue of $55,000 ....$	53,900 00
Proceeds debenture issue of $120,000	118,740 00
Proceeds debenture issue of $30,000	28,500 00
Interest, accounts and sundry credits	2,984 02
Frontage rates capitalized ..	19,048 45
Deficit	1,057 10

Expenditures.

Sec. A—From beds to west end of syphon ....$	4,602 26
Sec. B—Syphon	17,585 83
Sec. C—East end of syphon to west bank of river	10,451 07
Sec. D and E—Bridge and sewer to Thames street ..	13,514 32
Sec. F—Thames street to corner Grey and Richmond ..	15,026 69
Sec. G and H—Grey and Richmond to William and Hill	10,505 11
Sec. J—King and Ridout to Lichfield	21,237 74
Sec. K—Lichfield and Ridout to Mill and Richmond	18,118 90
Sec. L. M. N. O—Richmond and Mill to Egerton and Dundas	55,088 83
Sec. P—Wharncliffe, from Evergreen to Bruce	6,978 02
Sec. Q—Edward and Bruce to Wharncliffe	4,729 80
River street	1,193 57
Engineering salaries	5,551 66
General expense account	2,406 63
By-law expenses	707 67
Printing, advertising and plans	930 99
Brighton street	710,56
King street extension and protecting wall	521 03
Valve house	1,023 00
Proportion of cost of sewer to Canadian Packing Company's house	202 50
Land and right of way (80 acres)	17,847 25
Street repairs	7,058 08
Gullies, catch basins and manholes	2,450 42
Fencing grounds	177 72
Filtration beds ($736 of this not yet paid)..	7,109 92

Total .. ..$224,229 57   Total... ... ...$224,229 57

RECOMMENDATIONS.

Several matters of improvement in the sanitary interests of the city have been suggested during the year by the Board, but these have not been urged, because the estimates for the year had been prepared. But your attention is recalled to them, in order that they may go before the council of 1902. Among them are the following, and could they all be carried out the sanitary condition of London would be superior to that of any Canadian municipality:

1. That the necessary filtration beds for sewage disposal be completed, the number being at least three.

2. That a permanent isolation hospital be provided for cases of smallpox.

3. That the basement of the market building be placed in proper condition, the present filthy floor being removed and cement laid down.

4. That the police court building be repaired, or a new one erected. The building is a disgrace to a civilized community, and if a new one cannot be constructed the present one should be supplied with ventilation, drainage and heating.

5. That an efficient system of garbage collection and disposal should be adopted.

CL. T. CAMPBELL, Chairman Board of Health.

London, December 2, 1901.

STRATFORD.

REPORT OF DR. JOHN A. ROBERTSON, MEDICAL HEALTH OFFICER FOR
YEAR 1901.

To the Chairman and Members of the Local Board of Health, Stratford :

Gentlemen,—I hereby submit the annual report of the health department for the past year. You will find attached the report of the sanitary inspector of the work done during that time.

Contrasting the mortality of the city during the past year with that of the three years previous, we find there is an increase of seven deaths over that of any of these years. This may be accounted for ,by the number who have died from "old age." If the number of deaths "old age" stands boldly to the front, there being recorded twenty deaths from that cause. Consumption takes second place, claiming ten victims as its share. Pneumonia stands third in the list, eight having succumbed from that disease.

As a rule we generally find the mortality greater during infancy and childhood than that of old age, but the past year shows that thirteen died under one year old and five between one and ten, whereas forty died over sixty years of age. Tabulating the ages, we find that

11 died between 80 and 90	5 died between 30 and 40
11 died between 70 and 80	9 died between 20 and 30
13 died between 60 and 70	8 died between 10 and 20
9 died between 50 and 60	5 died between 1 and 10
7 died between 40 and 50	13 died under 1 year.

In the different wards we find that there were 11 deaths in Avon ward from all causes, 10 in Falstaff ward, 11 in Hamlet ward, 27 in Romeo ward and 37 in Shakespeare ward.

Number of deaths from Oct. 31st, 1897, to Oct. 31st, 1898. 89.

Number of deaths from October 31st, 1898, to October 31st, 1899, 86.

Number of deaths from October 31st, 1899, to October 31st, 1900, 89.

Number of deaths from October 31st, 1900, to October 31st, 1901, 96.

Premature or still births were not included in these. The slight increase in the death rate was not due to contagious diseases, as only seven deaths have been reported from all these.

It would be well if those registering deaths would be more specific in giving causes, for such vague entries as "inflammation" "decline," "dropsy," etc., fail to place the disease in the class to which it properly belongs. There were cases of scarlet fever reported with deaths. Thirteen cases of diphtheria, with three deaths, were reported, an increase over last year of six cases and two deaths. 97 cases of tphoid fever were reported, with four deaths, an increase of 49 cases over last year. This was due to the dry season, the water in the wells becoming low, and to defective plumbing and improper connections with the sewers. I cannot too strongly impress upon you the necessity of having framed and putting in force a suitable plumbing by-law for the licensing of plumbers. Some three or four years ago the City Engineer had same prepared under your instructions, and submitted to the council, but through some legal objections to its adoption it was laid over and has not since been brought up. The necessity of such a by-law cannot be questioned, for the careless and unsanitary condition with which plumbing has been done is a fruitful source of contagious diseases—a competent plumbing inspector should be appointed to supervise all such work.

I would also call your attention to the fact that the by-law regarding the connecing of house drains with the sewers has not been carried out. No connection should be made without applicaton in writing to the Board of works and its sanction given. such connections to be made under the supervision of one City Engineer or road commissioner. The houses in which contagious diseases were said to exist were examined, the well water tested and the surroundings inspected to ascertain whether proper cleanliness was observed. The cellar drains and sewer connections were examined and it was found that some had no sewer connection, others had sewer connection with no traps and no vent pipe. I shall not deal with the means to be taken for the prevention of death from old age, but must call your attention to the fact that not only in this Province, but throughout all the civilized world steps are being taken to limit the spread of consumption, on account of its prevalence and contagion, and the Provincial Board of Health at the last regular meeting instructed the committee on epidemics to issue a circular, containing, among other instructions a copy of a resolution that the Local Board of Health be urged upon to establish rules for the notification of cases of tuberculosis to the medical health officer or to the Secretary of the local board of the municipality. By carrying out this recommendation the Board would become aware of the number of cases in the municipality and could through the physicians in charge, supply them with short printed rules explaining the measures to be adopted for the benefit of the consumptive and for the protection of the other members of the household. Such rules to include directions for the destroying of expectorated matter, disinfecting of clothing, dispensing with unnecessary curtains and carpets in the room, proper ventilation, cleansing of floors and walls, the keeping of patients in rooms specially arranged for them, and a thorough disinfection from time to time of the rooms used by the sick. By having these rules carried out the Board, at a very little expense, would assist householders to take steps to limit the danger of infection, and houses once occupied by consumptives could be thoroughly disinfected before other families were permitted to occupy them.

The Legislature becoming aware of the prevalence of the disease, the danger of infection therefrom, its chronic character and unsuccessful results of home treatment, has passed an Act to encourage and assist municipalities in giving effective aid to persons affected with this disease. I would ask your Board to consider the advisability of taking steps towards the establishment of a sanatorium on a small scale, even to accommodate only four or five patients. It would be a nucleus for the foundation of an institution which would develop in size and resources as its needs might require. The co-operation of the different charitable institutions, charitably-disposed persons, religious denominations, societies and physicians might be enlisted and brought about. While dealing with this subject I would like to call your attention to the filthy habits carried on in our midst of spitting on the sidewalks and doorways by pedestrans and loungers about these places in the evenings. Such habits are not only disagreeable and annoying to the community, but dangerous to the public health--sputum is the chief means by which this disease is communicated, and I would ask you to consider and devise some means whereby such could in a manner be controlled. The same may be said regarding all public buildings.

The sewer committee deserve credit for the rapidity with which they are progressing with the disposal works. It is gratifying to know that the success of the system is now beyond doubt and from reports received from the Provincial Board of Health, after recent analysis of the sewage, it is found that the results are nearing perfection. The Provincial Board has expressed itself as perfectly satisfied with the workings of the system and has every confidence in it ultimately, when the additional beds are completed, arriving at the Government standard of purity. Too much praise cannot be given to the Chairman, Ald. Savage, for his untiring zeal, steady observation and intelligent supervision of the works.

In view of the presence of smallpox throughout the Province during the past year and from the fact that vaccination is the only preventative from the disease, I would ask you to consider the advisability of having all children attending school vaccinated. Very little vaccination has been done in the city for the past eight years, consequently a large number of children attending school have never been vaccinated.

I cannot close this report without again, as I have done for over ten years, asking you to render your assistance to procure, in whatever manner you consider practicable, a hospital for the isolation and care of those affected with contagious diseases, as it would prove the chief factor in the prevention and spread of such infection, and the guarding of the interests of the community, as well as securing the better chance of recovery of those requiring treatment. In the absence of any serious epidemic it is difficult to impress upon the public that such might occur at any time, and it is wiser to be prematurely prepared than to be caught napping. Some 63 heads of families in which contagious diseases had existed during the last two years, were approached and asked to express their opinion as to the necessity or desirability of such an institution, and also to state as to whether they would be willing to send their children, were they again afflicted with a severe contagious disease. They almost all admitted its necessity. Some 43 would take advantage of treatment there, and some expressed their willingness to contribute thereto. Eight were undecided and eleven refused. Some of these had only one child and felt it could be treated at home.

I am pleased the public are becoming alive to the advantage of hospital treatment, as is evidenced from the fact that 53 were treated in that institution during the past year. Respectfully submitted.

. J. A. ROBERTSON, M.H.O.

Sanitary Inspector's Report.

To the Chairman and Members of the Local Board of Health :

Gentlemen,—I have the honor to submit to you my annual report of the work done for the year ending October 31st, 1901.

I had a letter box put in the health and relief office, City Hall, for anyone having complaints to make, as I have very little time to spend in office, owing to so much outside work. Last April I had two hundred notices printed and posted in the city, in which I had a clause inserted calling attention to anyone having complaints to leave same at health office, and that they will receive prompt attention.

There was scarcely a day but what there were a number of complaints, but I have kept no record of them. I would be pleased if the Board would furnish me a daily journal, so that I could keep a record of every complaint.

I inspected all cellars, yards and lanes in the business part of the city early in the season. I found the majority of cellars in good sanitary condition, and in other cases I had considerable trouble to enforce cleanliness, had yards all cleaned and rubbish removed, and also several closets in rear of stores on Ontario street cleaned and buildings removed, as they were a public nuisance, and could find no one to be responsible as to their sanitary condition.

I also notified all parties having grates on sidewalks to have them cleaned and to use disinfectants freely, as I think they are a source of danger to the public, as mostly everyone, no matter with what malady he may be afflicted, uses them as a receptacle for expectorating. All complaints, from anyone, were promptly investigated, and wherever any nuisance was found to exist prompt action was taken to have same abated. I endeavored to carry out all instructions from your Board or the medical health officer to the best of my ability. I placarded thirty-five dwellings during the year, twenty-three for scarlet fever and twelve for diphtheria. In all cases they were thoroughly disinfected before removing placard; all cases of consumption are also disinfected. In company with the M.H.O. Dr. Robertson and I inspected the milk supply of the city, visited all dairies, inspecting barns, as to ventilation and general surroundings, took samples of water from wells where cattle were watering as well as that used for washing cans.

I also inspected a number of houses and surroundings where typhoid fever existed, to try to ascertain the cause.   I find in a number of cases they were connected with public sewers and laterals trapped but not vented and others where they have neither trap nor vent—nothing that I could find to prevent the accumulation of gas in sewers to escape through cellar connection and from there through the whole dwelling.

All of which is respectfully submitted.   Your obedient servant,

GEORGE DURST, Sanitary Inspector.

ST. CATHARINES.

REPORT OF DR. E. GOODMAN, CHAIRMAN OF BOARD OF HEALTH.

To the Mayor and Council of the Corporation of the City of St. Catharines :

Gentlemen.—In accordance with the requirements of the Public Health Act I have the honor herewith to submit my annual report of the sanitary condition of St. Catharines for the year ending the 15th day of November A.D. 1901.

It will be seen by the accompanying reports of the Medical Health Officer, the Secretary and the Sanitary Inspector that the city has been comparatively free from contagious diseases of a serious type during the past year, and that zymotic affections, dependent upon impure atmosphere from defective drainage, unsanitary surroundings, tainted milk, or unwholesome drinking water have not prevailed to any considerable extent although typhoid fever has not been entirely absent.   In this connection the Board would strongly recommend the adoption of some method by which the upper reservoir of the city waterworks may be made available for our water supply, for domestic and fire protection purposes, whenever it is found necessary to thoroughly clean out the lower reservoir, which, under present conditions, cannot be accomplished. The Board has much pleasure in recognizing the efforts of the Committee of Public Works of the City Council to extend the system of sewers and drains, which are such important factors in maintaining a high standard of public health.   The Board hopes it may be found possible during the coming year to construct a sewer on Church street and to continue the sewer on St. Paul street to a point below the swing bridge leading to the great western hill.   The flow of water now at that point is much greater than formerly owing to the increased volume of the Twelve Mile Creek since the establishment of the Cataract Company's works near De Cew Falls.   So that no apprehension need be felt of unsanitary results from any accumulation of sewage taking place at that outlet.   The present outlet of this sewer into the raceway is in many respects more objectionable.   Since my last annual report an additional flush tank has been installed at the junction of George and Louisa streets.   This tank, and all the others, are in good working condition, and have been recently inspected by Mr. O'Neill, cleaned out and treated to a new coat of cement in order to maintain their impermeability, and to prevent leakage.   In consequence of the rootlets of the willow trees on the Ontario street margin of the park having forced their way into the interior of the flush tank at the junction of Adams and Ontario streets, and also, on two occasions, into the sewer pipe in that vicinity, the Board, with regret, felt compelled to advise the Council to remove these ornaments of the park, as they were a constant source of danger.   No additional flush tanks were installed this year, for financial reasons, owing to the expense connected with the isolation and treatment of the three imported cases of smallpox, which were, fortunately, of a mild type.   Next year, however, it will be advisable to install at least three more of them where experience has shown that they are needed.   These smallpox cases and the attendant expense to the city, and hardship to citizens in whose houses the patients were necessarily quarantined, impressed the Board with the urgent need of an isolation hospital for the treatment of contagious diseases. The small building originally designed for that purpose being at present utilized for the accommodation of friendless and helpless paupers, is not available, and, if it were, is hardly suitable. It is to be hoped, therefore, that the council will take steps to meet this requirement on sanitary, humanitarian and financial grounds. The present method of confining patients in the houses where they happen to be taken ill, while at present a necessary course to pursue, is productive of hardship to those other occupants of the premises who are not affected with the contagious malady, but who have been exposed to it, and must, in consequence thereof, be kept isolated until all danger of communicating the virus to others has passed away. It also involves considerable expense, as sanitary guards have to be engaged to keep "watch and ward" night and day, and the infected houses have to be partially refurnished and renovated, to make good the loss arising from the necessary destruction of tainted articles, that if left in situ might convey the disease to others. It is important that the clause of the Public Health Act requiring that all typhoid fever cases be reported to the Local Board of Health should be enforced, in order that steps may be taken to ascertain and, if possible, remove the cause or causes on which the existence of the disease depends, whether from foul surroundings, impure milk, unwholesome well water or other unsanitary agencies.

The Anti-spitting By-law passed by the council at the request of the Board has produced good results already, and if the police will promptly act whenever they observe a violation of its provisions, they will materially aid in abating a disgusting nuisance, and in arresting the spread of tuberculosis. The Provincial Board of Health, following in the footsteps of similar sanitary organizations in other countries, has recommended that all cases of tuberculosis should be reported to the Local Board of Health. It is not intended to give publicity to these cases, nor to placard the houses, but merely to keep a careful supervision of them, to ascertain as far as possible the cause of contagion, and to aid and assist the medical attendants in adopting precautions to limit the spread of the disease by improving the sanitary surroundings. It is considered necessary to disinfect the tainted premises, to destroy contaminated articles of clothing, bedding, etc., that may have become saturated with the secretions containing the tubercle bacillus, that is now generally conceded to be the exciting cause of the fatal malady that carries off in the prime of life such a large percentage of our population. In the absence of suitable sanatoria for the care and treatment of tubercular consumption, everything practicable should be done by the Board and local medical practitioners to instruct the citizens as to the proper course to pursue, and the necessary steps to be taken to prevent the invasion and extension of this disease, the most deadly and insidious of all maladies to which mankind is exposed. As soon as the Board is made acquainted with the existence of any case of tuberculosis within the corporate limits of the city I should recommend, with the concurrence of my colleagues, that a copy of the suggestions of the Provincial Board of Health for the management of such cases be forwarded by the Secretary of our local board to the head of the household of which the patient is a member. I am convinced that these suggestions and recommendations of the Provincial Board of Health are admirably conceived, and would prove of the greatest service if faithfully observed and systematically carried out.

The services rendered by the Medical Health Officer, the Secretary and the Sanitary Inspector have met with the perfect approval of the Board. And the fact that the smallpox was stamped out, having been confined entirely to the two infected houses, should be satisfactory evidence of their efficiency in protecting the citizens from exposure to a dreaded, disfiguring and loathsome disease. The members of the medical profession, the school trustees and the teachers in all the schools of the city have cordially co-operated with the Board in securing the successful vaccination of all those who were found not to be immune, with a fair measure of success. The number of deaths which have occurred in the city from all causes amounts to 174 for the year ending the 15th November, 1901. Deducting from this number the deaths from old age, premature births, accidents, non-residents dying in hospital and suicide,

I find the rate of mortality, calculated upon a basis of population of 10,590, to be 11.80 for each 1,000 of the inhabitants, which is a satisfactory indication of the favorable sanitary condition of the city.

All of which is respectfully submitted.

E. GOODMAN, Chairman Local Board of Health.

REPORT OF THE MEDICAL HEALTH OFFICER.

To the Chairman and Members of the Board of Health :

Gentlemen,—I have the honor to submit my report on the sanitary condition of the city for the year ending November 15th, 1901.

It affords me great pleasure to report that the city is entirely free from those contagious diseases which have to be reported to the Secretary.

During the year there has been no serious epidemic. Forty-three cases in all have been reported, with four deaths, not including those from typhoid fever or tuberculosis, compared with one hundred and fifty cases reported, and three deaths, last year.

Of the forty-three cases, twenty were scarlet fever, twenty were diphtheria and three were smallpox.

Of the twenty cases of scarlet fever, only one died, showing the remarkably low mortality of 5 per cent.

Of the twenty cases of diphtheria, three died, of the three cases that died I had personal knowledge that two were of a most malignant type. It would be interesting to know in what percentage of these .cases antidiphtheritic serum was used.

This municipality has had three cases of smallpox during the past year. One came from Hamilton, the other two from Princeton, Ontario. All were of the mildest type, with little or no constitutional disturbance. One case was peculiar in that the disease first attacked the mucous membrane of the mouth, the cutaneous :.anifestations being limited to a half dozen very typical vesicles. This patient was the mother of a child who was first attacked after being in the city three days, having arrived from the village of Princeton to visit friends here. I attribute the peculiarity in her case to the fact that she persisted in defying the instructions and in allowing the child to place his hands in her mouth and to kiss her.

It affords me great pleasure to report that, owing to prompt isolation and vaccination of those exposed to the disease none of our citizens contracted the disease.

When we take into consideration the number of cases in other parts of the Province, the number of cases in the United States, and our proximity to the borders of that country and the Pan-American Exposition, it is a matter of congratulation that we escaped with so few cases.

These cases were all isolated in the private houses in which they happened to be found. This method of procedure was very unsatisfactory to your officers and inconvenient to the owners of the dwelling places. The presence of these cases only emphasizes the pressing need of an available isolation hospital. The need of an institution of this kind is felt not only in cases of smallpox, but also in cases of other contagious diseases. I think it is the opinion of all medical practitioners that there are cases of contagious diseases constantly arising that could be more satisfactorily handled in an isolation hospital, both in curing the patient and in preventing the spread of the disease.

I daresay the members of this Board will be surprised to find that while only one case of typhoid fever has been reported, yet the mortuary statistics show eleven deaths from that cause. I suppose such a condition arises from carelessness on the part of the medical practitioners. I would suggest that the Secretary be instructed to call the attention of the medical fraternity in this municipality to their duties and responsibilities in this regard.

There was an endeavor on the part of a section of the city press to "raise a scare" on account of a supposed prevalence of typhoid fever in the city, due to impurity of the city water. We can form no exact opinion of the prevalence of typhoid this year, compared with other years, owing to the incompleteness of the returns, but from general inquiries, I do not believe that there were any more cases in the city this year than last, and in regard to the condition of the city water, I may say that the Superintendent of the waterworks submitted several samples to the Government bacteriologist for examination. The report was that our city water ranks No. 1.

The deaths during the past year from tuberculosis were 25, 22 of these were pulmonary, three peritoneal. This is an increase of seven as compared with the previous year. This fact should impress all thinking persons with the hope that the time will speedily arrive when this disease will be treated in Sanatoria specially constructed for the purpose, and when, as strict measures will be adopted to prevent its spread as are usd in the case of all other contagious diseases.

This Board is to be congratulated on being in the very front rank of Local Boards of Health in this Province, in having secured the adoption of a bylaw to prevent spitting in public places, and in recommending the appointment of a committee of the City Council to confer with committees of adjacent municipalities in regard to the erection of a Sanatorium for consumptives.

Several complaints have been made this autumn as to the method of disposal of the refuse material from the various canning factories. This is a question of considerable importance from a sanitary point of view, and it will in all probability be necessary for the Board to formulate some regulations for the disposal of such refuse during this next season.

It seems to me that the system of scavenging in this city can be improved. The objection I have with the present system is that the scavengers are not responsible to anyone for the performance of their duties. They get their pay from multitudinous sources, and in many cases get no pay at all other than the refuse matter to feed their pigs. Consequently we find them sometimes dropping their duties for a time, according to their own convenience.

This can only be remedied by this Board adopting some systematic plan, with definite pay, from a definite source, and with responsibility for doing good work resting in a definite place.

It has been a source of gratification to me as Medical Health Officer to find that a number of new sewerage connections have been established this year, yet the fact remains that there are many dwelling houses in parts of the city where sewerage connections are possible, where occupants must still use the privy pits of olden times. I would impress on this Board the advisability, from a sanitary aspect, of having sewerage connections established in as large a number of houses as possible.

The McLean and Pinder complaints, which have been pending for some time, have been settled satisfactorily to all parties concerned.

The Sanitary Inspector has been faithful in the performance of his duties in assisting me in attending to the various cases which came under my notice.

All of which is respectfully submitted.

R. H. SMITH, M.B., M.H.O.

Report of the City Clerk.

E. Goodman, M.B., Chairman Local Board of Health :

Dear Sir,—I have the honor to submit to you herewith the annual statement of the number of deaths in the City of St. Catharines, from November 15th, 1900, to November 15th, 1901, and the causes thereof, together with a statement of the number of contagious diseases reported for the same period as per medical returns :

Alcoholic Paralysis	1	Marasmus	4
Anaemia	3	Meningitis	2
Apoplexy	3	Nephritis	2
Appendicitis	3	Ovarian tumor	2
Asphyxiation (gas)	1	Paralysis	3
Asthenia	1	Perforation of Stomach	1
Bronchitis	4	Peritonitis	5
Burn Shock	1	Pneumonia	15
Cancer of Bowel	3	Puerperal Convulsions	1
Cancer of Liver	3	Premature Birth	4
Cancer of Uterus	2	Pulmonary Tuberculosis	22
Cerebral Hemorrhage	4	Pyaemia	2
Cholera Infatum	5	Scarlet Fever	1
Chronic Salpingitis	1	Senility	7
Congenital Weakness	1	Septicaemia	1
Congestion of Lungs	1	Softening of Brain	1
Consumption of Bowels	3	Spina Bifida	1
Convulsions	1	Still Born	7
Diphtheria	3	Suicide	1
Drowning	2	Syncope	3
Empyema	1	Typhoid Fever	11
Enteritis	6		
Fits	1	Total	174
General Debility	2	Contagious Diseases Reported :	
Hemorrhage of Lungs	1	Scarlet Fever	20
Heart Disease	10	Typhoid Fever	1
Hepatitis	2	Dyphtheria	20
Inflammatory Croup	1	Smallpox	3
Injury and Accidents	8		
Intestinal Obstruction	1	Total	44

Your obedient servant,

JOHN S. McCLELLAND, City Clerk.
City Clerk's Office, St. Catharines, 16th November, 1901.

To the Chairman and Members of the Local Board of Health of the City of St. Catharines:

Gentlemen,—I have the honor herewith to submit my Annual Report as Sanitary Inspector to your Honorable Board, for year ending November 15th, 1901, and would say I have visited and inspected the following places: City and county cow-byres, slaughter and hide houses, city livery and hotel stables, canning and other factories ; and have pleasure in saying all are well kept and in good sanitary condition.

I have regularly tested the milk from the licensed milk vendors and the register has not been below 90. The streets and yards have received my strict attention. The city scavengers have removed 850 barrels of night soil, and they have performed their duties satisfactorily. I have made 890 house to house visits, and have placarded 42 houses during the year, in compliance with the medical returns of contagious diseases. I have fumigated 23 houses where contagion had existed, also the basement of the Court House, the Norris' Ward in the City Hospital and the Free Library.

All of which is respectfully submitted,

A. BOULDEN, Sanitary Inspector.
St. Catharines, November 15th, 1901.

WINDSOR.

REPORT OF DR. JOHN COVENTRY, MEDICAL HEALTH OFFICER, FOR YEAR 1901.

To the Chairman and Members of the Board of Health :

Gentlemen,—I have much pleasure in reporting to you for the year 1901, and in doing so have to repeat what I said in my last two reports, as to the very satisfactory condition of the city's health.

In looking over the Secretary's report, you will notice the very small number of scheduled diseases reported, and I am satisfied he is correct in stating the number would be greater if the attending physicians would do what is clearly their duty, viz., to report all their cases.

Only two deaths from scarlet fever, and one from smallpox, is a record-breaker in the matter of scheduled diseases, and, when it is explained that the smallpox patient was brought in from an outside municipality, the death rate is reduced to two in a population of 12,129. The total death rate from all causes during the year is 15 per 1,000.

Although scheduled diseases have been fewer, other mild epidemics have been present, such as mumps, rotheln and whooping cough. There have been several hundred cases of mumps during the last three months. The form is very mild, and my experience with this disease leads me to the belief that we should not attempt to control it in infancy and childhood, as it generally runs a mild course, whereas it is liable to be much more severe in adolescence and manhood.

Early in the year the School Board adopted a regulation by which, if a child was absent from school a week, readmission could only be secured by a physician's certificate. When no physician had been in attendance I examined the child and gave a certificate. While the result has been highly satisfactory from a sanitary point of view, it has had an unlooked-for effect in securing regularity in the attendance of pupils.

When parents found that their children had to undergo the ordeal of a physician's examination to get them into school again, they have been more careful in keeping them at school. It is perhaps the first time that this regulation has been tried in Ontario, and it has resulted in satisfaction to all concerned.

The public ice supply came under the notice of the Local Board of Health early last summer. Sandwich ice dealers had harvested a large supply, although they had been notified not to distribute it in Windsor for domestic purposes. Under the pretext of using it for cooling purposes, they got consumers to sign a contract not to use it for culinary purposes, and the Board, not wishing to do an injustice to innocent parties who had invested money without knowing the regulations, took no action. A committee of the Board visited the locality from which ice had been harvested and found it to be a bay of shallow water, colored red with dye stuffs from a fur factory near by, and it contained the sewage of Sandwich and Windsor, and was probably contaminated by Detroit sewage as well. This year all parties are warned that ice cut below the Walkerville Wagon Works will not be allowed to come within the municipality for either cooling or domestic purposes.

An examination of 50 samples of milk showed an average of 1.032 specific gravity, the standard being 1.029, and the butter fat averaged 3.87½ per cent., the standard being 3.50 per cent. The test confirmed my opinion that the people of Windsor are being supplied with good milk. A few dealers, who have been supplying water and skimmed milk, have been notified that if they continue to sell an inferior article, their licenses will be cancelled.

The attention of the Ontario and Dominion authorities has been called to the great expense we have been put to in maintaining smallpox patients, who came here from the United States, and our local representatives will be asked to introduce legislation, which will secure a grant of money to such municipalities as have provided themselves with hospitals for the care of these patients. We have been doing this kind of quarantine work and sanitary police work for the Dominion for many years, at the expense of the rate-payers of Windsor. It is only reasonable to ask the Government for some assistance, when it is pointed out that they spend thousands of dollars annually quarantining places that are not one-thousandth part as much exposed as Windsor is.

The Inspector, Mr. Grieves, has been indefatigable in the performance of his duty, and as a result much permanent improvement has been accomplished in plumbing and house drainage.

All of which is respesctfully submitted.

JOHN COVENTRY, M.H.O.

Windsor, December 15th, 1901.

December 6, 1901.

To the Chairman and Members of the Board of Health :

Gentlemen,—I have the honor to place before you for your consideration the statements required by your by-law, namely :

1. The deaths and their causes reported from the 15th of December, 1900, to the 6th inst., inclusive ;

2. The number and nature of the contagious diseases reported for the same period.

With respect to the first of these tables, a professional man would doubtless reduce the number of causes therein given ; and in respect to table No. 2, I think I am warranted in assuming that all the cases have not been reported—that in some instances, when the attending physician has reported a family in which a contagious disease has been developed, and other members of the same family have subsequently contracted the disease, no report of these latter cases has been made. If I am correct in this, it is plain that for statistical purposes the table is unsatisfactory.

I am, gentlemen, your obedient servant.

STEPHEN LUSTED, Secretary.

Deaths registered from December 15, 1900, to December 6, 1901, inclusive, showing the causes of death reported.

Accident	5	Heart Disease—various	15
Alcoholism	1	Haemoptysis	1
Anaemia	3	Hemorrhage Nephritis	1
Appendicitis	1	Infantile Convulsions	1
Apoplexy	5	Indigestion—various	2
Arterio Sclerosis	1	Inflammation of Bladder	1
Brain Fever	1	La Grippe	2
Brights' Disease	2	Malnutrition	1
Bronchitis	8	Marasmus	4
Broncho Pneumonia	2	Meningitis—various	6
Cancer	1	Mollities Cerebri	1
Cardeal Slenosis	1	Nervous Exhaustion	1
Cerebral Lesions	1	Non-Assimilation	1
Cerebral Hemorrhage	1	Obstruction of Bowels	1
Concussion of Brain	1	Old Age (Senile Decay)	13
Cholera Infantum	1	Oldema of Glottis	1
Congestion of Lungs	1	Overdose of Morphine	1
Congestion of Brain	1	Paralysis—various	8
Continued Fever	1	Peritonitis	4
Convulsions	1	Phthisis	2
Cystitis	2	Phthisis, Pulmonalis—Consumption	11
Cirrhosis of Liver	1	Premature Labor	1
Cerebral Thrombus and Shock	1	Pneumonia	2
Caries	1	Premature Birth	6
Debility	1	Scarlet Fever	2
Diabetes	2	Septicaemia	5
Diarrhoea	1	Shock	1
Dropsy	3	Simple Atrophy	1
Eclamsia	2	Smallpox	1
Eclamsia and Atrophy	1	Spasmodic Croup	1
Embolism Cerebral	1	Still Born	11
Endocarditis-Rheumatic	1	Suicide	1
Epilepsy	1	Typhoid Fever	5
Epithelioma of Lip	1	Uraemia	3
Found Dead	2	Whooping Cough with Pneumonia	1
Gangrene	1		
Gastritis	2	Total Deaths	183
General Asthenia	1		

Contagious Diseases.

The number of cases reported is 52

The number of houses placarded 41

Number of cases of scarlet fever 46

Number of cases diphtheria   5
Number of smallpox cases   1
The statement of "deaths registered" discloses the number of the above cases that proved fatal.

WOODSTOCK.

REPORT OF MEDICAL HEALTH OFFICER, FOR YEAR 1901.

To the Mayor and Members of the Council of the City of Woodstock :

Gentlemen,—Permit me to submit the following as my annual report, re sanitary matters, for the year ending November 30th, 1901 :

I am pleased to inform you that the health of our citizens during the year has been above the average. No epidemic has visited our city, and for the past three months only one house has been placarded.

Early in the year every precaution was taken by your Health Board and its officers to encourage a rigid cleaning up, and I am pleased to inform you that our citizens generally complied with our efforts and request, and to-day our city is in as good a sanitary conditon as any city in the Province.

Your Board has adopted a system for the removal and disposal of night soil. We nave met with some difficulty in properly enforcing it, but as two or more scavengers have now the proper appliances we fully expect less friction in the future.

Your Board has also placed in conspicious places signs, requesting our citizens to avoid spitting on sidewalks. I am pleased to say that they are generally complying with our request.

Milk has been carefully tested twice during the year, and found to be good; also herds, byres, etc., properly inspected by Dr. Rudd, Vet. His report was very satisfactory.

We congratulate you on the extension of our sewer and cement sidewalk systems, and trust that in the near future the southern portion of our city will have a proper sewer, thereby adding to the comfort and health of our citizens.

An outbreak of scarlet fever, attended by one death, took place at Woodstock College during the summer, and as a consequence the college was closed for two months, thereby entailing a financial loss to both college and many of our citizens. Had we had an isolation hospital, the college would not have been closed.

Smallpox has been very contiguous to our city during the year. Every precaution was taken by our Mayor and your Board to prevent it spreading to our city.

Number of deaths during the year 103, or about 11 per 1,000. Several of those died in the hospital who belonged to outside municipalities. Number of deaths from consumption, 7 (much less than in former years); pneumonia, 14; typhoid fever, 5; diphtheria, 5; arlet fever, 1; measlés, 0; heart disease, 11; cholera infantum, 1, a great decrease; old age, 10.

All of which is respectfully submitted.

A. McLAY, M.H.O.

Woodstock, November 30th, 1901.

S H.

CHATHAM.

REPORT OF DR. W. R. HALL, MEDICAL HEALTH OFFICER FOR THE YEAR 1901.

Gentlemen,—Nothing of special importance has occurred during the past year on which to report until the smallpox outbreak occurred. Writing at this late date I would say that the smallpox outbreak in the city of Chatham is ended. The last case was dismissed from our Isolation Tents on Tuesday, March 16th, 1902.

The disease was first discovered here on December 17th, 1901, in a family of six persons, named La Bute. Two children were sick with the disease. The father was working at a large factory here, a son in another, and one child attending public school. Ou December 19th, 1901, a second family of seven persons, named Dauphin, was discovered. In this case two of the children were attending public school. These two families and the people coming from Dover and adjoining townships during the Christmas Holidays infected a number of our citizens.

The Local Board of Health went promptly to work, and rigid quarantine was enforced of all infected persons, and on December 23rd "compulsory vaccination" was proclaimed. Ou December 25th, 1901, three large isolation tents, and a cook's tent, were raised and furnished, a physician, trained nurses, cook and porter employed; also an additional inspector and several guards.

Total number of cases, forty-five ; representing 74 families, or 24 points of infection, and 104 people or exposed persons in the families. Thirty-one houses were quarantined in all ;, 24 houses in which the disease was discovered, and four quarantined for chicken pox and three for exposure to the disease.

Three families resisted vaccination and removal to the isolation tents, as follows: La Bute family, six inmates, five cases ; Dauphin family, seven inmates, six cases ; Hock, family, seven inmates. seven cases ; a total of eighteen cases in three families.

Of the remaining 31 families there were no other cases occurred after the disease was discovered, and precautions. such as vaccination, disinfection and isolation taken. In each of two families two patients were seized at the same time. In one family five cases existed one week before discovered. They were mingling with the public very freely, and a number of people were, I think, infected, but prompt vaccination of the exposed stopped the development of the disease. In each of the other families only one case occurred.

One hundred and sixty-four people were quarantined in all ; fourteen of this number were quarantined because they were exposed to the disease.

The total expense incurred in connection with the epidemic will probably be about $3,842.30. For part of this we have assets, worth probably $1.000, which consist of tents, iron beds, bedding, tables. chairs, stoves, dishes and other furniture. Total amount paid for medical attendance, consultations. etc., $602. Amount paid for enforced vaccinations by public vaccinators, $85.65.

Our experience in this epidemic proves the efficacy of vaccination in a very marked degree. In not a single instance did the disease occur where vaccination had been successfully done, but four instances occurred where a vaccinated person escaped when all the other members of the family took the disease.

There were no deaths.

I am yours truly,

WM. R. HALL.

OTTAWA.

REPORT OF DR. ROBT. LAW, MEDICAL HEALTH OFFICER, FOR THE YEAR 1901.

To the Chairman and Members of the Board of Health :

Gentlemen,—I beg leave to lay before you the Annual Report of the Health Department for the year ending 31st October, 1901. The records show that it has been an exceptionally busy one for the department.

The close of the year finds us with several cases of smallpox of the prevailing mild type in our city. In all, since the commencement of the disease, on August 13th, we have had seventy-three cases, none of which have terminated fatally.

Your Board is to be congratulated on the prompt manner with which you have met this threatening epidemic, having rapidly provided comfortable hospital accommodation and good care for such cases on Porter's Island. The prompt removal of all cases from their homes greatly lessened the spread of the disease, but the great check is your recommendation for a general vaccination, and the provision of means for its ready accomplishment. It is estimated that so many are complying with the order of council that the fear of an epidemic of serious magnitude is greatly lessened; but it is most regrettable that prejudice has prevented so many from availing themselves of this great safeguard against the dread disease. Do what we may, surrounded as we are by the disease on all sides, it will continue to be brought into the city and develop in this unprotected remnant, thus needlessly prolonging a trouble that might be promptly stamped out.

The accommodation for scarlet fever, long overtaxed, is so absolutely inadequate that I trust Council, recognizing the extreme urgency of the case, will now grant us a suitable site, so that, if deemed necessary, we may erect a temporary structure thereon at once, and allow us to commence the erection of a permanent building early next year, so that our next annual report may include one from a thoroughly first-class hospital for contagious diseases, the great need of which has so long been urged by Dr. Robillard.

In conclusion, I beg to express my sincere appreciation of the kind and ready counsel of Dr. Robillard, whom Council has so wisely retained as consultant in the consideration of the many difficult points that arise in this department. I must also especially mention the good work done by Dr. Craig on Porter's Island, which has been managed most successfully. Despite the number of cases treated not one death has yet occurred from smallpox. I also wish to express my thanks to all the members of the staff and of our office and the hospitals for the ready way in which they have responded to the increased demand made upon them during the busy time through which we are now passing.

Respectfully submitted,

October 31st, 1901.   ROBERT LAW, M.D.

Table I.

Total Mortality from All Causes for the Year 1901.

Diseases.	November.	December.	January.	February.	March.	April.	May.	June.	July.	August.	September.	October.	Total.
Abcess							1	·1		1	1		4
Accident or violence :													
Burn							4	2					6
Drowning								4	1		2		7
Electricity	1									1			2
Explosion											1		1
Exposure											1		1
Fall	1	1				2			2			1	7
Poisoning		1	1										2
Railway	1				1								2
Shooting		1											1
Stabbing		1											1
Suffocation			1								1		2
Alcoholism				1	1								2
Anaemia			2	2	1			2	1	2			10
Apoplexy	3		1		1		3	1	3				12
Appendicitis			1		3		1				1		6
Ascites					1								1
Asthma	1						1	1					3
Bronchitis	1	1		1	2	7	8	1	2	1	2		26
Cerebral Hemorrhage				1		2	1		1		1		6
Cerebral Tumor						1						1	2
Cirrhosis of Liver	1		1	1	2		1		2			2	10
Convulsions	3	3	3	6	9	6	6	11	11	4	10	1	73
Congenital Defect			4			2	2	3	3	1	5	1	21
Debility, Infantile	4	3	7	3	3	5	7	3	14	8	10	5	72
" Senile	2	4	7	4	9	8	6	6	3	4	3	7	64
Diabetes		1	2						1				4
Diarrhœa and diseases incidental to dentition	1	2	4	5	3	5	3	25	76	30	9	3	166
Diphtheria	3	5	2	5	12	8	3	6	1	1	12	7	65
Dyspnoea			2		2		1	1		1	3	1	1	12
Eclampsia		1		1			1	1		1		1	6
Eczema			1										1
Embolism							1	1		1	1		4
Erysipelas												1	1
Erythema Multiforme					1								1
Gangrene	1	1											2
Gastric Ulcer	1			1	2								4
Hemorrhage			1		2								3
Heart Disease	7	5	6	6	10	8	7	8	5	11	8	7	88
Influenza		1			2	3							6
Intestinal Obstruction	1		1		1		1	1	2	3	2		12
Intestinal Rupture						1							1
Malignant Growth	4	3	3	1	1		3	6	3	3	5	5	37
Mastoditis			1										1
Measles			1	1		2	5	14	3	2		1	29
Meningitis	5	6	3		5		5	7	1	4	3		39
Nephritis		3		5	4	4	2	4	1		1	4	28
Neurasthenia				1									1
Paralysis	2	3	2		4	3	3	2	1	1	5	1	27
Pemphigus													1
Peritonitis						1					1	1	2	5
Pomphylyx									1				1
Pneumonia	8	7	12	22	11	10	1	7	2	3		7	102
Premature Birth	2	4	6	4	5	2	♦	3	7	4	2	4	45
Rachitis				1	1								2
Rheumatism				1	2	1					1		5
Scarlet Fever	1	1		4	4	8	4	9	5	6	6	4	52
Shock, Post Operative						1		2	1				4
Septicaemia	1	1		1			2			1	1	1	4	12
Syphilis		1							1				2
Tetanus								1					1
Typhoid	3	2	1					1		1	2	2	12
Tuberculosis	4	12	12	15	14	9	11	12	11	6	14	5	125
Whooping Cough	3	3		1			1			3	1		12
Unknown causes	1	1	1	2	1	1				1	1		1	10
Total	67	79	89	98	122	105	110	140	170	105	112	76	1,273
Exclusive of Still Births	2	4	13	3	12	6	8	9	5	4	4	3	73

Table II.

Showing number of cases treated in Hospital for Contageous Diseases during 1901.

	Protestant Annex.		R. C. Annex.	
	Diphtheria.	Scarlet Fever.	Diphtheria.	Scarlet Fever.
Admitted	108	149	166	152
Discharged	90	122	137	126
Died	12	10	22	10
In hospital 1st Nov., 1901	6	17	7	16
Of these from outside	11	8	10	1

Table III.

Showing Infectious Diseases reported during 1901.

Diseases.	No. of cases.
Diphtheria	258
Scarlet Fever	391
Smallpox	73
Total	722

Table IV.

Record of House of Bethlehem for the year 1901.

How disposed of.	No. of cases.
Admitted	241
Placed outside or returned to parents	102
Died............................	102
Remaining in Home on 1st November, 1901	37

(1) Algoma.	(2) Is there general sanitary inspection? Is it repeated at intervals every year, or is action taken only on complaint.	(3) Contagious diseases, cases of. Number of deaths.	(4) Is isolation of contagious diseases systematically carried out? Does any isolation hospital exist?	(5) Is diphtheria anti-toxine in common use by physicians? Are results satisfactory?	(6) Is disinfection after contagious diseases carried out under the personal supervision of an officer of the Board.	(7) Does the Board make inspection of public schools? Are new school children vaccinated?
Towns & Villages:						
Gore Bay	No	None	No	No	No	No ....
S. S. Marie	Yes	Smallpox, 44 cases, 1 death; scarlatina, 2 deaths; diphtheria,1 death; typhoid, 11 deaths; tuberculosis, 3 deaths.	Yes ; no	Yes	Yes........	Yes ......
Thessalon Village.	....	Smallpox, 24 cases, diphtheria,1 death; typhoid, 5 cases, 2 deaths; tuberculosis, 3 deaths.	Yes ; no	No	Yes	No ; no.....
Fort William ..	Yes ; yes	Smallpox, 1 case; scarlatina, 6 cases; typhoid, 5 cases,1 death; tuberculosis, 7 cases, 7 deaths.	Yes ; yes.......	Yes	No	No ....
Little Current..	Action on complaint.	Smallpox, 8 cases typhoid, 15 cases; tuberculosis, 1 death.	Yes ; yes ; for smallpox.	No diphtheria.	Yes	No ....
Townships :						
Billings	Only on complaint.	Smallpox, 1 case.	No	Don't know	Yes	No ....
Cockburn Island	On complaint.	None	No hospital.....	No	No	No ... ..
Gordon.........	Only on complaint	None	No cases ; yes, if necessary.	....	....	No ....
Hallam	On complaint.	Yes	Yes	Yes	Yes	Yes........
Howland	At intervals..	Smallpox, 60 cases; typhoid, 10 cases, 3 deaths.	Yes ; no hospital.	No diphtheria.	Yes	No ; yes....
Hilton	When complaint is made.	Tuberculosis, 1 case.	No	No	Yes	No ....
McDonald	....	None	No	No	Not in use..	No . ...
Nairn and Lorne	On complaint.	Smallpox,2 cases	Yes ....,...	Yes	Yes	Sometimes .
Prince	....	....	Yes	Yes	....	No ....
Sandfield	Action taken on complaint	None	No	....	.. ..	No ....
Thessalon Tp...	Action on complaint.	Smallpox, 2 cases tuberculosis, 2 cases, 2 deaths.	Yes; no hospital.	No diphtheria.	Yes	No ....
Tehkummah....	On complaint.	None	No	....	Yes	Yes ....
Assignack	Yes ; yes ; no.	Typhoid, 2 cases, 1 death; tuberculosis,1 death.	Yes ; no	No	Yes	No ; no.....

(8) Are forms for notification supplied to teachers and M. H. O.?	(9) Is there public water supply? If from wells give usual depth of water bearing stratum.	(10) Is there systematic inspection of dairy cows? Have cases of tuberculosis occurred? and state whether tuberculin test has been used.	(11) Are slaughter houses licensed? How is offal disposed of? Is there inspection of carcasses by any officer of the Board?	(12) Is there systematic removal of garbage and night soil?	(13) Is there a public sewerage system?	(14) State No. and kind of noxious trades. See sec. 72, Public Health Act. How licensed and regulated.
No	Spring water ...	No	No	No	No.	
No	Yes		Slaughter houses not inspected.	Yes	Yes, in part of the town.	None.
No	Yes, from Lake Huron.	No	No, some buried.	No	No	None.
Only physicians.	Yes ; no typhoid	Yes ; no	None	Twice a year night soil and garbage are removed.	Yes	None.
To physicians.	Well, 10 to 15 ft. deep.	No	None allowed in the corporation.	Yes	No	None.
No	No	None	None	None	None	None.
No	Creeks and wells	No ; no	None	None	None	None.
No	Well, no typhoid	No ; no	None.			
Yes	Wells, 15 ft	None	No	No	Yes	No.
Yes	No	No	No	No	No	No.
Yes	Springs and Creeks.	No	No	No	No	None.
Yes	From wells	No	No	No	No	None.
Yes	Wells 12 to 16 ft.	No	No	No	No	None.
	Wells & springs	No	No	No	No	None.
No	Springs, creeks and wells.	No ; no	None	No	No	None.
No	Wells, 10 ft.; no cases of typhoid.	Cows not inspected; no tuberculosis.	None	No	No	None.
No	Yes, from wells.	No	None	No	No	None.
No	No; 10 ft. and Bay ; no.	No	No	No	No	None.

	(2)	(3)	(4)	(5)	(6)	(7)
Canarvon	No	None	Yes, when it is necessary.	No	Yes	No ....
Garden River etc	No	Tuberculosis, 5.	No	No	No	No ....
S. S. Marie..... BRANT. City & Towns:	....	Smallpox, 2 cases typhoid, 1 death; consumption, 2.	Yes	No	Yes	No ....
Brantford	Yes ; yes	Smallpox, 17 cases ; scarlatina, 21 cases, 1 death ; diphtheria, 4 cases, 1 death ; typhoid, 67 cases, 7 deaths ; tuberculosis, 24 deaths.	Yes ; yes	Yes	Yes	Yes ......
Paris.	Yes ; yes	Scarlatina, 4 cases.	Yes ; no........	Yes ; yes...	Yes	Yes ......
Townships :						
Burford	Yes, action on complaint.	Smallpox, 58 cases ; diphtheria, 4 cases ; tuberculos i s, 5 cases, 5 deaths.	Yes ; no........	Yes	Yes	Yes ....
Dumfries, S	Yes ; yes	Scarlatin a, 17 cases; diphtheria, 2 cases, typhoid, 3 cases.	Yes, houses placarded ; patients isolated.	Yes	Yes	Yes ; No ...
Brantford	Yes ; yes	Scarl a t i n a, 2 cases; diphtheria, 2 cases ; typhoid, 2 cases ; consumption, 2 cases, 2 deaths.	Yes ; no........	Yes ; yes ...	No	No ; no ....
Onondaga	Action only on complaint.	Tuberculosi s, 3 cases, 1 death.	Yes, isolation of house.	Yes	Yes	Yes ....
BRUCE. Towns and Villages: Chesley	Yes ; yes.....	Scarlatina, 10 cases; diph., 3 cases, 2 deaths; tuberculosis, 2 cases, 2 deaths.	Yes ; no........	Yes	Yes	No ; no ....
Kincardine.....	Once a year ..	Tuberculosis, 1.	Patients isolated in their homes; no.	Yes ; yes...	Yes..	No. ....
Lucknow........	Inspection in May of each year.	None	Yes ; no hospital	....	No..........	No..........
Paisley....... ..	Yes ; yes.....	Diph., 8 cases, 2 deaths ; typhoid, 21 cases; tuberculosis, 3 cases, 3 deaths.	Yes ; no........	Yes ; when required.	No...... ..	No..........
Port Elgin	At intervals..	Scarlatina, 2 cases; diph., 1 case; tuberculosis, 1 case.	Yes ; no..	Yes ; yes...	Under supervison of attending physician.	No ; no ....

(8)	(9)	(10)	(11)	(12)	(13)	(14)
No	No	No ..., ...	No ....:	No	No	None.
No	No	No	No	No	No	None.
No	No, wells 15 to 20 feet.	No	No	No	No	None.
Yes	Yes, typhoid mostly in districts where wells are used.	Yes	None in city....	Night soil regularly removed, garbage before 15th May.	Yes	1 varnish factory, 1 hide storehouse, both outside city.
To teachers by M.H.O	Yes, from springs not this year.	Yes, by veterinary; yes.	None in town...	Not garbage but night soil by contract.	A beginning was made this year.	None.
Yes	Wells and springs.	No ; yes..........	Not licensed, offal fed to hogs.	No	No	No.
Yes	No ; no..........	Yes ; no.........	Yes ; no........	No ....:	No	None.
Yes	Well, 20 to 60 ft.	Yes	No	No	No	None.
No	No ; wells	No	One ; yes ; no...	No	No	None.
Yes........	No ; 12 to 40 ft.	No..............	None in municipality.	Yes........	No.........	None.
Yes........	Yes ; also wells ; no typhoid.	No ; annual......	Inspected ; offal burried ; no.	No	No.........	1 tannery & slaughtering hogs.
No.........	Wells, 20 ft	No ; no..........	None	Each householder attends to it.	No........	None.
M.H.O. only	Wells, from 12 to 50 feet.	No ; no..........	No ; burried ; no	Yes........	No...	1 pork packing house.
No	No ; Wells, 10 to 30 ft.	No.....	None	Yes........	No.........	None.

	(2)	(3)	(4)	(5)	(6)	(7)
Southampton...	Yes..........	Typhoid, 5 cases; tuberculosis, 1 case, 1 death.	Yes ; no........	Yes	Yes........	Yes ; yes...
Teeswater......	Yes ; yes	Diph., 1 case ...	Yes ; no........	Yes ; yes...	Yes.......	Yes........
Walkerton	Yes ; yes	Typhoid, 2 cases; tuberculosis,11 cases, 5 deaths.	Yes ; no	Yes ; yes...	Yes........	No ; no ....
Wiarton	Yes ; yes	Diph., 1 death; tuberculosis, 4.	Yes ; no........	Yes ; yes...	Yes........	Yes ; yes...
Townships:						
Albermarle.....	Only on complaint.	Tuberculosis, 1 case.	No ; no........	Yes	Yes........	Yes ; yes...
Amabel........	Yes ; yes.....	Scarlatina, 15 cases; typhoid, 3cases,1 death; tuberculosis, 4 cases, 4 deaths.	Yes ; no........	Yes ; yes...	Yes........	Yes ; yes...
Brant..........	Yes ; yes ; no.	....	Yes ; no hospital	Yes	Yes........	No ; no ....
Carrick	Yes ; once a year.	Scarlatina, 10 cases; diph., 6 cases, 2 deaths; typhoid,1 case; tuberculosis, 3 cases, 3 deaths.	Yes ; no...... ..	Yes	Yes........	Yes; when request is made by parents or trustees.
Culross	Inspection once a year.	Tuberculosis, 2 cases, 2 deaths.	Yes	....	Yes........	Yes........
Elderslee.......	Yes ; yes.....	Tuberculosis, 2 deaths.	Yes ; no........	Cannot say.	Yes........	Yes ; no ...
Greenock.......	General sanitary inspection yearly.	Scarlatina, 10 cases ; diph., 1 case, 1 death; typhoid, 8 cases 2 deaths; consumption, 2 cases, 2 deaths.	Yes ; no........	Yes ; yes ..	Yes........	Yes; not by the Board.
Huron	At intervals ..	Diph., 1 case, 1 death; typhoid 1 case ; consumption, 5 cases, 5 deaths.	In diphtheria, scarlatina and smallpox ; no.	No.........	Yes ; by M. H. O.	No ; no ....
Kincardine.....	At intervals and always on compl'nt.	Typhoid, 4 cases; Tuberculosis, 2 cases, 2 deaths.	Yes	No cases ...	Yes	No ; no ....
Kinloss	On complaint.	Typnoid, 1 case; tuberculosis, 6 deaths.	Yes ; no........	Yes ; yes...	Yes........	No ; no ....
Linsday and St. Edmund.	....	Scarlatina, 1 case.	Yes ; no........	....	Yes........	No ....
Saugeen........	On complaint.	Typhoid, 1death; tuberculosis, 1 death.	As ordered by M.H.O.	Yes ; not always.	Yes........	Only when required.

(8)	(9)	(10)	(11)	(12)	(13)	(14)
Yes	Wells, 8 to 25 ft.	No ; no	No ; burried ; yes.	No.........	No.........,	Slaughter'ng animals, extracting oil from fish.
Yes........	Wells, 40 to 70 ft	No......	No ; .ffal burried ; no.	No....... ..	No.........	None.
Yes........	Yes ; some wells 14 ft.; no.	No ; no..........	No ; cooked and fed to hogs.	Yes........	Yes......:.	None.
Yes........	Yes.............	Yes. ; no	None	Yes........	No.........	None.
No	No ; wells, 10 to 80 feet.	No ; no	None	No.........	No.........	None.
Yes	No ; wells, 20 ft; no.	No ; no..........	No ; burried ; no	No.........	No.........	None.
No	Wells	Yes ; no	Yes ; boiled or burried.	No.........	No.........	Slaughter-houses.
No..........	No ; wells, 20 to 30 ft; no deaths from typhoid.	No	No.............	No.........	No.........	None.
Yes........	Wells, 20 to 70 ft	No.....	No ; no			None.
Yes........	Wells, 30 ft.....	No ; no	Only a few small ones.	Yes	No.........	No.
Yes........	No ; wells, 20 ft.	No ; no	Yes ; burried ; no.	No.........	No.........	None.
To physicians only.	Wells, 20 to 40 ft	No ; no	Yes ; burried ; no.	No........	One sewer in village of Ripley.	None.
M. H. O's. only.	Wells, 25 ft ; no.	No ; no	No ; can't say ; no.	No.........	No.........	None.
No	Wells, 20 to 40 ft	No ; no..........	No	No.........	No.........	None.
Yes........	Wells, 12 ft.....	No . ...,....	None		No.........	None.
When requested.	Wells ; Saugeen river & creeks; no.	No...............	Yes ; licensed ; offal fed to hogs ; no.	Removed by householder.	No........	Slaughterhouses and beef rings all kept in sanitary condition.

	(2)	(3)	(4)	(5)	(6)	(7)
CARLETON. *City and Towns:*						
Ottawa	General sanitary inspection.	Smallpox, 73 cases, no deaths; scarlatina, 391 cases, 52 deaths; diph.,258 cases 65 deaths; typhoid, 12 deaths; tuberculosis, 125 deaths.	Yes	Yes ; good results.	Yes....... .	No ; no ....
Ottawa East....	General inspection.	Smallpox,6cases; scarlatina, 9 cases, 2 deaths; diph., 3 cases; tuberculosis, 4 cases.	Yes ; no........	Yes	Yes.........	Yes........
Townships:						
Fitzroy	Action on complaint.	Typhoid, 1 case; tuberculosis, 1 death.	Yes ; no........	Yes ; yes ..	Yes........	No ; no ....
Gloucester....	Regular sanitary inspection.	Smallpox,9cases; Scarlatina, 30 cases, 1 death.	Yes ; no hospital	Yes ; yes..	Yes.........	No; 240 children vaccinated...
Goulborne......	Only on complaint.	Scarlatina, 2 cases ; diph., 12 cases, 2 deaths ; tuberculosis, 2 deaths.	Yes ; no........	Yes; yes...	Yes..	No ; no ....
Malborough ...	No ; no ; yes.	Scarlatina,1case; tuberculosis, 2 cases, 2 deaths.	As far as possible ; no.	Yes	Yes	No ; no ....
March.........	At intervals..	Scarlatina, 25 cases, 1 death; tuberculosis, 2 cases, 1 death.	Yes ; no	Yes ; yes...	No ; only as physician directs.	No ; no ....
North Gower ..	No...........	Tuberculosis, 2 cases.	No	Yes	Yes........	No ; no ....
Nepean	On complaint.	Smallpox, 31 cases, 1 death ; Scarlatida, 25 cases, 1 death ; diph., 45 cases, 5 deaths ; typhoid, 3 cases.	Yes ; no	Yes ; yes...	Yes.......	None.......
DUFFERIN. *Towns and Villages:*						
Grand Valley ..	Yes ; yes ; no.	Typhoid, 4 cases.	Yes ; no	Yes ; yes...	Yes	Yes; no ....
Orangeville.....	Yes ; repeated at intervals.	Scarlatina, 15 cases ; diphtheria,14 cases; 4 deaths.	Yes ; no........	Yes ; yes ; when used early.	Yes	Yes ; yes...
Shelbourne	Repeated inspection.	Diphtheria, 13 cases, 3 deaths,	Strict quarantine, ; no hospital.	Yes ; yes...	Yes	Yes ; yes...
Townships:						
Garafraxa, E...	No ; yes ; no.	....	Yes ; no........	Yes	Yes	No ; no ....

(8)	(9)	(10)	(11)	(12)	(13)	(14)
Yes........	Yes.............	Yes...............	None in city....	Yes........	Yes........	None.
No.........	No : 15 to 20 ft.; no.	Owners have had them inspected; none.	Yes ; carted away and buried.	Night soil only.	No.........	....
Not always.	Wells, 12 to 20 ft	Yes..............	None	No.........	No.........	None.
No...	No ; 25 to 50 ft	No ; no...........	Yes.............	No.........	No.........	Mfg of dynamite piggery and slaughter-houses.
No....	No ; wells......	No ; no	None	No.........	No........ ...	None.
No.........	Wells, 20 ft ; no.	No ; no	No ; no	No.........	No.........	None.
Yes........	Wells of all depths.	No ; no	None	No.........	No.........	None.
No.........	Wells, about 17 ft ; no.	No ; yes...........	No ; no	No.........	No.........	Slaughtering animals.
Yes........	No ; wells.	No ; no	Yes; carted away by farmers no.	Yes.........	No.........	....
Yes	No ; 30 ft ; no..	No ; no	No ; buried ; no	No.........	No.........	None.
Yes	Yes	No	None	Yes	No.........	None.
Yes	Artesian wells, 500 ft. deep ; tower system ; no typhoid.	No	None	Not a complete system.	No.........	None.
No	Wells, 20 to 60 feet.	No	None	No.........	No...... ..	None.

	(2)	(3)	(4)	(5)	(6)	(7)
Luther, E....	Slaughter houses inspected monthly; other cases on complaint	Typhoid, 2 cases; tuberculosis, 2 cases, 2 deaths.	Yes ; no	Yes ; when used early.	Yes	No ; no ....
Melancthon ,...	Action taken only on complaint.	Scarlatina, 1 case; diphtheria, 7 cases ; tuberculosis, 2 cases.	Yes ; no........	Yes ; yes...	No	No ; no ....
Mono..........	....	3 deaths from consumption.	No..............	No..........	No	No ....
ELGIN. *City and Towns :*						
St. Thomas.....	Action on complaint.	Scarlatina, 57 cases, 5 deaths.	Yes; hospital for smallpox only.	Yes ; yes...	Yes	No ; no.....
Aylmer	Yes ; yes	Scarlat'na, 1 case; typhoid, 1 case; tuberculosis, 9.	Yes ; no........	No..........	Yes	No ; yes....
Port Stanley ...	General inspection.	Scarlatina, 2 cases, 1 death; tuberculosis, 2 cases, 1 death	Yes ; no........	Yes ; yes...	Yes	No ; no ....
Springfield	Yes ; yes	Typhoid, 1 case, 1 death,	Yes ; no........	Yes	Yes	No ; no ....
Vienna	Action on complaint.	Typhoid, 1 case; tuberculosis, 1 case, 1 death.	No hospital.. ..	Yes	No	No ; no ....
Townships .						
Aldborough	Yes ; yes	Scarlatina, 12 cases, 1 death; tuberculosis, 6 cases, 6 deaths.	Yes ; no........	No cases this year.	Yes	Yes ; no ...
Dorchester, S...	Action on complaint.	None..........	No ; no	Yes ; fair ..	Sometimes..	No ; no ....
Southwold	Yes, annually.	Scarlatina, 2 cases; tuberculosis, 3 deaths.	No ; no	Used some times.	Yes	Yes ; yes...
Yarmouth	Action on complaint.	Scarlatina, 7 cases; typhoid, 4 cases ; tuberculosis, 6 cases, 6 deaths.	Yes ; no hospital	Yes	Yes	Yes ; yes...
ESSEX. *City and Towns :*						
Windsor	Going on all the time.	Smallpox, 1 case, 1 death; scarlatina, 38 cases, 2 deaths ; diphtheria, 5 cases; typhoid, 4 deaths ; tuberculosis, 6 deaths.	Yes ; yes......	Yes ; yes...	Yes	No ... .

(8)	(9)	(10)	(11)	(12)	(13)	(14)
No	No ; wells, 20 ft.	No·	No ; buried ; no.	No.........	No.........	None.
No	Wells ; no......	No	None	No..........	No..........	None.
No	No	No	No.............	No.........	No.........	None.
No	Y e s ; typhoid has . not been reported.	No; cannot say...	Only at pork packing establishment.	No.........	Yes	Stor a g e of hides, soap works, tallow melting slaug h t e r-house, g a s works.
No	Wells, 8 to 12 ft.	No ; no............	....	Yes	No.........	None.
No	Wells, 12 to 18 ft,	No	No ; offal fed to hogs.	No.........	No.........	None.
No	Wells, 50 ft.; no.	No ; no...........	Yes ; buried; no.	No..........	No..........	None.
Yes	Wells, 20 to 30 ft.; no.	Don't know	None	Yes	No........	None.
No	Wells ; no ty-phoid.	No ; no	No ; no	Yes	No.........	4 slaughter-houses.
Don't know.	No ; 25 ft	No...............	None	No.........	No.........	None.
None.......	Wells, 20 feet ; none.	Yes ; none	No ; offal fed to hogs.	Gene r a l l y burned.	No.........	None.
Yes	Wells, about 20 ft.; no.	N o ; inspection when required.	Yes; offal buried	Yes, f r o m p u b l i c schools.	....	... .
Yes	Yes ; no wells..	No ; yes	None	Yes	Yes	None.

	(2)	(3)	(4)	(5)	(6)	(7)
Belle River.....	Action on complaint.	Diphtheria, 3 cases, 2 deaths; tuberculosis, 3 cases.·	No..............	Yes ; yes...	Yes	No ....
Kingsville......	Yes ; at intervals during the year.	Smallpox, 1 case; tuberculosis, 2 cases, 2 deaths.	Yes ; no	Yes ; yes ..	Yes	No ; no.....
Leamington	Several times a year.	Scarlatina, 15 cases, 1 death.	No ; no.........	No diphtria.	Yes	Yes ; no....
Walkerville	Yes ; by sanitary inspector.	Smallpox, 2 cases, 1 death ; scartina, 9 cases ; diphtheria, 1 case, 1 death.	Yes ; yes	Yes ; results satisfactory	Under direction of M H.O.	Yes; yes ...
Sandwich	....	Scarlatina, 6 cases, 1 death; diphtheria, 1 death; typh'id, 1 death.	Yes ; no hospital	Yes	Yes	Yes ....
Townships:						
Anderdon	When complaint is made.	Tuberculosis, 8 cases, 8 deaths.	Yes ; no........	Yes ; yes...	By attending physician.	No; no.....
Colchester, S ...	On complaint only.	Scarlatina, 1 case; diphth'a, 25 cases, 2 deaths ; typhoid, 10 cases; tuberculosis, 4 cases, 1 death.	No..............	No..........	Yes	No ; no.....
Gosfield, N.....	When complaint is made.	Typhoid, 10 cases; tuberculosis, 3 deaths.	Yes ; no hospital	Yes ; results good.	Yes	Yes ....
Malden	Action on complaint only.	Tuberculosis, 3 deaths.	No ; no	Yes ; yes...	No	No ; no.....
Maidstone	On complaint.	Diphtheia, 2 cases, 1 death.	Yes	....	Yes	....
Mersea	Action taken on complaint.	Scarlatina, 12 cases, 1 death ; diphthria, 8 cases, 1 death; typhoid, 21 cases, 1 death ; tuberculosis, 5 cases, 5 deaths.	Yes ; no........	Not much used.	Yes	Yes; yes....
Gosfield, S......	Only on complaint.	Tuberculosis, 3 deaths.	Not required; no	Yes ; yes...	Yes	No ....
Sandwich, S	Only on complaint.	Typhoid, 1 case, 1 death; tuberculosis, 1 death.	Yes ; no	Yes ; yes...	Yes	No ; no ....
Rochester	Action taken on complaint	None	Yes; no hospital	.No..........	Yes	No ; no ....
Sandwich, W...	....	Typhoid, 1 case.	No..............	Yes ; yes...	Yes	No ; no ....
Tilbury,'N	On complaint only.	Tuberculosis....	Yes ; no........	No occasion.	Yes ; by M. H. O.	No. ....

(8)	(9)	(10)	(11)	(12)	(13)	(14)
Yes	Wells, 10 ft.; no.	No.....	No; fed to hogs; no.	No.........	No.........	None.
No	Yes ; lake water and wells ; no.	No ; no	None	No.........	No.........	None.
Yes	Wells, 50 ft	No ; no	None	No.........	No..... ...	None.
Yes	Yes ; no	Yes, by M.H.O...	None	Yes	Yes	Not any.
Yes	Yes, ; from river Detroit.	No ; no	None	No.........	In part.....	None.
No	Wells, from 30 to 60 ft. in a few cases.	No ; no	None	No.........	No.........	None.
No	Wells, 10 to 30 ft.; no.	No...............	No.............	No.........	No..... ...	None.
Yes	No	No ; no	No........... ..	No.........	No.	None.
No	Wells, 75 ft.; no.	No ; no	No : fed to pigs ; no.	No.........	No..... ...	None.
....	Wells	None	....	No.........	No........	None.
Yes	Wells ; yes.....	No ; no	No : no	Yes	No.........	None.
To M.H.O..	From wells ; no.	No ; no	None in the Tp.	No.........	No...... .. .	None.
No.........	No; some surface wells and some artesian ; typhoid comes from former.	No ; no	No ; fed to hogs	No	None	No.
No...... ..	Wells, 10 to 15 ft.	No ; no	Not licensed ; offal generally fed to hogs.	No	No	Slaughter houses.
Yes	Wells, 12 ft.; no.	No	Inspected	No	No	None.
Yes	No ; wells about 18 feet; yes, about 3 years ago.	No	None	Yes	No	None in Tp.

9 H.

	(2)	(3)	(4)	(5)	(6)	(7)
Tilbury, W....	Yes ; yes	Typhoid, 1 case.	No............	Yes ; yes...	Yes	Yes ; no....
FRONTENAC. *City and Towns* :						
Garden Island..	Yes ; yes	Scarla t i n a, 21 cases; typhoid, 1 case; tuberculosis, 1 case, 1 death.	Generally taken to Kingston hospital.	....	Yes	Yes ; no....
Portsmouth	General inspection.	Typhoid, 1 case, 1 death; tuberculosis, 8 deaths.	Yes ; yes.......	Yes	No.........	No ; no ....
Townships : Bedford...	Action taken on complaint.	Tuberculosis, 1 death.	N o contagious diseases in Tp.	Not required.	When necessary.	No ; no....
Clarendon a n d Miller.	Inspection on complaint.	None	Yes; no hospital.	....	Yes	....
Hinchinbrook ..	Action on complaint.	Scarla t i n a, 15 cases; diphtheria, 2 cases.	No ; no	Yes ; yes...	No.........	No ; no ....
Kingston	No re'gular system.	Consumption, 3 deaths.	No ; no	Don't know.	No.........	No.........
Kennebec	Yes ; yes.....	None	Yes ; no........	Yes ; yes ..	Yes	No ; no ....
Olden	Inspection twice a year	Diph t h e r i a, 5 cases; typhoid, 2 cases.	Yes; no hospital.	Yes ; yes ..	No : no	No ; no ....
Oso	Only on complaint.	Smallpox,6 cas's; tuberculosis, 1 death.	Yes ; yes	Yes ; yes ..	Yes	No ; yes....
Palmerston, etc.	When complaint is made.	Diph t h e r i a, 1 death.	Yes ; no ....'.. .	Don't know.	Yes	No children were vaccinated in 1900.
Pittsburgh . ..	Yes; no; action taken on complaint.	Tuberculosis, 2 deaths.	Yes ; no	Don't know.	By order of physici a n in charge	No.........
Portland.......	....	Typhoid, 5 cases.	No.	No..........	No.........	Yes ......
GREY. *Towns and Villages* : Durham........	....	Diphtheria, 25 cases, 2 deaths.	Yes ; no	Yes ; yes...	Yes, by M. H. O.	Schools a r e inspected.
Hanover'.......	Yes ; yes	Diph t h e r i a, 8 cases.	Yes ; no	Yes ; yes...	Yes	Yes ; no....
Owen Sound....	Yes ; yes	Scarlatina, 1 case ; diphtheria, 3 cases, 2 deaths ; typhoid, 20 cases, 2 deaths.	Yes	Not often required; results satisfactory.	Yes	No ....

(8)	(8)	(10)	(11)	(12)	(13)	(14)
No.........	No; wells 125 ft.; yes, from surface wells.	No	No	No ....,	No	None ......
No.........	Lake water used.	No ; no	None	Only night-soil.	No	None ......
No.........	Wells	No	None	Yes	No	None ......
No...	Wells & springs.	No ; no	None	Yes	No	None .....
No.........	Wells & springs.	No inspection	None	Yes	No	None ......
No.........	Wells,10 to 15 ft.	No ; no	None	No	No	None ......
No.........	Wells	Yes ; no..........	None	No	No	None ......
No.........	Wells, from 10 to 20 feet.	No	No	No	No	None ......
No.........	Wells, about 10 ft.	No ; no	No ; offal buried; no inspection.	Yes	No	None .....
Yes	....	No ; no	No ; no ; yes....	Yes	No	None ......
Yes	No	No ; no	None	No	No	None ......
No..........	No; wells ; don't know.	Yes ; no...	No slaughter-houses.	No	No	None ......
No.........	Wells, 10 to 75 feet.	No	None	No	No	None ......
....	Wells,15 to 60 ft.	No ; no	None	Nightsoil is removed.	No	None.
Yes.	Waterworks in course of construction.	No	No ; buried ; no.	No	No	None.
Yes	Yes ; no........	No	Yes; boiled and fed outside town limits.	Not thorough.	Yes	Storing hides, tallow melting, tanning hides, m'fg. gas, slaughtering animals.

	(2)	(3)	(4)	(5)	(7)	(7)
Townships :						
Artimesia	No general inspection.	Diphtheria, 1 case, 1 death; typhoid, 2 cases, 1 death; tuberculosis, 2 cases, 2 deaths.	Isolation carried out when notice is given.	Not used to any extent.	Yes	No ; yes....
Bentinck	Yes; and spec'l inspection when required.	Diphtheria, 1 case ; tuberculosis, 2 cases, 2 deaths.	Yes ; no.	Yes ; satisfactory.	Yes	No; don't know.
Derby..........	Yes ; yes	None	No occasion	Don't know.	No	Yes ; no....
Egermont	No ; action taken on complaint.	Typhoid, 2 cases; tuberculosis, 2 cases.	No ; no	Yes ; yes...	No ; only by order of Dr.	No ....
Euphrasia	On complaint.	Smallpox,.1 case; scarlatina, 6 cases ; diphtheria,13 cases.	Yes	Yes ; fairly so.	Yes	No ....
Glenelg	On complaint.	Diphtheria, 8 cases,3 deaths; typhoid, 6 cases, 1 death,; tuberculosis, 2 cases, 1 death.	Yes ; under attending physician's directions.	Yes ; no ...	Yes	Yes ; no....
Normanby	Partial inspection.	Scarlatina, 1 ; 1 death ; diphtheria, 2 cases, 1 death; typhoid, 2 cases, 2deaths; tuberculosis,1 death.	As well as circumstances will permit; no hospital.	Yes ; results good,when used[early.	Yes	No ....
Osprey	Action on complaint.	Typhoid, 8 cases; tuberculosis, 4 cases, 2 deaths.	Yes; no hospital.	Yes	Yes	No ....
Sarawak	....	Tuberculosis, 2 deaths.	No ; no	No cases ...	Not required.	Yes . .....
Sullivan........	Yes ; yes	....	Yes	... .	Yes	Yes ; no....
Sydenham	Action on complaint.	Tuberculosis, 1 death.	Yes ; yes	No	No ; no	Yes ....
HALDIMAND. *Towns and Villages*:						
Caledonia	No ; only on complaint.	None	Yes ; no	Yes ; yes...	Yes ; by M. H. O.	No ....
Cayuga	Yes ; yes.....	Typhoid, 9 cases.	Yes ; no	Yes ; yes...	No	No ; no.....
Dunnville	None during the year.	Scarlatina, 3 cases, 1 death ; diphtheria, 1 case; tuberculosis, 4 deaths.	Isolated in residence.	Yes ; yes...	Under the supervision of attending physician.	Not this year.
Townships :						
Canboro........	Only on complaint.	....	....	....	....	No ....

(8)	(9)	(10)	(11)	(12)	(13)	(14)
Yes	No ; about 35 ft.	No ; no............	No	No	No	None.
Yes	No ; wells, about 20 ft.	No ; no............	No; no	No	No	None.
Yes	No ; wells, 15 to 40 ft.	No ; no............	Yes; don't know.	No	No	Two slaughter houses, licensed.
Yes	wells, about 20 to 30 ft.	No ; none	No ; only o n e slaughter house.	No	No	None.
No	Wells, 20 ft.....	No	No	No	No	No.
Yes	No ; wells......	No; no	No	No	No	None.
Yes	No ; wells, 13 to 35 ft.; no.	No; no	Yes ; offal cooked ; no.	No	None	No.
Yes	Wells	No	No ; offal fed to hogs.	No	No	None.
Yes	No ; no typhoid.	Yes; no	Yes	No	No	None.
Yes	No ; wells.....	....	Yes	No	No	None.
....	Wells, from 10 to 40 ft.	No, no	None...........	No	No	None.
Yes	Wells, 18 ft.; no.	None	No; offal fed to hogs.	No	No	None.
No	No ; very f e w wells, mostly rain w a t e r used.	No	No ; no...... ..	No	No	None.
None t h i s year'	Yes; no typhoid.	No	None in municipality.	No	No	None.
....	No	No	No	....	....	....

	(2)	(3)	(4)	(5)	(6)	(7)
Cayuga, S......	Only on complaint.	Scarlatina, 2 cases; tuberculosis, 2 cases.	Yes; no hospital.	Yes	Yes	No ....
Cayuga, N	....	Smallpox, 2 cases.	Yes; no hospital.	Yes; yes...	Yes	Think not..
Dunn	Action on complaint.	Scarlatina, 2 cases, 2 deaths; diphtheria, 2 cases, 1 death.	No; no..........	Yes; yes...	No	No; no ....
Moulton.	No; no	Tuberculosis, 2 cases, 2 deaths.	No; no..........	Yes; yes...	Yes	No; no ....
Rainham., ...	....	Tuberculosis, 2 cases.	No	Don't know.	No	No ....
Sherbrooke	Action on complaint.	None	No occasion	No	No contagious diseases.	No ....
HASTINGS. *Cities and Towns:* Belleville.......	Yes; yes.....	Scarlatina, 25 cases; diphtheria, 13 cases.	Yes; yes.......	Yes; yes....	Yes	Yes ......
Madoc	Yes; yes.....	Tuberculosis, 3 deaths.	No............	Yes; yes....	Yes	Yes; no ....
Trenton........	Yes; yes.....	Scarlatina, 1 case; diphtheria, 1 case; typhoid, 4 cases.	Yes; no	Yes; yes...	Yes	Yes; no ....
Tweed	Yes; yes.....	Scarlatina, a few mild cases; tuberculosis, 1 case, 1 death.	Yes; no	Yes; no....	M. H O. attends to it.	Yes; no ....
Stirling	Yes; yes.....	Tuberculosis, 2 deaths.	Yes; no	Yes; yes....	Yes	No ....
Townships: Carlow	No; only on complaint.	None	No.	Not reported.	No contagious diseases	No; yes....
Dungannon	No	Tuberculosis, 1 case.	No; no	Yes; yes....	Yes	No; no .....
Faraday........	Sanitary inspection annually.	None	Yes; no	No	Yes	No; no .....
Hungerford	Only on complaint.	Diphtheria, 7 cases, 2 deaths; typhoid, 1 case; tuberculosis, 1 case, 1 death.	....	....	....	....
Huntingdon.....	No	....	No; no	Yes; yes	No	No; no .....
Limerick.	On complaint.	Tuberculosis, 1 case, 1 death.	No; no	Some physicians use it	No	No; no .....
Madoc.	Action taken on complaint.	Diphtheria, 1 case.	....	Not required	Yes	No; no .....
Marmora and Lake.	Action taken on complaint.	Smallpox, 1 case.	Fairly; no......	Yes; yes....	Yes	No; no .....
Mayo	....	None ....:....	No cases........	No	....	General vaccinati'n last year.

(8)	(9)	(10)	(11)	(12)	(13)	(14)
No	No	No	None .... No	No	No	None.
No	No ; wells and cisterns.	Think not........	There are none.. Yes		No	None.
No	Wells, 10 to 24 ft.	No; no	None in Tp..... No		No	None.
No	No ; 5 to 15 ft. ; no.	No; no	No ; said to be No .... cooked and fed to hogs ; no.		No	None.
No	No	No	No .... No		No	None.
No	No; 12 to 16 ft..	No	None .... No		No	None.
Yes	Waterworks; yes	Yes; no	None in city limits.	Yes	Partially ...	None.
No	No; 15 to 30 ft..	No ; no	No ; no	Yes	No	Ncne.
No	Waterworks and some wells.	Yes; no	None...	Yes	No	None.
No	Wells only	Yes ; by veterinary surgeons ; no.	No; carted away; no	No ; only by household-ers.	No	None.
No	No ; 25 ft	No	Yes	Yes	No	Ncne.
No	Wells &streams; no.	No	No; carted away; no.	No	None.......	None.
No	Wells ; 12 ft. ; no.	No; no	None in Tp.....	No	No	None.
No	Water from wells; from 10 to 30 ft. ; no typhoid.	No ; none........	No ; fed to hogs, no.	No	No	None.
....	....	No ; no............	No ; fed to hogs; no.	No	No	None.
No	Wells	No	No ; don't know.	No	No	None.
No	Springs gener-ally.	No	None in Tp	No	No	None.
No	No; about 20 ft.; no.	No ; no	None in Tp	No	....	None.
No	No; from 15 to 25 ft.	No	None in the Tp.	No	No	None.
No	Wells; from 3 to 50 ft.	No	None in Tp	....	No	None.

	(2)	(3)	(4)	(5)	(6)	(7)
McClure, Bangor and Wicklow.	Only on complaint.	None	Yes; no	Yes; yes....	By M.H.O.	No ....
Sidney	Yes, as to schools, factories & slaughter houses.	Scarlatina, 4 cases; diphtheria, 2 cases, 1 death; typhoid, 12 cases, 3 deaths; tuberculosis, 6 d'ths.	Yes; no	Yes	Yes	Yes; no ....
Tyendinaga	Only on complaint.	Tuberculosis, 5 cases.	When necessary; no.	I think so .	Yes	None.......
Rawdon........	Yes	Typhoid, 2 cases; tuberculosis, 6 cases.	No............	Yes; yes....	Yes	No ....
HURON. *Towns and Villages:* Bayfield.......	Yes ; only on complaint.	Scarlatina, 1 case; typhoid, 7 cases; tuberculosis, 2 cases, 2 deaths.	Yes; no	No cases ..	No	No; no .....
Brussels..	Yes ; twice a year.	Diph., 2 cases; tuberculosis, 4 deaths.	Yes; no	No	Yes	Yes ....
Clinton	Gen'ral inspection every spring and repeated at intervals.	Smallpox, 1 case; scarlatina, 8 cases; diphtheria, 2 cases, 2 deaths ; typhoid, 5 cases, 1 death; tuberculosis, 2 d'ths.	Yes; no hospital.	Yes; no	Yes	No; no; the Board will not agree.
Goderich	Yes ; at intervals.	Diphtheria, 4 cases, 1 death; typhoid, 10 cases; tuberculosis, 8 deaths.	No ; no	Yes; yes....	Yes, in some cases.	No; no .....
Seaforth	Yearly inspection.	Scarlatina, 14 cases; typhoid, 10 cases; tuberculosis, 2 d'ths.	Yes; yes........	No...........	No	No ....
Wroxeter	No.	None	No......	No..........	No	No ....
Wingham	Action on complaint.	Tuberculosis, 4 deaths.	Yes	Yes	Yes	No ....
Townships: Ashfield........	Only on complaint.	....	No ; no	Don't know.	M. H, O. or attending physician.	No; no .....
Colborne	Only on complaint.	None	No ; no	Think so ...	Yes, by M. H.O.	No; no .....
Goderich	On complaint.	Typh.id, 1 case.	None	No..........	Yes	Yes; no ....
Grey	Yes ; action on complaint.	Tuberculosis, 4 deaths.	Yes; no	Yes; yes....	Yes	No; no .....
Hay	School houses, slaughter houses, etc., inspected.	Diphtheria, 2 cases; tuberculosis, 4 cases.	Yes; no	Yes; yes....	Yes	Once during June; no.

(8)	(9)	(10)	(11)	(12)	(13)	(14)
No	Wells; no	No ; no	None..	....	No	None.
No	No	No	No	....	No	None.
No	Wells; various depths; cannot say.	No	No ; fed or buried ; no.	No	No	None.
No	No	No	No	No	No	No.
No	Wells	No ; no	None.....	No	No	None.
Yes	No; Wells; 12 to 35 ft.; no.	No ; no	None in town...	Yes	No	None.
Yes	Yes ; wells, 40 ft. ; artesian wells, 125 ft. ; no.	No ; no	No ; fed to hogs; no.	Yes	No	None.
No	Yes	No	No ; fed to hogs; no.	No	Yes	None.
No	No; wells; 15 to 30 ft.; no evidence that such was the case.	None within municipality.	None within municipality.	Each householder attends to his own.	No	Rendering tallow.
No	No; wells ; no..	No	None in the municipality.	No	No	None.
Yes	Wells ; 12 to 30 ft. deep.	No ; no	None..........	No	No	None.
No	Wells	No ....,........	No ; no	No	No	None.
No	Wells; 30 to 40 ft.	No ; no	None in Tp	No	No	None.
No'	Wells ; don't know.	No ; no	....	....	....	....
Yes	No; no	No ; no	No : don't know ; no.	No	No	None.
No	No; wells from 20 to 100 ft.	None in Tp.......	No ; fed to hogs; no.	No	No	None.

	(2)	(3)	(4)	(5)	(6)	(7)
Howick	Yes ; yes ; no.	Smallpox, 1 case; scarlat i n a, 6 cases.	Yes ; no	Yes	Yes	No ....
Hullett	Action taken on complaint.	Tuberculosis, 1 case.	No	Not c o m-m o n l y used.	No	No ....
McKillop	On complaint.	Tuberculosis, 4 deaths.	No ; no	Don t know.	No	Yes ....
Stanley	Yes ; action on complaint.	Tuberculosis, 3 deaths.	Yes ; no........	Yes	Attending physic i a n gives directions.	Partially ...
Stephen	No ; no ; yes..	Small pox, 24 cases; typhoid, 1 case, 1 death; tuberculosis, 3 cases,3 deaths.	Yes ; yes.......	Yes	No; no.....	No ....
Turnberry..*....	Yes ; on complaint.	Typhoid,3 cases.	In so far as isolation at homes can be carried out ; no.	Don't know.	Under direction of M. H. O.	N o : about 450 vaccinated during the summer.
Usborne........	Action taken on complaint.	Scar l a t i n a, 9 cases, 1 death ; diphtheria, 2 cases ; tuberculosis,3 cases, 2 deaths.	No hospital; isolated as far as practicable in their homes.	Yes ; yes...	Yes	Yes ; no....
Wawanosh, E ..	Action taken on complaint.	None	No hospital	....	....	No ....
Wawanosh, W..	When c o m-plaint is made.	Tuberculosis, 1 death.	Yes; no hospital	Yes	Yes	No; yes ....
HALTON. Towns and Villages :						
Acton..........	General and on complaint.	Tuberculosis, 1 case.	No	No cases reported.	Yes	No ; no.....
Georgetown	General sanitary inspection.	Tuberculosis, 1 case.	No hospital, tent provided if required.	Yes; yes....	Yes	Yes; no ....
Oakville........	Yes ; yes ; no.	Dipht h e r i a, 3 cases; tuberculosis, 1 case.	Yes ; no........	Yes	Yes	Yes; no ....
Townships : Nassagawega ..	No ; no	Typhoid, 1 case; tuberculosis, 1 case.	No ; no	No cases ...	No ; no.....	No; no .....
Esquesing	Yes ; yes	....	Yes	Yes	Yes	....
HALIBURTON. Townships : Anson & Hinden	Only w h e n complaint is made.	None	Yes ; no........	No occasion.	When necessary.	No; no .....
Dysart..........	No	Scar l a t i n a, 4 cases.	Yes; no........	No	Yes	No; no.....
Glanmorgan ...	No ; no ; only on complaint.	....	Yes, house infected is isolated.	No; no	Yes	No; no .....

(8)	(9)	(10)	(11)	(12)	(13)	(14)
No	No	No	No; fed to hogs.	No	No	None.
No	No ; wells 20 ft. deep ; no.	No	No	No	No	None.
Yes	Wells, 20 to 30 ft.	No; no	No ; no	No	No	None.
....	Wells, 20 to 40 ft.; no.	No ; no...........	None in Tp......	No	No	None.
No	No ; wells 12 to 120 ft.	Yes	No'; fed ; no....	No	No	Slaughter houses.
Yes	Wells, 20 to 25 ft.; no.	No; no	No ; boiled and fed to pigs; no.	No	No	None.
Yes	Wells, 15 to 55 ft.	No; no...........	No ; offal is fed to h o g s, or buried.	No	No	None.
....	....	No	None in Tp.....	....	....	....
Yes	....	No	None	....	....	....
No	Wells, about 20 ft.	No'; no..........	None in town ..	No	No	None.
Yes	Waterworks....	None in village...	No	Yes	No	None.
Yes	Wells, 14 to 30 ft.	No	No; offal buried.	No	No	None.
No	Yes; 30 ft.; no..	No	No ; don't know; no.	....	No	No.
....	Wells	No	....	....	No	....
No	Wells, 12 to 20 ft.; no.	No; no..........	None in Tp....	No	No	None.
No	No; wells 20 ft.; no.	No; no..........	No ; none ; no..	No	No	None.
No	Wells	No ; no..........	No'	No	No	None.

	(2)	(3)	(4)	(5)	(6)	(7)
Lutterworth....	Only on complaint.	Tuberculosis 2 deaths.	No	Yes	Yes	No; no.....
Minden	Only on complaint.	Typhoid, 12 cases; tuberculosis, 4 deaths	Yes; no........	Yes; yes...	Yes	....
Monmouth	No; no; yes..	None	No; no	Yes	No	No; no.....
Stanhope	On complaint.	None	Yes, in house; no.	No cases....	Yes	No ....
KENT. *Towns and Villages:* Bothwell	General inspection and when complaint is made.	Typhoid,5 cases, 1 death.	No	Yes	Yes	No ....
Dresden........	Yes; not unless ordered by the Board.	Scarlatina, 2 cases; diphtheria, 6 cases, 1 death; tuberculosis, 4 deaths.	Yes; no	Yes; yes...	Yes	Yes; yes....
Ridgetown	Action only on complaint.	Tuberculosis, 1 death.	Yes; no........	Yes	Yes	No ....
Thamesville	When complaint is made.	None	No; no	Yes; yes....	Under instructions of attending physician.	No; no.....
Tilbury	General inspection.	Smallpox, 5 cases; scarlatina, 1 case, 1 death.	As well as possible in private houses.	Yes; yes....	Yes	Yes; yes....
Townships: Camden	Action taken on complaint.	Typhoid,1 death; tuberculosis, 3 deaths.	No; no.........	Yes; yes....	No	No; no .....
Oxford	On complaint.	Tuberculosis, 14, chiefly Indians.	Yes; no........	Yes; yes....	M.H O. sees provisions enforced.	Yes ....
Raleigh	On complaint.	Scarlatina, 1 case, 1 death; diphtheria, 4 cases; tuberculosis, 4 cases, 3 deaths.	Yes; no.	Yes; yes....	Yes	No; yes ....
Romney........	Action on complaint.	Tuberculosis, 1 case.	No hospital; no contagious diseases.	Yes; yes...	None to disinfect.	No; no....
Zone	Yes; yes.....	Yes; no	Yes; yes	Yes	Yes	Yes; no ...
LAMBTON. *Towns and Villages:* Alvinston	Yes...........	Scarlatina,1 case; tuberculosis, 1 death.	No; no	Yes; yes...	Yes	Yes; no ...
Arkona	Once each year	Tuberculosis, 2 deaths.	Yes; no	Yes; yes...	Yes	Yes; no ...

(8)	(9)	(10)	(11)	(12)	(13)	(14)
No	No	No	None in Tp....	No	No	None.
No	Spring w a t e r; no.	No ; no	None in Tp....	No	No	None.
No	No ; wells and springs ; no.	No ; no	None in Tp....	No ...,....	No	None.
No	Wells, 20 to 40 ft.; no.	No ; no	None in Tp....	No	No	None.
No	Wells, about 14 ft.	None	None in t o w n limits.	No	No	None.
Yes	Wells, about 30 ft.; no.	None kept in the corporation.	None in town ; meat inspected by sanitary inspector.	No	No	None.
Yes	From wells, 10 ft. deep.	No	Outside of corporation.	Yes	No	None.
Yes	No; drive wells, 15 ft.	Yes	No ; no	No	No	None.
Yes	No ; wells 10 to 12 ft.	No ; no	No	No	Yes	None.
No	No : cannot say.	No; yes	No ; don't know; no.	No	No	Some slaughter houses.
Yes; yes....	No ; wells, good water.	No ; no	No	No	No	None.
Yes	No; wells, 90 ft.	No	No	No	No	None.
No	No : wells 120 to 140 ft.; no.	No dairy system here ; no.	No	No.........	No.........	None.
No	Yes ; about 10..	No ; no	No ; fed to pigs.	No.........	No..........	None.
No	No ; wells 12 to 14 ft.	No ; no	Offal fed to hogs	Yes	No..........	No.
No	No ; about 20 ft.	No ; no	None in the village.	Yes, by each householder.	No...	None.

	(2)	(3)	(4)	(5)	(6)	(7)
Petrolia	Yes ; yes ...	Scarlatina, 10 cases, 1 death; diphtheria, 3 ; tuberculosis, 6 deaths.	Yes ; no	Yes ; yes...	Yes	Yes ; no ...
Sarnia	General inspection in the spring.	Scarlatina, 4 cases ; diphtheria, 1 case ; typhoid, 5 deaths ; tuberculosis, 9 cases, 9 deaths.	Yes ; yes	Yes ; yes...	No	No ; yes ...
Thedford	Regular inspection annually.	Scarlatina, 1 case	Yes	Don't know.	Yes	Yes , yes...
Point Edward	On complaint.	Scarlatina, 1 case	No ; not required.	Don't know; no cases.	Yes	No ....
Bosanquet	On complaint.	Scarlatina, a few cases ; typhoid 1 case ; tuberculosis, 6 cases, 6 deaths.	No	Not used...	Yes, by M. H. O.	No ; no ....
Brooke	Action on complaint.	Scarlatina, 18 cases; typhoid, a few cases ; tuberculosis, 2 deaths.	Only by placarding ; no.	....	Don't know.	No ; no ....
Enniskillen	General inspection; on complaint.	Scarlatina, 5 cases ; diphtheria, 3 cases; tuberculosis, 2 deaths.	House placarded ; no hospital.	Yes ; yes...	Yes, in some cases.	No ; no ....
Euphemia	On complaint.	Tuberculosis, 3 cases.	No ; no........	Yes ; yes...	No	No ; no ....
Moore	Action on complaint.	Diphtheria, 2 cases ; typhoid 2 cases; tuberculosis, 1 death	Yes ; no	Yes ; yes...	Yes	Yes ; generally.
Plympton	No ; action on complaint.	Scarlatina, 3 cases.	No ; no........	Yes	No	No ; no ....
Sarnia	On complaint.	Scarlatina, 6 cases, 3 deaths; typhoid, 4 cases, 2 deaths; tuberculosis, 3 deaths.	Yes ; no	Yes ; yes...	Yes	No ; no . ..
LANARK. Towns and Villages: Lanark	Yes ; every spring.	None	No ; no	Used if required.	No contagious diseases	No ....
Smith's Falls	Yes ; yes	Scarlatina, 2 deaths ; tuberculosis, 6 deaths.	No.............	Yes	Yes	Yes ... ...
Townships: Bathurst	Action on complaint.	Diphtheria, 6 cases, 1 death.	Yes ; no	Yes ; yes...	Yes	No ....
Darling	Action on complaint.	None	No ; no........	Yes ; yes...	No	No ....

(8)	(9)‟	(10)	(11)	(12)	(13)	(14)
Yes	Waterworks....	Yes, twice a year.	No ; offal fed to hogs.	Yes	Partial	None.
Partially so.	Yes	Yes ; no	None in town ..	Yes	Yes	1 oil refinery ; 1 hide warehouse; 1 gas manufactory.
....	No ; from wells 25 to 60 ft.	Yes ; no	None in town ..	....	No........	None.
Yes	Partial ; some wells 22 ft.	No ; no	None in the corporation.	Yes	No.	None.
No.........	Wells ; yes ; 1 case typhoid.	No ; no..........	No ; offal carted away.	....	....	None.
No..:	No ; 10 to 70 ft.	No...	No ; burried ; only when complaint is made.	No.	No........	None.
No.	No ; wells 50 to 100 ft.	No..............	No offal is fed to hogs.	No.........	No........	None.
No.........	No............	No.............	No.............	No.	No...... ..	None.
Sometimes..	No wells ; yes, 1 case.	No..............	No ; offal is fed to hogs.	No.........	In some villages there is.	Some slaughter houses.
To M.H.O. and physicians only.	No ; wells 15 to 30 ; no.	No ; no cases reported.	No ; offal fed to pigs and burned ; no inspection.	No.........	No.........	None.
No.........	No........... .	Yes	No ; burnt ; no.	No.........	No.........	None.
Yes	No ; no........	No..............	No systematic inspection.	No...........	No.........	None.
Yes	Waterworks ; no typhoid.	Yes	None allowed in corporation. ‛	Yes	Yes	None.
No.........	No ; wells......	No	No.....	No.........	No.........	None.
No.........	Wells 18 ft.: no.	No ; no	None in the corporation.	No.........	No.........	None.

	(2)	(3)	(4)	(5)	(6)	(7)
Dalhousie & N. Sherbrooke...	No ; no ; only on complaint	Tuberculosis, 3 deaths.	Yes	No cases this year.	No, under M. H. O's. instruct'n.	No ; no ....
Drummond.....	Action on complaint.	Tuberculosis, 8 deaths.	Houses placarded; no hospital.	Yes ; yes ..	Not usually.	No ....
Elmsley, N.....	On complaint.	Diphtheria, 1 case, 1 death.	Yes ; no........	Yes ; yes ..	Yes	No ; no ....
Lanark	Inspection every spring.	Diphtheria, 20 cases; tuberculosis, 2 deaths.	Yes ; no........	Yes ; yes ..	Yes	No ; no ....
Lavant.........	Only on complaint. ·	None	....	....	....	No ; no ....
Ramsay........	Yes ; on complaint.	Tuberculosis, 2 deaths.	Yes ; no........	Yes ; cannot say.	No	No ; no ....
Sherbrooke, S ..	Only on complaint.	Smallpox, 2 cases.	Yes ; no........	No diphtheria.	Yes	School children are not all vaccinated
LENNOX & ADDINGTON. *Towns and Villages.* Bath	Yes ; yes.....	None.....	Yes ; no........	Yes ; yes ..	Yes	No ....
Napanee	General in the spring; action on complaint.	Scarlatina, 17 cases ; diphtheria, 2 cases; tuberculosis, 8 deaths.	Under direction of attending physician.	Yes ; yes ..	No	No ; general vaccination this year.
Adolphustown..	Yes	....	Yes	.. ..	No	....
Amherst Island.	No ; no	Tuberculosis, 2 deaths.	No ; no	Has not been tried.	Yes, in case it is required.	No ....
Denbigh, A.&A.	Action taken when complaints are made to Board.	Scarlatina, 30 cases ; diphtheria, 7 cases, 1 death ; typhoid, 1 death.	As well as circumstances will permit.	Yes ; yes...	Yes	No ; no ...
Ernestown	Only on complaint.	Typhoid, 5 cases; tuberculosis, 10 cases, 8 deaths.	No ; no	Yes ; yes...	Yes	Only on complaint ; no
Fredericksburgh South	When complaint is made.	None	Yes ; no........	....	Yes	School children are generally vaccinated
Kaladar, A.& E.	Action on complaint.	Smallpox, 4 cases ; scarlatina, 10 cases, 2 deaths; diphtheria, 9 cases, 4 deaths ; tuberculosis, 2 cases, 2 deaths.	Yes ; no........	Yes ; yes...	Yes, by doctor in charge.	No ; no ....
Richmond......	Action on complaint.	Scarlatina, 1 death.	Yes ; no........	No.	Yes	No ; no ....
Sheffield	Action on complaint.	Scarlatina, 2 cases ; diphtheria, 5 cases, 1 death ; typhoid, 7 cases; tuberculosis, 6 deaths.	Isolated in their homes; no hospital.	Partially ...	Yes, by M. H.O.	No ....

(8)	(9)	(10)	(11)	(12)	(13)	(14)
No.........	Wells & springs; no.	No ; no	None in township.	No..........	No...... .	None.
Yes	Wells, 30 ft.; no typhoid.	No cases have occurred.	No; no	No	No	None.
Yes	Wells	No; no	No	No	No	None.
No	Wells, various depths.	No; no	No	No	No	None.
No	No ; wells......	No; no	None in township.	No	No	None.
No	From wells and springs; no.	No; no	No; fed to pigs .	No	No	None.
Yes	From wells, 20 to 25 ft.; no typhoid	No; no	No systematic inspection.	No	No	None.
No	Yes, Bay of Quinte; no.	No	No; fed to pigs .	Yes	No	None.
Yes	Not for drinking purposes ; 25 ft.; think not.	No ; not to my knowledge.	No; no	No	About 4 blocks only.	Gas works ; 1 tallow melting ; 1 slaughter house.
....	. ...	....	...........: ...	No	No	None.
No	No; lake water and some wells.	No; no	No	No	No	None.
No	Wells, from 10 to 20 ft.	No; no	None in township.	No	No	None
Yes	No; 20 ft ; yes..	No; no	No; fed to hogs; no.	No	No	None.
No	No; wells; no ..	No; no	No; no	No	No	None
No	No; about 12 ft.; no.	No; not known ..	None in township.	No	No	None.
No	No; no	No; no	No; yes	No	No	None.
No	No; from wells 10 to 15 ft.	No inspection	Not licensed ; don't know; no inspection.	No	No	None.

	(2)	(3)	(4)	(5)	(6)	(7)
LEEDS & GREN-VILLE. *Towns and Villages.*						
Brockville......	Yes ; yes.	Smallpox, 1 case; scarlatina, 24 cases, 1 death; diphtheria, 2 cases ; tuberculosis, 15 deaths.	Yes ; yes.......	Yes........	Yes, very strictly.	Yes ; yes...
Cardinal	Yes.........	Scarlatina, 1 case; diphtheria, 1 case, 1 death.	Yes............	Yes'	Yes	Yes ....
Kemptville.·....	Sanitary inspection. ·	Tuberculos's, 5 deaths.	No	No cases ...	Not been ce-cessary.	Yes ....
Prescott........	Yes·; yes.....	Scarlatine, 20 cases, 1 death ; tuberculosis, 6 deaths.	Yes ; no	Nt.	Yes	Yes ; no....
Townships. C:osby, N......	General sanitary inspection.	None	No hospital.....	No	Yes	No ; no ....
Crosby, S	Only on complaint.	....	No ....,.	Cannot say.	No; no cases	No ....
Edwardsburgh..	No	Diphtheria, 4 cases, 2 deaths; typhoid, 1 case, 1 death ; tuberculosis, 3 cases, 3 deaths	Yes ; no	Yes ; yes ...	Yes	No ....
Elmsley, S	Action on complaint.	Tuberculosis, 4 deaths.	No	Yes ; yes...	No	No ; no ....
Gower, S.......	Action on complaint.	None	Not aware of any.	No	No	No ....
Leeds and Lansdown Front ..	Action taken on complaint.	....	No necessity; no.	Yes ; yes...	Not in all cases.	No ; no ....
Oxford	No	None	No	No .... ..No	No	No ... .
Yonge & Escott Front	Action on complaint.	Tuber ulosis, 3 deaths.	No	No	No	No ....
LINCOLN. *Cities and Towns:*						
St. Catharines..	General and systematic ; carried on from day to day.	Smallpox, 3 cases; scarlatina, 20 cases, 1 death ; diphtheria, 20 cases, 3 deaths ; tuberculosis, 22 cases, 22 deaths.	Yes; no, but one is being built.	Yes; opinion somewhat divided, but generally favorable.	Yes.........	Yes... ...
Beamsville	Once a year and on complaint.	Typhoid, 1 case, 1 death ; tuberculosis, 1 death.	No	No	No ...·.....	Yes........
Port Dalhousie .	Yes.........	....	Yes	Yes	Yes.......	....
Townships : Caistor	At intervals...	Typhoid, 2 cases; tuberculosis, 3 cases, 1 death	No ; no	Yes	No	Yes........
Gainsboro	Only on complaint.	Scarlatina, 10 cases.	No	No	No	No ....
Grantham	Only on complaint.	Tuberculosis, 1 case.	Yes	Don't know.	No	No ; no ....

(8)	(9)	(10)	(11)	(12)	(13)	(14)
Yes	Yes ; very few wells.	Yes	No; boiled and fed to hogs ; yes, by veterinary inspector.	Yes	Yes	Tannery, Oak Belting Co., Light & Power department, gas works.
No	Yes; no typhoid.	No; no	No; not permitted within corporation.	No	No	None.
....	Wells; no;......	No	None within corporation.	No	No	None.
No	Yes; no	No dairy in town .	None within corporation. -	No	No .. ....,	None.
No	Wells, 20 ft.; no	No	No offal fed to pigs.	No	No	None.
No	No; wells, 30 ft.	No; no :..........	No; no	No	No	Nore.
No	Wells, various depths.	No	No	No	No	None.
No	Wells, 20 to 40 ft.	No, none reported.	No ; hurie1 or burned.	No	No	No.
No	No	No	None	No	No	No.
No	Wells, 12 ft.; no.	No..............	No ; burned and fed to hogs; no	No	No	None.
No	No; wells, 20 ft.	No	No	No	Nc	No.
No	Wells	No	No	No	No	None.
Yes	Waterworks....	Yes; every month; no.	No, but under supervision of sanitary inspector.	Yes	Yes	Three tan neries, one soap factory, two hide houses.
Yes	Waterworks; none reported.	No	None in the corporation ; no.	Removed on complaint; no system.	No	None.
....	....	No	....	....	No	None.
Yes	Wells and cisterns ; no.	No ; no	No ; boiled ; fed to hogs.	Only householders.	No	None.
No	No	No'	No..............	No	No	None.
No	Wells, 12 to 30 ft.	No ; no	No	Don't know.	No	None.

	(2)	(3)	(4)	(5)	(6)	(7)
Grimsby, N.....	When complaint of nuisance is made.	Diphtheria, 8 cases; typhoid, 6 cases.	Yes	Yes; yes...	Yes	No ....
Grimsby, S.	General inspection.	Scarlatina, 8 cases; typhoid, 1 case.	Yes; no........	Yes,if necessary.	No, but is carried out under instructions.	No ....
Louth	General sanitary inspection.	Typhoid, 6 cases.	Yes	Yes; yes...	Yes	Yes; no....
MIDDLESEX. *Town & Villages.*						
Ailsa Craig.....	Yes; yes.....	Diphtheria, 3 cases, 1 death.	Partially; no hospital.	No	Generally left to medical attend-ant.	No; yes....
Glencoe........	General inspection and on complaint.	....	No; no	Yes; yes...	Yes........	No ....
Parkhill........	Annual inspection and on complaint.	Smallpox, 1 case; scarlatina, 12 cases; tuberculosis, 3 deaths.	Yes; no	Yes	Yes.... ...	Yes ......
Strathroy	On complaint only.	....	No	No	Yes........	No ....
Townships:						
Adelaide	....	Scarlatina, 2 cases, 2 deaths; diphtheria, 2 cases, 2 deaths; typhoid, 1 case, 1 death.	Yes; no hospital.	Yes; yes...	Sometimes..	No; majority are.
Caradoc	Yes; twice yearly.	Diphtheria, 4 cases, 3 deaths; typhoid, 5 cases, 1 death; tuberculosis, 3 deaths.	Yes; no hospital.	Yes; yes...	Yes.	Whenever inspector complains.
Delaware	Twice a year and on complaint.	Scarlatina, 5 cases; typhoid, 5 cases; tuberculosis, 3 deaths.	Yes; no hospital	Yes; yes...	No	No; no ....
North Dorchester	On complaint only.	Smallpox, 5 cases; diphtheria, 10 cases; typhoid, cases, 1 death; tuberculosis, 5 deaths.	Yes; no........	Yes	Yes	No ....
Ekfrid	On complaint only.	Tuberculosis, 3 cases.	No; no	Not used ...	Generally ..	No.........
London	No; on complaint.	Smallpox, 11 cases; scarlatina, 9 cases; diphtheria, 2 cases, 1 death; typhoid, 2 cases; tuberculosis, 4 cases, 4 deaths.	No; no	Yes; yes...	Sometimes..	No; no ....
Lobo	No; on complaint only.	Typhoid, 1 case, 1 death; tuberculosis, 1 case, 1 death.	No	To a certain extent....	When complaint is made.	No ....

(8)	(9)	(10)	(11)	(12)	(13)	(14)
No	Wells, 20 ft.....	No ; no	No ; no	No	No	None.
No	No ; from 10 to 100 ft.	No ; no	No; offal buried ; no. .	Yes	No	None.
No	No ; from wells, 15 to 30 ft.	No	No...	No	No	None.
No	No ; 2 to 10 ft.; not of late.	No ; do not know.	None in municipality.	Yes	No	None.
Yes..... ..	About 20 ft.; a few rock wells, 150ft. in depth;	No ; no	None inside corporation ; no.	Yes; scavengers employed by Board of Health.	Not a complete one.	None.
Yes	About 120 feet to rock; operated by wind mills.	No	None in municipality ; no.	Yes	No	None.
Yes........	No	No	No	Yes........	No	None, unless canning factory.
No	No ; from 20 to 60 ft.	On complaint only; not known to have occurred.	No ; 2 fed ; 3 by sanitary officer	Yes; by private parties.	No	None.
Yes........	No; 20 ft.; yes..	No ; no	No ; generally fed to hogs.	No	No	None.
Yes........	No ; from wells, 15 ft.; yes.	No; not observed..	2 Licensed; fed; no inspection.	No	No	None.
Yes........	Wells, 30 ft.....	No	Yes ; boiled and fed to hogs.	No	No	None.
Yes........	No ; 12 to 20 ft.; none during year.	No ; no	No ; no	No	No	Slaughter houses.
No	No; wells, 40 ft..; no.	No ; do not know.	Yes ; after inspection, fed to hogs ; no.	No	No	2 Bone boiling; licensed.
Not lately..	No	No	No ; no	No	No	None.

	(2)	(3)	(4)	(5)	(6)	(7)
Metcalfe	On complaint only; schools and cheese factories at intervals.	Scarlatina,1case; typhoid, 1 case.	Yes ; no	Think so ..	No	No ....
McGillivray ...	Yes	None..........	Yes ; no........	Yes ; yes...	Yes	No ....
Nissouri.......	Yes ; 3 times a year.	Diphtheria, 3 cases ; scarlatina, 2 cases ; typhoid,2 cases; tuberculosis, 5 deaths.	No ; none	....	No	No ....
Westminster ...	Cheese factories, etc , inspected yearly.	Smallpox,2cases; tuberculosis, 3 cases.	Yes ; no..... ..	Yes ; yes...	No	No ; no ....
MUSKOKA. *Towns and Villages :* Bracebridge....	Yes, on complaint.	Smallpox,2cases; Scarlet fever, 3 cases; diphtheria, 23 cases ; tuberculosis, 2 cases.	Yes ; no	Yes ; yes...	Yes	Yes ; not as a rule.
Port Carling ...	....	None.....	Yes, if necessary; no.	No occasion	Yes, if required.	Yes ....
Townships : Cardwell.......	No, on complaint only.	None..........	Yes	No...... .	Yes	No ....
Chaffey	....	None	Yes ; no........	Yes ; no ..	Yes.... ...	No.........
Draper.	When complaint is made.	Diphtheria. 2 cases, 1 death.	....	Yes	Yes, when necessary.	No.........
Medora & Wood.	....	Smallpox, 1 case.	Yes, at their homes.	No.........	Yes	Yes........
Monck	Action on complaint.	Diphtheria, 2 cases; typhoid, 1 case, 1 death.	No	Yes	Partly so...	Some are vaccinated.
Muskoka.... .	No action except when contagious diseases exist	Tuberculosis, 4 deaths.	Yes ; no........	Yes ; yes...	No..........	No ....
Oakley	Action on complaint.	No ; no	No....	Not required.	No	No...... ..
Ryde	Action on complaint.	None..........	Yes ; no	....	Yes	No.........
Stisted	No	None..........	No	No	Yes	No.........
Macaulay	Only on complaint.	None..........	No occasion	Don't know.	Yes	No ....
Watt	Yes ; repeated on complaint.	Diphtheria, 1 case.	Yes ; no........	Yes ; yes...	Yes........	No ....

(8)	(9)	(10)	(11)	(12)	(13)	(14)
No	Rock wells, 60 to 120 ft.; no.	No , no	None in municipality.	....	No	None.
Yes	....	No	....	.. ..	... .	....
Yes	No; 20 ft... ...	No ; can't say	Yes; fed to hogs.	No	No	None.
Yes	No; 30 lt.......	No; no	Yes; don't know.	No	No	None.
Yes	Yes; no........ ..	No; no	Yes	Yes	Yes........	2 tanneries, 2 slaughter houses.
No.	Some wells; mostly lake water; no.	None.............	Yes	Yes..... ..	No	None .....
Yes	No ; no typhoid.	No; none	None in Tp.....	No	No.........	None .....
No	No; yes........	No	None in Tp.....	No	No	None ......
No	Wells, 12 ft.; no.	None.............	Nore in Tp.....	No	No	None ......
No	Wells, 10 to 20 ft.	No; no	No; buried.....	No	No	None.......
Don't know.	Supplied from wells,10 to 24 ft	No	No	None.......	No	None.......
No	Wells	No................	No ; offal fed to pigs; no.	No	No	None.......
No	No	No; none	None in Tp	No	No	None.......
No	No	No	No; fed to hogs.	No	No	None.......
No	Wells, 4 ft.; no..	No	None in Tp.....	No	No	None.......
No	Wells. about 4 ft.	No	None in Tp.....	No ,.......	No	Nore.......
No	From wells; no.	No; none	No ; no	No	No	None.......

	(2)	(3)	(4)	(5)	(6)	(7)
NORFOLK. *Towns and Villages* :						
Delhi	Inspection twice a year.	Scarlet fever, 20 cases; typhoid, 1 case : tuberculosis, 3 cases, 1 death.	Yes ; no.	Yes ; yes...	Yes	Yes; no....
Port Dover.....	Action on complaint.	Typhoid, 2 deaths; consumption, 3 deaths.	Yes; no........	No cases ...	No	No; yes....
Port Rowan....	Once in each year.	Tuberculosis, 1 death.	No ; no	Yes ; yes...	No cases....	No; some ..
Simcoe	General, and on complaint.	Diphtheria, 1 case.	Yes, except typhoid and tuberculosis.	Yes ; yes...	Yes	Yes; no....
Waterford	Yes, once a year.	Typhoid, 1 death	No ; no	Don't know.	No	No ; no ....
Townships : Charlotteville ..	General inspection.	Diphtheria, 1 case ; typhoid, 2 cases, 2 deaths ; tuberculosis, 1 death	Yes ; no........	Yes ; yes...	Yes	Yes ; no....
Houghton.	Only on complaint.	Tuberculosis, 1 death.	No ; no	Don't know	Yes..	No; no ....
Middleton......	Only on complaint.	Diphtheria, 4 cases; typhoid, 1 case.	Yes; no.... ...	No .. .. ,.	No	No ....
Townsend	No	Typhoid, 2 cases, 2 deaths; tuberculosis, 2 cases, 2 deaths.	No	Don't know	Yes.........	No ....
Walsingham, S.	....	Smallpox, 1 case, diphtheria, 7 cases; typhoid, 6 cases, 1 death; tuberculosis, 2 cases, 2 deaths.	No	Yes	Yes	No ....
Woodhouse.....	Action on complaint.	Diphtheria, 1 case; typhoid, 3 cases, 2 deaths ; tuberculosis, 2 cases, 2 deaths.	Only partially; no.	Used by some physicians; yes.	No....... ..	No inspection unless complaint is made ; 85 per cent of children vaccinated
NORTHUMB'LAND AND DURHAM. *Towns and Villages* : Bowmanville ...	Yes ; yes ; and repeated at intervals.	Diphtheria, 6 cases; typhoid, 3 cases, 1 death; consumption, 2 deaths.	Yes; no hospital.	Yes ; yes...	No ; partial.	Yes, new school children are not compelled.
Brighton	Only on complaint.	Diphtheria, 1 case ; tuberculosis, 2 cases, 1 death.	Yes, except typhoid and tuberculosis.	Don't know.	Yes	M.H.O. inspects schools; no.

(8)	(9)	(10)	(11)	(12)	(13)	(14)
No	No; wells 20 to 35 ft.	No dairy cows here; no.	None in the village.	No	No	None.......
No	No; wells, 15 to 20 ft.	No; no	No; offal fed to hogs.	No	No	None.......
No	Wells, about 27 ft.; no.	No dairy cows here.	Not allowed within the corporation.	No	No	None.......
Yes	Artesian wells, 10 to 30 ft.; no.	No	None in municipality.	No	No	Canning factory; gas plant.
No	Wells & springs.	No	None in the municipality.	Night soil removed ev'ry spring	No	None.......
Yes	No; wells; no..	No; occasionally..	No; buried and fed to hogs.	No	No	None.......
No	Wells, 15 to 20 ft.	No; no	None in Tp.....	No	No	None.......
No	Wells, 5 to 30 ft.	No	Yes; yes......	No	No	None.......
No	No.............	No	No	No	No	None.......
No	Wells, 18 ft.; no.	No	No	No	No	None.......
No	No; depth of wells varies; not definitely.	No; no	Yes; boiled and fed to hogs; no	No	No	Slaughtering of animals; cheese factories, hog pens in connection.
Yes	Wells, usually from 25 to 30 ft.; no.	Yes; no cases of tuberculosis reported.	No; but under the control of the Board; offal buried; no.	Yes	Yes; in the congested part of the town.	Slaughtering of animals.
Yes	Wells, 15 to 20 ft.	No	No; no inspection.	No	No	None.......

	(2)	(3)	(4)	(5)	(6)	(7)
Cobourg.......	Yes..........	Scarlatina. 33 cases ; dipl theria, 1 case ; typhoid, 4 cases ; tuberculosis, 2 deaths.	Yes, as far as practicable; no hospital.	Yes ; under supervision of sanitary inspector.	No......	No ....
Colborne	General in spring, then on complaint	Diphtheria, 2 cases; typhoid, 3 cases.	Yes ; no........	Yes ; yes...	Yes	No ; no ....
Hastings.......	Yes...... ...	Tuberculosis, 1 death.	No	No occasion to use it.	Yes, if necessary.	Yes ; yes...
Millbrook	Yes...........	Scarlatina, 1 case ; tuberculosis, 1 case.	Yes ; no........	Yes	Yes	Yes ....
Port Hope	Yes	Diphtheria, 1 case, 1 death ; typhoid, 3 cases, 3 deaths; tuberculosis, 7 deaths.	No	Don't think so.	No	No ; yes....
Townships: Alnwick....... ..	Action on complaint.	Tuberculosis, 4 cases.	Yes ; isolated in their homes.	Yes ; yes...	No	No ....
Brighton	Only on complaint.	Scarlatina, 40 cases, 1 death; diphtheria, 12 cases. 1 death ; typhoid, 7 cases, 1 death: tuberculosis, 7 deaths.	Houses are isolated ; no hospital.	Yes........	Generally by M.H.O.	No ; no ....
Cartwright	Gen'l sanitary inspection annually, also on complaint	Scarlatina. 2 cases; typh id, 1 case, 1 death; tuberculosis, 1 death.	Systematically carried out.	No	Yes, under supervision of M.H.O.	No ; vaccination not compulsory.
Cavan.........	No ; no ; only on complaint.	Tuberculosis, 3 deaths.	Yes ; no	Yes ; yes...	Yes	No ; no.....
Clarke	Yes ; yes	Diphtheria, 3 cases, 1 death	Yes ; no	Has been used with good results.	Under direction of physician in charge.	Yes ; no....
Cramahe	On complaint.	Small pox,1 case; typhoid, 6 cases, 1 death; tuberculosis, 2 deaths.	Yes	Yes ; yes..	No	No ....
Darlington	Yes, and on complaint.	Scarlatina, 20 cases ; diph theria,10 cases, 2 deaths; typhoid,16 cases, 2 deaths.	Yes ; no	Yes ; yes...	Partially ..	No ....
Haldimand.....	No ; no	Small-pox, 2 cases ; scarlatina, 16 cases ; diphtheria, 5 cases, 1 death ; typhoid, 4 cases ; tuberculosis,9 cases, 5 deaths	Yes ; no........	Yes ; yes...	In some cases only.	No ; vaccination done once in 7 years.

(8)	(9)	(10)	(11)	(12)	(13)	(14)
No	Yes; some wells 12 to 15 ft; no ported.	Yes; no cases of tuberculosis re-ported.	No; burning and feeding to hogs; no.	Yes; once a year.	Yes	Storing of hides.
No	No; 12 ft; cases exceptional.	No; no	No; buried.....	No organized system.	No	None.......
Yes	No; from wells, 12 to 14 ft.	No; no	None within the corporation.	Yes	No	None.......
No	Artesian wells, no.	No	None inside corporation.	No	No	None.......
Yes	Yes; some wells, 80 ft.; yes.	No; do not know of any.	None allowed within municipality.	No	Partial system.	Storing hides; bone boiling; a glue factory; gas house.
No	No; about 20 ft.	No	No	No	No	None.......
No	Generally from wells; sometimes.	No; no	No; offal is fed to hogs.	No	No	None.......
Yes	No; wells; subject to inspection.	No; no	No; offal buried.	No	No	None.......
Yes	Wells, about 20 ft.	No; have not heard of any.	No; boiled and fed to hogs.	No	No	2 slaughter houses, not licensed.
To physicians only.	Wells, 20 to 40 ft	No; no	No; buried and fed to hogs.	Each householder removes his own.	No	None.
....	....	No; no	No; buried	No	No	None.
No	Wells, about 30 ft.; yes.	No; no	No; fed to hogs.	No	No	None.
To physicians.	No; wells, 10 to 40 ft.	No; no cases reported.	No; fed to hogs	No	No	None.

	(2)	(3)	(4)	(5)	(6)	(7)
Hamilton	General sanitary inspection.	Scarlatina, 6 cases; diphtheria,4 cases; typhoid, 3 cases.	Yes ; no........	Yes ; yes...	Yes........	Yes ; no....
Manvers	Action only on complaint.	Scarlatina, 1 case; tuberculosis, 6 deaths.	Yes ; no........	No	Yes; under supervision of M.H.O.	No ; no ....
Monaghan, S...	Action on complaint.	Scarlatina, 2 cases ; tuberculosis, 1 death.	Yes ; no.......	Yes; yes..	Yes........	No; no ....
Murray	Yes ; general inspection.	Scarlatina, 5 cases, 1 death ; diphtheria, 4 cases, 1 death ; tuberculosis, 6 cases, 6 deaths.	Yes ; no........	Yes; yes...	Yes........	No ; no ....
Percy	Inspection made on complaint.	Small-pox, 1 case ; scarlatina, 6 cases ; typhoid,1 case	Yes ; no........	Yes; yes...	Yes........ •	No ; no ....
NIPISSING. *Towns and Villages* : North Bay	Yes ; yes, and on complaint.	Small-pox, 1 case ; scarlatina, 7 cases, 1 death ; diphtheria, 4 cases. 1 death; tuberculosis, 3 deaths.	Yes............	Yes........	Yes........	No ; no ....
Sturgeon Falls..	....	Small-pox, 5 cases; scarlatina, 14 cases, 4 deaths ; typhoid, 1 case ; diphtheria, 4 cases,2 deaths: tuberculosis, 1 death.	Yes ; yes......	Yes; yes...	Yes.	Yes ; yes...
Townships : Eayfield	General sanitary inspection in April and May.	Small-pox, 3 cases ; diphtheria, 2 cases, 1 death ; typhoid, 1 case.	Yes	....	Yes ; under supervision of M.H.O.	No ....
Cameron	Only on complaint.	None	No	....	By physician in attendance.	No ....
Calvin	Action on complaint.	Small-pox, 2 cases ; scarlatina prevalent; tuberculosis, 1 death.	Only in cases of small-pox.	....	Only after small-pox.	No .. ..
Dymond	No: no; action on complaint.	Small-pox 4 cases	Yes ; no........	Not used...	No	No ....
Mattawan......	Action on complaint.	Tuberculosis, 1 death.	Yes ; yes	No occasion to use it.	Yes, when necessary.	Yes; don't know.

(8)	(9)	(10)	(11)	(12)	(13)	(14)
Yes	Wells, all depths; yes.	Yes, once a year ; no.	Yes ; no	No	No	None.
Yes	Springs & wells, 10 to 60 ft.	No ; no	No ; no	No	No	None.
No	Wells, 20 to 60 ft.	No	None	No	No	None.
To physicians only.	No ; wells, 20 ft.; no.	No ; no	Yes ; buried ; no	No	No	None.
No	Wells, 20 to 30 ft.; no.	No ; no	No ; buried ; no.	No	No	None.
No	Yes	No	None in the corporation.	No	No	None.
Yes	No ; wells, 12 to 20 ft.	No	No ; buried ; no.	No	Being constructed.	None.
No	No ; from 12 to 20 ft.	No	None within Tp.	Household ers remove garbage and night soil.	No	....
No	No ; springs; no	None	No	No	No	None.
No	No	No	None in Tp	No	No	None.
No	No ; wells, about 14 ft.; no.	No ; no	No	No	No	None.
No	No ; wells ; no .	No ; no	No	No	No	None.

	(2)	(3)	(4)	(5)	(6)	(7)
McKim	Yes; not repea'ed.	Small-pox, 37 cases; diphtheria, 10 cases,2 deaths; typhoid, 45 cases,6 deaths	Yes; yes	Yes; yes...	Yes, by M.H.O.	No; no ....
Papineau	Action on complaint.	......	Yes; no	No	No occasion.	No; no ....
Springer	Action taken on complaint	None	Yes; no	Do not know	Yes, generally.	Yes; all children vaccinat·d
Wildifield ONTARIO Towns and Villages:	On complaint.	Scarlatina, 26 cases,3 deaths; typhoid,1 case.	Yes; no	Yes	Yes	No ....
Beaverton	Yes; twice a year.	Typhoid, 1 case; tuberculosis, 2 cases,2 deaths.	Yes; no	Yes; yes ..	Yes	No ....
Cannington	Two inspections yearly.	Diphtheria, 2 cases; tuberculosis, 1 case.	Yes; no	Yes	No	No ....
Oshawa	Yes; yearly, also on complaint.	Scarlatina, 13 cases; diphtheria, 3 cases; typhoid. 3 deaths; tuberculosis, 7 deaths.	Yes; no	Yes; yes ..	Under the supervision of M.H.O.	No ....
Port Perry	Action on complaint.	......	By placarding; no.	Yes..	Yes...	No ....
Uxbridge	Yes	Diphtheria, 15 cases,3 deaths; typhoid, 8 cases,3 deaths; tuberculosis, 1 death.	Yes; no	Yes; yes ..	Yes	Yes; no....
Townships: Brock	General once a year.	Scarlatina, 6 cases, no deaths; diphtheria, 6 cases, 3 deaths; tuberculosis, 1 death.	Yes; no hospital	Yes; yes ..	Yes	Yes; no....
Pickering	Village school houses and slaughter houses inspected; action taken on complaint.	Scarlatina, 8 cases,1 death, diphtheria, 11 cases; typhoid, 7 cases; tuberculosis, 8 deaths.	Yes; no	Yes; yes ..	Yes...	Yes; n· ....
Rama	No; no; only on complaint	None	Yes; no	Yes; yes ..	Yes	No; no ...
Reach	Only on complaint.	Diphtheria, 2 cases; typhoid, 1 death; tuberculosis, 5 deaths.	Only when case is reported ...	Yes; yes ..	Yes	Yes; not general.

(8)	(9)	(10)	(11)	(12)	(13)	(14)
Yes........	No ; wells, very shallow ; no.	No	No ; no	No	No ....:....	None.
No	No; streams; no.	No ; no	No ; no	No	No	None.
No	Water from wells, 8 to 12 ft.	No ; no	None in Tp	Yes, partially.	No	None.
No	Wells,15 to 20 ft.	No ; no	No	No	No	None.
No	From wells,average 17 ft.	No	None in municipality ; no.	Yes	No	None.
Yes........	No; wells, 16 to 30 ft.; no.	No ; no	No ; none......	Yes, semi-annually.	No	None.
Yes, to physicians.	No ; wells, 12 to 25 ft.; supposed cause.	No ; nonereported.	No ; fed to hogs; no.	Yes........	No	None.
No	No ; no	No	None in the corporation	No ; no ....,	No	None.
No	No : 25 to 30 ft .	No	No ; offal removed ; no.	No	No	None.
No	No ; wells......	No ; no	No; offal buried; no.	No	No	None.
Yes	No ; average of 30 ft.; no.	No ; 2 cases......	Yes ; buried and fed to hogs ; no.	No	No	None.
No	No	No ; no	None in Tp	No	No	None.
No	Wells,average 25 ft.	No ; no	No	No	No	None.

	(2)	(3)	(4)	(5)	(6)	(7)
Scott..... ...	Action on complaint only.	None	As far as practicable.	No ...:......	No	No ....
Scugog	Action taken on complaint.	Tuberculosis, 1.	No	No cases.....	No	No ....
Thorah	When complaint is made.	Small-pox, 1 case; scarlatina, 13 cases; diphtheria, 3 cases; typhoid, 4 cases.	Yes; no hospital.	Yes; yes ..	Yes......	No; no ....
Uxbridge	Only on complaint.	Scarlatina, 12 cases; diphtheria, 4 cases; typhoid, 20 cases; tuberculosis, 1 case.	Yes; no...... .	Yes; yes ..	Yes......	No......
Whitby East ..	No; no; action on complaint.	Tuberculosis, 3 cases,3 deaths.	Yes; no........	No	No	No; no ....
Whitby	No; only when notified.	Diphtheria, 1 case; typhoid, 1 case; tuberculosis,2 cases.	When reported; no	No	Not required	Yes; no....
OXFORD *Towns and Villages*:						
Embro	General inspection yearly and at intervals.	Scarlatina, 1 case; diphtheria, 1 case	Yes; as well as possible; no.	Yes; yes ..	By M.H.O.	Yes; yes ..
Norwich	General inspection and when complaints are made.	Diphtheria, 2 cases. 1 death; tuberculosis, 2 deaths.	No; no	Yes; yes ..	Under supervision of Sanitary Inspector	No; yes....
Tilsonburg	Yes; yes	Typhoid,6 cases, 4 deaths; tuberculosis, 2 cases.	Yes; no.......	No cases....	Yes.	No ....
Woodstock	Yes	Scarlatina, 1 case; diphtheria,5 cases; typhoid, 5 cases; tuberculosis,7 cases.	Yes	Yes........	Yes.........	Yes; yes ..
Townships: Blandford	Action on complaint.	1 case tuberculosis.	No; no	Yes; yes ..	No; left to attending physician.	No; no ....
Blenheim	General inspection of schools and slaughter houses; action taken on complaint.	Small-pox, 1 case; scarlatina, 14 cases, 1 death; diphtheria,10 cases, 1 death; typhoid, 3 cases; tuberculosis, 3 deaths.	Yes, except tuberculosis; no.	Yes; yes ..	Yes.........	Yes; no....
Nissouri E	Action only on complaint.	Small-pox, 1 case; scarlatina, 2 cases; diphtheria, 4 cases,2 deaths; typhoid, 2 cases; tuberculosis,1 death.	Only as occasion requires; no.	Yes; yes ..	Yes.........	No; no ....

(8)	(9)	(10)	(11)	(12)	(13)	(15)
To physicians only.	No	No	No	No	No	None.
No	Wells,20 to 30 ft.	No ; no	None in Tp	No	No	None.
No	From wells, 18 to 30 ft.; not certain.	No ; inspection by Govt. Inspector on request.	No ; buried or boiled ; no.	No	No	None.
Yes........	From wells, 15 to 120 ft.; yes.	No ; no	None	No	No	None.
No	No; wells, 25 ft.; yes.	No ; no	No	No	No	None.
No	Wells	No	No ; fed to hogs; no.	No	No	None.
Yes........	No ; wells,30 ft.; no.	No ; no	No ; usually buried or burned ; yes.	Yes........	No	None.
Yes..	Wells, 12 to 40 ft.; no.	No ; yes..........	None in the corporation.	Each householder looks after his own.	No	None
Yes........	No ; 12 to 15 ft.; no.	No ; no	No ; none ; no..	Yes........	No	None.
Yes........	Yes....	Yes	None within the corporation.	Yes........	Partial system.	None.
M.H.O.only	No ; wells, 25 to 100 ft.	No ; not this year.	No ; fed or buried ; no.	No	No.	None.
Physicians only.	No ; wells,about 30 ft.	No ; no	No ; boiled, fed to hogs ; no.	No	No	None.
For M.H.O.	From wells ; no.	No ; no	No	No	No	One tannery, one slaughter house.

11 H.

	(2)	(3)	(4)	(5)	(6)	(7)
Oxford N	Yes; yes; no.	Small - p o x, 10 cases.	Yes ; no........	Yes ; yes ..	In cases of small-pox, the druggist disinfects.	Yes . .....
Oxford E	General inspection by Sanitary Inspector.	Scarlatina, 1 case ; typhoid, 1 case.	Yes ; no........	Yes........	Yes........	Yes ; yes...
Oxford W......	General inspection and on complaint.	Small - p o x, 35 cases ; scarlatina, 6 cases ; diphtheria, 1 case ; typhoid, 2 cases ; tuberculosis,1 death.	Yes ; no...... ..	Yes ; yes ..	Under M.H.O.	Yes ; nearly all.
Zorra E	Yes ; yes ...	Small-pox, 2 cases ; scarlatina, 3 cases, 1 death; typhoid, 7 cases, 1 death; tuberculosis,6 cases, 5 deaths.	Yes ; no........	Yes ; yes ..	No	Yes; no....
PEEL. Towns and Villages : Brampton	Yes	Small-pox,1case; scarlatina, 6 cases ; diphtheria, 13 cases, 2 deaths. Tuberculosis. 3 deaths.	Yes ; no........	Yes : yes...	Yes	Yes; yes ...
Bolton	Only on complaint.	.. ..	Yes ; no........	Yes ; yes...	Yes	No; yes....
Streetsville	House to house inspection.	None	No	Yes ; yes...	Yes	Yes........
Townships: Caledon	Action on complaint.	Scarlatina, 6 cases ; diphtheria,11 cases; typhoid, 4 cases.	Yes ; no........	No..........	Not always.	No; no.....
Chinguacousy ..	Only on complaint.	Diphtheria, 5 cases.	Yes ; no.......	....	Yes	No.........
Toronto Gore...	Creameries & butter factories are inspected.	None	No occasion	Not in common use.	No...	No.........
Toronto	Yes	Scarlatina, 3 cases ; diphtheria,16 cases, 1 death. Typhoid, 16 cases, 1 death. Tuberculosis, 4 deaths.	Yes; no........	Yes ; yes...	No	Yes; no....
Albion	General in spection.	....	Yes	Yes	Yes........	....
PERTH. Towns and Villages : Listowel	Yes : Yes	Scarlatina, 5 cases; typhoid, 4 cases,1 death. Tuberculosis, 2 cases, 2 deaths.	Yes ; no........	Yes ; yes...	No, left to attending physician.	Yes ....

(8)	(9)	(10)	(11)	(12)	(13)	(14)
No	Wells, 24 ft.; no	No ; no	Permitted by council ; cooked ; no.	No	No	None.
No	No ; 30 ft.; no.	No	No	No	None	None.
Yes	Wells, from 20 to 125 ft ; no.	Not on farms unless on complaint ; no.	No, but inspected ; offal boiled.	As well as possible.	No	None.
Yes........	Wells, 20 to 30 ft.; yes.	No	Yes ; buried or burned.	....	No	None.
Yes........	Yes	Yes ; no...........	Yes; boiled and fed to hogs; no	No	No	Gas pl'nt not licensed.
Yes........	Wells 15 to 30 ft.	No	Offal boiled and fed to hogs.	No	No	
Yes........	Wells 30 ft. ; no.	Yes: no...........	Yes ; offal fed to hogs ; no.	No	No	None.
Yes.... ...	Wells and spring	No	No; inspected on complaint.	No	No	None.
....	No...............	No	No	No	No	None.
Yes........	Wells 20 to 50 ft.	No	No	No	No	None.
Yes........	No	No	No	No	No	None.
No.........	Wells	.. ..			No	None.
No..... ...	Wells; mostly attributed to water.	No; no	None in corporation	No; removed by private parties.	No	Gas works ; storing hides

	(2)	(3)	(4)	(5)	(6)	(7)
Milverton	Yes and on complaint.	No; no	....	No.	No.	No; no ....
Townships :						
Blanchard......	Yes; yes; on complaint.	Scarlatina, 1 case; typhoid. 6 cases. .	Yes; no........	Yes; yes...	Yes	Yes; yes...
Downie	Committee from Boards inspects.	Scarlatina, 2 cases, 2 deaths. Typhoid, 4 cases; tuberculosis, 1 case.	Only in their own homes; no.	No cases this year.	Yes, by M. H. O.	Partial; no.
Easthope S	No; no; action on complaint	None......	No; no	dont know .	Yes, by M. H. O.	No; no.....
Ellice	Only on complaint.	Scarlatina, 7 cases; tuberculosis, 2 deaths.	Yes	Yes; yes...	Yes...	No; no.....
Elma	Not gen'l. action on complaint.	Scarlatina, 2 cases; tuberculosis, 6 cases.	Yes generally; no hospital.	Yes........	No.	No. ....
Hibbert	Action on complaint.	Scarlatina, 1 case; diphtheria, 1 case; typhoid, 6 cases.	Yes generally; no.	Yes; yes...	Yes, by M. H. O.	No; no.....
Logan..........	Only when complaint is made.	Scarlatina, 69 cases, 1 death. Diphtheria, 2 cases.	Isolated in their homes.	Yes; yes...	Yes	No; no.....
Mornington .	Yes; yes.....	Scarlatina, 11 cases; diphtheria,12 cases, 2 deaths. Typhoid tuberculosis, 3 deaths.	Yes; no........	When necessary.	No	Not this year
Wallace	No regular inspection.	None reported..	Yes: no........	Yes; yes...	No	No; no.....
PETERBORO. *Towns and Villages:*						
Norwood	Yes; yes	Small-pox, 2 cases.	Yes; no	No..........	Yes	Yes; yes...
Peterboro	Yes and repeated.	....	Yes	Yes		....
Townships :						
Belmont and M.	No; no; yes..	Small-pox, 5 cases.	Yes; no	Yes; yes...	Yes...... ..	No; no ....
Chandos	On complaint.	None	No cases.......	....	No..........	No..........
Douro..........	No; on complaint only.	Tuberculosis, 3 deaths.	Yes; no........	No..........	Yes	No; no ....
Dummer ...:..	Only on complaint.	Small-pox, 1 case; tuberculosis, 3 deaths.	No; no....:...	No..........	No	No; no ....
Ennismore	Action on complaint.	Scarlatina, 4 cases; typhoid, 2 cases; tuberculosis, 2 deaths.	No; no.........	Yes; yes....	No...... ...	No; no ....

(8)	(9)	(10)	(11)	(12)	(13)	(14)
No.........	Wells 10 to 20ft.; no.	No; no	No; fed to hogs.	No	No '........	Piggery in connection with cheese factory.
Yes	....	No	No; burned ; no.	....	....	
No.........	No; no	No; no.	No; no	No	No	Slaughter houses.
Yes	From wells 15 to 40 ft.; no.	No	No; feed to hogs; no.	No	No	Slaughter houses.
Yes........	No; from 30 to 120 ft.; no.	No; no	Don't know; no.	Yes.... ...	....	None.
No.........	No; from wells 15 to 20 ft.; yes	No; none	No; partly boiled	No	No	None.
No.........	No ; from 20 to 30 ft.; no.	No; no	None in Tp ...	No	No	None.
No.........	No: wells; no.	No; no	None in Tp...	No	No	None.
No.........	No; about 50 ft	No; no	No; burned generally.	No	No	None.
Yes... ...	Wells; yes.	No; no	No buried ; no.	No	No	None.
Yes........	Wells; 30 ft.; no.	No; no	No; no ; offal fed to pigs.	No	No	None.
Yes........	Waterworks....	....	....	Yes........	No	None.
No........	No; 20 ft ; no.	No; no	No; burnt; no.	No	No	None.
No...... ..	No	No	None	No	No	None.
Yes........	No ; wells 30 ft.; no.	No	None in Tp.....	No	No	None.
Yes........	No ; wells 20 ft.	No	No	No	No	None.
No.........	No; wells 10 to 40 ft.; yes.	No: no	None in Tp.....	No	No	None.

	(2)	(3)	(4)	(5)	(6)	(7)
Galway	Action taken on complaint	Scarlatina, many cases; diphtheria, 2 cases, 1 death.	No; no.........	Not enough cases to give it a fair trial.	Yes.........	No.........
Harvey	Action on complaint.	Diphtheria, 2 cases, 1 death. Tuberculosis, 1 case,1 death.	Yes; no........	Yes; yes...	Yes.........	No; no.....
Monaghan N. ..	No; no; yes..	....	Yes; yes, in Peterboro t'wn	No; no....	Yes.........	No; no.....
Otonabee.. ..	When complaint is made.	Scarlatina, 13 cases; diphtheria, 5 cases; tuberculosis, 3 deaths.	Yes no	....	Yes..	No; no.....
Smith	No	None reported..	No hospital	Dont know.	Under instructions by attending physiciau.	-No ....
PRESCOTT AND RUSSEL. *Touns and Villages*:						
L'Original	Only on complaint.	None	Yes; no........	Yes; yes...	Yes.........	No; no ....
Vankleek Hill..	Gen'l sanitary inspection, repeated at intervals.	Diphtheria, 1 case; Tuberculosis, 2 deaths.	Yes; no........	Yes; yes...	Yes.........	No; no ...
Townships :						
Alfred	On complaint.	Small-pox, 4 cases; scarlatina, 25 cases, 1 death; diphtheria,15 cases; tuberculosis, 4 cases.	Yes; no........	Yes; yes...	Yes.........	On complaint; yes.
Clarence	Yes, once a year and on complaint.	Tuberculosis, 3 cases.	Yes; no.	Yes; generally.	Yes.... ...	No; yes....
Caledonia	Action taken on complaint	Tuberculosis, 2 cases.	No	Yes; yes...	Yes.........	No ....
Hawkesbury E.	On complaint only.	Scarlatina, 6 cases, 2 deaths; tuberculosis, 2 cases.	No; no hospital.	Yes; yes...	Yes...... ..	No; yes....
Plantagenent S.	Yes; No; Yes;	Small-pox, 17 cases; diphtheria, 11 cases; tuberculosis, 6 cases.	Yes; no........	Yes; yes...	Yes, by M. H. O.	Yes; partly; no.
Cambridge	Only on complaint.	Diphtheria, 3 cases; typhoid, 3 cases	Yes, in cases of diphtheria.	Yes; yes...	Yes	No; no.....
PRINCE EDWARD. *Towns and Villages* :						
Wellington	Yes..........	Yes............	Yes; no........	Yes.... ...	Yes.........	Yes; Yes ..
Townships:						
Ameliasburgh ..	Yes, every year.	Tuberculosis, 3 cases.	Yes; yes	Yes	Yes.........	No; no.....
Athol	No; action on complaint.	Tuberculosis, 1 case.	Yes; no........	Yes	Yes	No; no.....

(8)	(9)	(10)	(11)	(12)	(13)	(14)
No.........	No; wells various depths; no.	No; no	None	No	No	None.
Yes to M.H.O.	No; from wells 30 ft.; no.	No; no	None in Tp.....	No; only in schools.	No	None.
No.........	No; no.	No; no	Yes; boiled and fed to hogs.	No	No	None.
No.	No; 20 ft.	No; no	No; fed to hogs; no.	No	No	3 slaughter houses.
No.........	No; wells 10 to 30 ft.	No; no	No	No	No	None.
Yes	Wells; don't know.	No; no	No	No	No	None except slaughter houses.
Yes..... .	Wells, 15 to 24 ft.; don't know as to typhoid.	No	No; offal buried; no.	No	No	One slaughter house.
No	No; well,12 ft. in some cases.	No; no	No; buried; yes.	No	No	None.
No	No; wells, 10 to 15 ft.; no.	No; no	No; no	No	No	None.
No	No	No; no	No; no	No	No	None.
No	No; no; no	No; no	No	No	No	None.
No	No; don't know; no.	No; no	No; burned; no.	No	No	None.
No	Don't know.....	....	No	No	No	None.
Yes........	No; about 12 ft.	Yes; no..........	None in Corp'n.	Yes........	No	None.
Yes........	No; wells, 10 to 40 ft.	No; no	Yes; buried; no.	Yes........	No	None.
No	No; from wells 8 to 30 ft.; no.	No; no	None in Tp	No	No	None.

	(2)	(3)	(4)	(5)	(6)	(7)
Hallowell	Action on complaint.	Diphtheria, 1 case ; tuberculosis, 2 cases.	Isolated in their homes; no hospital.	Yes	Yes	No ....
Hillier	No	....	No ; no	Yes ; yes...	Yes	No ....
Marysburgh, S.	On complaint.	Scarlatina, 1 case, 1 death ; tuberculosis, 4 deaths.	Yes ; no........	Yes ; yes...	Yes	No ; no.....
Marysburgh, N.	Gen'l sanitary inspection at intervals.	Tuberculosis, 1 case.	Yes ; no........	Yes ; yes...	Yes	Yes ; no....
Sophiasburg	No; no; action on complaint.	None	No hospital	Yes	Yes, by attending physician.	No ... ..
PARRY SOUND DISTRICT. *Towns and Villages* :						
Burk's Falls....	Yes; yes; yes;	Scarlatina, 4 cases, 1 death ; diphtheria, 8 cases, 1 death ; tuberculosis, 1 death.	Yes ; no	Yes ; yes...	Yes	Yes ; no. ..
Sundridge	Yes ; one yearly inspection & action on complaint.	Typhoid, 7 cases, 4 deaths; tuberculosis, 1 death.	Yes ; no........	Yes ; yes...	Yes	Yes ....
Townships :						
Armour	Only on complaint.	None	No cases ; no....	....	Yes,if necessary.	No ....
Chapman	No ; action on complaint.	Scarlatina, 7 cases.	No hospital; contagious diseases are isolated.	No	....	....
Carling	Action on complaint.	None	No hospital	....	....	No ; no.....
Christie........	....	None	Yes ; no........	Yes	No	No ....
Hagerman......	Yes, in spring & when complaint is made.	Scarlatina, 1 case, 1 death.	Yes ; no........	Yes	Yes	No ....
Himsworth N ..	Yes	1 scarlet fever ..	Yes	Can't say...	Yes	No ....
Himsworth S ..	Yes, twice yearly......	Scarlatina, 16 cases ; diphtheria, 30 cases, 1 death ; tuberculosis, 3 deaths.	Yes : no........	Yes ; yes...	Generally ..	No ....
Joly	On complaint.	None	No	....	No diseases.	No ; no.....
Macher	No; only on complaint.	None	No ; no	No physician in Tp	Yes	No ....
McDougal	Action on complaint.	None	No	No	No	No ....
McKellar	No	None	No	No	No	No ....
McMurrch	No	None	Yes	No cases ...	No	Yes ; no....
Nipissing	....	None	Yes	No	Yes	No ....

(8)	(9)	(10)	(11)	(12)	(13)	(14)
No	No	No	No	No	No	None.
Yes, to M.H.O.	No;15 to 20 ft; no	No	No	No	No	None.
Yes..	Wells, 10 to 40 ft.; no.	No	None in Tp	No	No	None.
No	No; no.	No; no	None in Tp	No	None	No.
No	No; wells, 20 ft.; don't know.	No; no	No; offal buried; no.	No	No	None.
No	No;wells average 15 ft ; no.	No; no	No; fed to hogs; no.	No	No	None.
No	No; wells and spring, from 3 to 12 ft.; no.	No; no	No; buried ; no	Yes	No	None.
Yes	Wells,all depths; no.	None	No; buried ; no.	No	No	Slaughter houses.
	No	No	None in Tp	No	No	None.
No	No	No; no	None in Tp	No		None.
No	No; 5 to 20 ft ; no.	No	None in Tp	No	None	None.
No	From wells about 15 ft.; no	No	No; no inspection.	No	No	None.
No	No ; wells from 12 to 30 ft.; no	No	No; no	No	No	None.
No	From wells ; no.	No	No ; fed to hogs	Generally once a year.	No	None.
No	No; wells, 20 ft.; no.	No; no	None in Tp	No	No	None.
Yes	No ; wells, 16 to 25 ft.	No ; no	None in Tp	No	No	None.
No						
No	Wells	No; no	None in Tp	No	No	None.
No	No	No	None in Tp	No	No	None.
No	No; wells about 18 ft.	No ; no	No	No	No	None.

	(2)	(3)	(4)	(5)	(6)	(7)
Ryerson........	Action on complaint.	Tuberculosis, 1 case.	Yes............	In diphtheria.	Yes........	No; no.....
Strong.........	When complaint is made.	Typhoid, 2 cases.	Yes ; no........	No	Yes........	No ....
RENFREW, Towns and Villages:						
Eganville	Yes ; yes.....	Smallpox, 1 case; scarlatina, 2 cases.	Yes	Yes; yes...	Yes	No; no .....
Pembroke	Yes ; yes.....	Smallp'x,7 cases; scarlatina, 12 cases; diph.,23 cases, 4 deaths; typhoid, 137 cases, 4 deaths.	Patients isolated from other members of the family; hospital for smallpox only.	Yes; yes....	In smallpox only, for other diseases attending physician disinfects.	
Renfrew	General 'sanitary inspection.	Smallp'x,4 cases; scarlatina, 7 cases; diph., 5 cases; typhoid, 2 cases; tuberculosis,7 cases, 5 deaths.	Yes; yes	Yes; yes....	Yes	No ....
Townships:						
Admaston	When complaint is made	Smallpox, 34 cases; typhoid, 1 case; tuberculosis, 1 case.	Yes; no	Yes; yes....	Yes	No; no .....
Algona, S......	No ; no ; yes..	Typhoid, 1 case, 1 death.	Yes; no	Yes; yes....	Yes	No ....
Bagot & Blythfield.	Only on complaint.	Smallpox, 15 cases; diph., 1 case; tuberculosis, 2 deaths	Smallpox only ; no hospital ...	No; no	No	No ....
Bromley	When complaint is made	Scarlatina, 2 cases; typhoid, 8 cases; tuberculosis, 3 d'ths	Yes; no	Yes; yes....	Yes	Yes; no ....
Brudenell & Lyndock.	No	None	When necessary; no.	Yes; yes....	Yes	Vaccination is generally observed.
Grattan........	Action taken	Smallpox, 11 cases; tuberculosis, 3 cases, 3 deaths.	Yes; no	Yes; yes....	Yes	No; no .....
Griffith & M....	Action on complaint.	Smallpox, 13 cases.	No	Yes; yes....	Yes	No; vaccination carried out this year.
Haggerty, etc ..	Action taken on complaint.	Diph., 2 cases, 2 deaths.	Yes; no	Yes	Yes	No; no .....
Horton........	Only taken on complaint.	Smallp'x,2 cases; diph., 2 cases, 1 death.	Yes; no	Yes; yes....	Yes	No; yes ....
McNab	Action only on complaint.	Smallp'x 6 cases; scarlatina, 10 cases reported, 1 death; diphtheria, 5 cases, 2 deaths; typhoid, 4 cases, 2 deaths.	Yes	Have not heard of its use.	Under M.H. O.and sanitary inspector.	No ....

(8)	(9)	(10)	(11)	(12)	(13)	(14)
No	No	No	No	No	No	None.
Yes	Mostly spring..	No	No	No	No	None.
No	No	No; no	No	No	No	None.
Physicians only.	Yes ; about 25 p.c.have wells.	None in town.....	None within limits of the town.	No, except by regulation of local B.H.	Yes	None within the town limits.
No	Yes	No; no	None allowed in the town.	Yes	Yes	None.
Yes	No ; don't know; no.	No; yes	No; fed to hogs ; no.	No	No	Slaughter houses.
Yes	Yes; about 20 ft.; no.	No; no	None in Tp.....	No	No	None.
No	Wells and lake water.	No	None in Tp.....	No	No	None.
No	No; from 12 to 30 ft.; no.	No; no	No; buried; no..	No	No	None.
Yes	Wells; no	No; no	None in Tp.....	No	No	None.
No	Wells, 10 to 12 ft ; no	No; no	No; fed to hogs; no.	No	No	None.
No	Spring water ...	No	No	No	No	None.
No	Wells ....:	No	None in Tp.....	No	No	None.
No	No; wells; don't know.	No	None in Tp.....	No	No	None.
....	Wells & springs.	Yes; no .....'	No; offal buried.	Yes	No	None.

	(2)	(3)	(4)	(5)	(6)	(7)
Pembroke	No	Smallpox, 2 cases	Yes; no	Yes; yes....	Yes	No ....
Radcliffe and R.	....	None......... ..	Yes	. ...	Yes	....
Rolph, B. & W.	....	Tuberculosis, 2 cases, 2 deaths.	No	....	....	....
Sebastopol	On complaint only.	None..........	No	No cases ...	No cases....	No; no .....
Stafford	Only on complaint.	Diph., 1 case...	No	Yes; yes....	Yes, under M.H.O.	No ....
Westmeath.....	....	Diph., 3 deaths.	No	Yes; yes....	....	No ....
Wilberforce and North Algona.	No	Diph., 1 case; tuberculosis, 3 cases, 3 deaths.	Yes	Yes; yes....	Yes	No; no .....
RAINY RIVER DISTRICT. *Townships :* Chapple	No ; no	Diph., 18 cases, 3 deaths; typhoid, 2 cases.	Yes; no	Yes; yes....	Yes˙	Yes; no ....
Emo	Action on complaint.	Smallpox, 1 case.	Yes; when necessary; no.	Do not know	Yes	No; yes ....
Mikado & Shoal Lake.	No ; no	Typhoid, 16 cas's, 1 death.	Yes, generally..	....	Yes, under instructi'ns of physician	No; no .....
Regina Mine District.	No ; no ; yes..	None..........	No outbreak....	No outbreak	No outbreak	No ; school closed.
Wabigoon	No ; no.......	None..........	No	Yes; yes....	No	No ....
Wainwright and Dryden.	No ...:......	None......	No	Yes; yes...	No	No; no .....
THUNDER BAY DISTRICT. Port Arthur....	Yes ; yes.....	Smallp'x, 7 cases; diphtheria, 1 case; typhoid, 84 cases ; 7 deaths ; tuberculosis, 8 d'ths	Yes; yes........	Yes; yes....	Under Dr. attending.	Not this year ; no ; children vaccinated recently.
SIMCOE. *Towns and Villages :* Alliston	Yes, twice a year.	Smallp'x, 5 cases; tuberculosis, 1 case.	Yes; yes	Yes	Yes	Yes; yes ...
Barrie...	Yes; general inspection and repeated at intervals.	Scarlatina, 3 cases; diph., 6 cases, 2 deaths; consumption, 4 cases.	Yes; no	Occasionaly.	Yes	No; yes ....
Beeton	Yes; repeated.	Diph., 7 cases, no deaths; tuberculosis, 2 cases, no de'ths	Yes, as far as practicable in houses.	Yes; yes....	Yes	No; no .....
Collingwood	Yes, on complaint.	Smallp'x, 6 cases, diphtheria, 3 cases, 3 deaths.	Yes; yes........	Occasionally used.	Yes, by M.H.O.	No; no .....

(8)	(9)	(10)	(11)	(12)	(13)	(14)
No	No; 10 or 12 ft.; no.	No; no	No; buried; no..	No	No	None.
....	Wells; no	No	None in Tp.....	No	No	None.
No	No	No	None in Tp.....	No	No	None.
No	No; no	No; no	No; no	No	No	None.
No	No; no.........	No	None in Tp.....	No	No	None.
No; no	No; about 20 ft.; yes.	No	No	No	No	None.
No	No; 14 ft	None	None in Tp.....	No	No	None.
No	No ; rivers and streams.	No; no	None	No	No	None.
No	No; wells; no....	No ; no...........	No; no	Yes	No	None.
No	Lake water; no.	No ; no...........	None; offal buried.	Yes	No	None.
No	Whitefish Bay..	None	None	No	Yes	No.
No	Wells; 20 to 30 ft.; no.	No	No	No	No	None.
No	No; wells, 20 ft.; no.	No	None	No	No	None.
Yes	Wells, 10 ft.; no.	Yes, some few cases.	No; burned	Yes	Partial system.	None.
Yes	Wells, 20 ft.; no.	No ; no...........	No; cremated; no.	Yes, by household'r	No	None.
Yes	Yes; also wells, 125 ft.; no.	No ; no..........	No ; boiled. no..	Yes, of night soil.	Yes	None.
Yes	Yes	No ; no.....	No; buried; no..	Yes	No	None.
No	Yes; no wells...	No ; no...........	No; boiled and fed to hogs.	Yes	Partly on Main st.	None.

	(2)	(4)	(4)	(5)	(6)	(7)
Creemore.......	Generally twice a year.	Diph., 1 death..	Yes; no	Yes	Yes	No ... .
Midland........	... .	Scarlatina, 8 cases; diph., 1 de'th; typhoid, 1 death.	No; except small pox; yes.	No	Yes	No ....
Tottenham	Yes, yearly and on complaint.	None...........	Yes; no	Yes; yes....	No; Dr. in attendance disinfects.	No; no .....
Townships: Essa...........	....	None...........	No	Don't know.	No	Yes ....
Gwillimbury, W.	Only on complaint.	Tuberculosis, 1 death.	No occasion ...	No occasion.	....	No ....
Innisfil........	Action on complaint.	Scarlatina, 29 ; diph., 9 cases, 2 deaths ; typhoid,14 cases, 2 deaths; tuberculosis, 5 cases,3 deaths.	Yes, generally..	Yes; yes....	Yes, by M. H.O.	No; no .....
Matchedash	Action on complaint.	Diph., 4 cases, 2 deaths.	Yes	Yes	....	Yes; yes ...
Medonte	Inspection on complaint.	Smallpox, 10 cases ; scarlatina, 14 cases ; typhoid,3 cas's, 2 deaths.	Yes; yes........	Don't know.	Yes	No: no .....
Nottawasaga ...	Action on complaint.	Typhoid, 1 case; tuberculosis, 5 cases, 5 deaths.	Yes ; no hospital.	Dont' know.	Yes	No........
Oro	Action on complaint.	Scarlatina, 2 cases, 2 deaths; diph. 2 deaths.	No ; no........	Yes ; yes...	Yes	No....... ..
Orillia	Yes ; yes	Scarlatina, 1 case ; tuberculosis, 11 cases, 11 deaths.	No ; none......	Yes, by some physicians.	Under M H. O.	Yes ; no ...
Sunnidale	Yes..........	Diphtheria, 1 case reported, 1 death ; typhoid, 1 case.	No ; no	Yes...	Yes.......	Yes ; no ...
Tay	Only on complaint.	Smallpox, 17 cases; typhoid, 4 cases ; tuberculosis, 5 deaths.	Yes ; yes	Yes ; yes...	Yes	No ; no....
Tecumseth	Action on complaint.	Smallpox, 4 cases ; diphtheria, 2 cases; typhoid,1 case; tuberculosis, 1 death.	Yes ; no........	Yes ; yes ..	Yes ; by M. H. O.	No ; no....
Tossoronto	No ; no ; only on complaint	Smallpox, 1 case; typhoid, 15 cases, 1 death; tuberculosis, 3 cases, 2 deaths.	Yes ; no........	No occasion.	Yes	No ; no....
Tiny	No...........	None	No	Yes........	Yes	No.........
Vespra	Only on complaint.	None	Yes; when necessary.	....	Yes	When requested.

(8)	9)	(10)	(11)	(12)	(13)	(14)
Yes	Wells, from 10 to 15 ft.; no.	No	No; fed to hogs.	No	No	None.
No	At present water works are being put in.	No	None in corpora-tion.	No	No	None.
No	No; wells, 20 to 40 ft.; no.	No ; no...........	No; don't know; no.	Yes	No	None.
No	Wells, 30 ft	No	No; no	Yes	No	None.
No	Wells, 20 to 40 ft.; no.	No ; no...........	None in Tp.....	Don't know.	No	None.
Yes	No; from 20 to 40 ft.; no.	No ; no...	No; offal fed to hogs; no.	No	No	None.
Yes	Wells, 12 ft.....	No ; no......	None in Tp.....	....	No	None.
Yes	No; wells, 10 to 100 ft ; yes, 2 cases.	None	No; fed to hogs; no.	No	No	No.
No..........	Water from wells 30 ft.	No....	No.....	No..........	No........	None.
Not to teachers.	No ; 20 to 70 ft.; yes	No.....	No ; don't know.	No..........	No...	None.
No..........	No ; about 16 ft.	No ; none	No ; burned ; no.	No..........	No	None.
Yes	Wells, 20 ft.; no.	No ; no..........	None in township.	No..........	No....	None.
No........	No ; 20 ft.; no..	No ; no..	No; burried; no.	No.	Don't know.	None.
No..........	Water supply from wells, 25 to 35 ft.; no.	No..............	No.............	No..........	No..........	None.
No..........	From wells 15 ft.; no.	No ; no.........	No; don't know.	No..........	No.........	1 tannery.
....	No	None	None	No..........	No..........	None.
Yes	Wells from 20 to 100 ft.; no.	No..............	None	No..........	No........	None.

	(2)	(3)	(4)	(5)	(6)	(7)
STORMONT, DUNDAS & GLENGARRY. *Towns and Villages:*						
Alexandria	Action taken on complaint	Smallpox,7 cases; diphtheria, 48 cases, 5 deaths; typhoid, 10 cases.	Yes; no hospital.	Yes; yes; when administered early.	Only in cases of smallpox.	No; no....
Chesterville	Yes, after first inspection.	Typhoid, 1 case; tuberculosis, 1 death	Yes; no........	Yes; yes...	Yes........	No...... ..
Cornwall	Yes, at intervals during the summer.	Scarlatina, 6 cases; typhoid, 8 cases; tuberculosis, 11 deaths.	Yes; yes.......	Yes; yes...	Yes........	Yes........
Lancaster	Action on complaint.	None...........	Yes; when required.	Yes; yes...	Yes........	Not always.
Winchester.....	Yes, repeated at intervals.	Typhoid, 1 case; tuberculosis, 1 death.	Yes; no........	Yes; yes...	Yes........	No; no....
Townships: Charlottenburgh	Action on complaint.	Smallpox, 8 cases.	Under direction of M.H.O.	....	Under direction of M. H. O.	No........
Cornwall.......	General sanitary inspection.	Scarlatina,1case; diphtheria, 1 case; tuberculosis, 2 cases.	Yes; no........	Yes; when used early.	Yes........	No; no....
Finch..........	No, general...	Smallpox,1 case.	Yes; no hospital.	Yes........	Yes........	No...... ..
Kenyon........	No; no......	Diphtheria, 6 cases, 5 deaths.	Yes; no........	Yes; yes...	Yes; generally.	Don't know.
Matilda........	Only on complaint.	Typhoid, 2 cases, 2 deaths; tuberculosis, 3 deaths.	....	....	Yes........	No........
Mountain	Action on complaint.	Tuberculosis, 3 deaths.	No.............	No...... ..	No.........	No........
Osnabruck	On complaint only.	Tuberculosis, 8 deaths.	No hospital ; all contagious diseases isolated except consumption.	Yes; yes ..	Yes........	No; no....
Roxborough ...	Action on complaint.	Scarlatina, 30 to 40 cases; diphtheria, 9 cases.	Yes; as well as possible.	Yes; when used early.	Under the instruction of attending physician.	No; no ...
Winchester	No, action taken only on complaint	Tuberculosis 4 deaths.	Yes; no	Yes; yes...	Yes; by M. H. O.	No........
VICTORIA. *Towns and Villages:* Bobcaygeon	On complaint.	Scarlatina, 2 cases ; diphtheria, 4 cases.	Yes; yes	Yes; yes ..	By M.H.O.	No........
Lindsay........	....	Smallpox,2cases; Scarlatina, 9 cases ; diphtheria, 46 cases, 3 deaths ; typhoid, 8 cases.	Yes; no hospital	Yes; yes...	Yes........	Yes; no...

(8)	(9)	(10)	(11)	(12)	(13)	(14)
No.........	Yes ; no	No ; no........ ..	None in the corporation ; no.	No.........	No.........	None.
No.........	No ; 20 ft.; no..	Yes ; no	None in the village.	No.........	No.........	None.
No.........	Yes ; yes.......	No ; no..........	No ; but inspected ; offal buried ; no.	No ; removed as required.	Yes	Storing of hides; slaughtering of animals ; gas mfg.
Yes........	No ; wells 15 to 18 ft.; no.	No ; no........ ..	No ; burried; no.	No...... ..	No.........	None.
Yes	No ; cannot say; yes, one case.	No...............	None within the corporation.	Done by individuals ; no system.	No...	None.
No.........	Wells, average 30 ft.	No ; no..........	No ; no........	Does not apply to tp.	Does not apply to tp.	
M. H. O only.	Wells, depth 15 to 25 ft ; no.	No ; no.....	No; burried; no.	No.........	No.........	None.
Yes	Wells...........	No ; no..........	No..............	No.... ..	No.........	None.
Yes	Yes, from 6 to 20 ft.; no.	Occasionally ; no.	No ; offal burried ; no.	Not necessary.	Not necessary.	None.
Yes	Wells, average 25 ft.	No..............	No.............	No.........	No.........	None.
No.........	No ; wells, 10 to 40 ft.; no.	No.........	No.............	No.........	No.........	None.
No.........	Wells from 8 to 10 ft.	No..............	No.............	No.........	No....	None.
No........	No ; wells from 10 to 30 ft.; sometimes.	No ; yes, a few ...	No ; burried ...	No.........	No.........	None.
No	Wells, 25 ft.; no.	No..............	No........... ..	No.........	No.........	None.
No.........	A pipe from a spring and some wells.	No.	Are inspected occasionally.	No.........	No.........	None.
Yes ; no...	Yes ; wells, 8 to 20 ft.; yes.	No..............	None	No.........	No.........	None.

	(2)	(3)	(4)	(5)	(6)	(7)
Omemee	General sanitary inspection.	Tuberculosis, 1 death.	Yes ; no........	No.........	Yes........	....
Sturgeon Point.	General sanitary inspection.	None	Had no cases ...	No occasion.	No occasion.	No schools..
Woodville	On complaint.	Consumption, 1 case.	Yes ; no..	Yes ; yes...	Yes	No.........
Townships: Bexley	No ; no ; action on complaint.	Diphtheria, 2 cases; typhoid, 5 cases, 2 deaths ; tuberculosis, 1 case, 1 death.	Yes ; yes.......	Yes ; yes...	No ; under attending physician.	No ; yes....
Carden	....	Smallpox, 21 cases.	Yes ; no........	Some use it.	Yes	No ; no....
Dalton........	No...........	None	....	....	....	No.........
Emily..........	On complaint.	Scarlatina,1case; typhoid,1 case; consumption,1 case.	Yes ; no........	Yes ; yes...	Yes	No ; no....
Laxton, Digby, and L.........	Action on complaint.	None	Yes ; no........	Yes : yes...	Yes	No ; yes...
Ops.	Yes ; yes	Scarlatina, 2 cases ; diphtheria,11 cases, 1 death.	Yes ; as far as practicable in homes of patients.	Yes ; yes...	Yes	Yes ; no ...
Fenelon	Only when complaint is make.	Diphtheria, 2 cases : tuberculosis,1 death	Yes ; no........	Yes ; yes...	Yes	No. ....
Verulam	Not general, only on complaint.	Diphtheria, 1 case.	Yes ; no........	Yes ; yes...	Yes	No ; yes . .
WATERLOO. *Towns and Villages :*						
Berlin..........	Yes ; yes......	Scarlatina, 78 cases, 1 death. Diphtheria, 18 cases,2 deaths. Typhoid, 3 cases.	Yes ; yes.......	Yes ; yes...	Yes	No ; yes....
Elmira	Yes; general in May & Sept.	None	Yes ; no........	Yes ; yes...	Yes.......	No ....
Galt	Yes ; house to house inspection by inspectors.	Diphtheria, 21 cases ; typhoid,24 cases, 1 death. Tuberculosis, 16 deaths.	Yes ; no..	Yes ; yes...	Yes.........	Yes.........
Hespeler	Yes; action on complaint.	Typhoid, 1 case ; tuberculosis, 1 case.	Yes ; no........	Yes	Yes.........	Yes.........
Preston	Yes ; cn complaint.	Diphtheria, 15 cases, 1 death. Tuberculosis, 4 cases.	Yes, as far as practicable; no ·	Yes	Yes.........	Yes ; yes ...

(8)	(9)	(10)	(11)	(12)	(13)	(14)
Yes	No ; 15 ft.; no.	No.........	None	No........	No.........	None.
....	Wells, 10 ft.; no.	No...............	None	Yes	No.........	No.
No.........	No.............	No.....	None	No.........	No.........	None.
No.........	No ; wells, 25 ft.	No ; no.....	No; burnt and burried.	No.........	No.........	None.
No.........	No ; about 10 ft	No ; no..........	None in township.	No.........	No.........	None.
No	No.....	No.....	None	No.........	No.........	None.
Yes	No...........	No......	No.............	No.........	No.........	No.
Yes........	Wells ; no	No ; no..........	None	Generally ..	No.........	None.
Yes........	No ; wells, 12 to 50 ft.; no.	Yes ; no	Yes ; steamed or boiled ; fed to hogs.	No.........	No.........	None.
No.........	No ; 15 to 50 ft.; some typhoid when water becomes low.	No...............	No......	No.........	No.........	None.
No.........	Wells, 25 ft ; no.	No ; no.	None in township.	No.........	No.........	None.
Yes	Yes	No ; yes..........	No; used for fertilizing purposes ; yes.	No.........	Yes	None.
No.........	No ; from wells usu'l depth 30 ft	No ; no	No; offal thrown in the river ; yes.	No	No.........	None.
Yes	Yes ; no	Yes : no	None in corporation.	Yes	Partial	2 laundries ; 1 gasho'se.
Yes	From wells 20 to 40 ft.	Yes ; no ·.........	None within the town.	Yes	No..........	None.
Yes	No ; 15 to 30 ft.	No ; no dairies in corporation.	None in corporation.	No	No.........	None.

	(2)	(3)	(4)	(5)	(6)	(7)
Waterloo......	Yes	Scarla t i n a, 15 cases ; d i p h-theria,12 cases, 3 deaths. Ty-phoid, 6 cases, 2 deaths. Tu-berculo s i s, 4 cases,2 deaths.	Yes ; yes.......	Yes ; yes...	Yes..... ..	No , no ....
Townships :						
Dumfries N	Yes ; inspec-tion on com-plaint.	Diphth e r i a, 2 cases.	Yes ; no........	Yes ; yes...	Yes........ .	No ; no ....
Waterloo.......	Yes ; general inspection.	Sm a l l - p o x, 2 cases ; d i p h-theria, 20cases, 1 death. Ty-phoid,25 cases, 1 death. Tu-berculosis, 1 death.	Yes ; no........	Yes ; yes...	Yes.........	Yes ; yes...
Wellesley	Yes ; yes.....	Scarlatina, 10 cases, 1 death. Diphtheria, 18 cases; typhoid, 12 cases, 1 death.	Yes ; no........	Yes	Yes: yes...	Yes ; yes...
Wilmot	Yes	Diphtheria, 9 cases,4 deaths. Typhoid, 9 cases, 1 death.	Yes ; no........	Yes ; yes...	Yes.........	No ; no ....
Woolwich	Only on com-plaint.	Tuberculosis, 4 cases.	Yes ; nc........	No........	No	No ; no ....
WELLAND. *Towns and Vil-lages :*						
Bridgeburg	Yearly insp'tn	None	No	Do not know	Yes.........	Yes.........
Fort Erie	Gen. inspect n	Typhoid, 1 case.	Yes ; no........	Yes ; yes...	Yes.........	No ; no ....
Niagara Falls ..	Yes ; yes.....	Diphtheria, 10 cases, 1 death. Typhoid, 10 cases ; tuber-culosis, 3 d'ths.	Yes ; no........	Yes ; yes...	Yes........	Yes; no....
Niagara Falls South	Yes and action on compl'nt.	None	No occasion	Don't know.	....	No ; no ....
Port Colborne ..	No ; only on complaint.	Diphtheria, sev-eral cases, 1 death. Ty-phoid, 1 death.	Yes ; yes.......	Yes ; yes...	No	No ; no ...
Welland	Inspection is repeated.	Tuberculosis 3 deaths.	Yes	Cannot say..	Yes........	Yes.........
Townships :						
Bertie	Action only on complaint.	Scarlatina, 1 case ; typhoid, 2 cases ; tu-berculosis, 2 cases, 2 deaths.	As well as prac-ticable without isolation hos-pital.	....	Yes, by di-rection of M.H.O.	No; vaccina-t i o n i s general.
Crowland	On complaint.	Diphtheria, 1 case ; typhoid, 1 death.	No occasion	Don't know.	Yes, by M. H.O.	No ; no ....

(8)	(9)	(10)	(11)	(12)	(13)	(14)
Yes	Yes ; no	Yes : no..........	No; carted away; no.	No........ .	Yes	1 tannery ; 1 1 gasho'se ; 2 sl'ter h'ses
Yes	Wells & springs 30 ft.; no.	Yes ; no..........	No ; cooked and fed to hogs.	No.........	No	None.
Yes	No ; yes....... ..	Yes ; no...	Yes ; buried or fed.	No.........	No	None.
No.........	Yes ; wells 20 to 40 ft. ; no.	No ; no	No ; buried ; no.	Yes	No.........	Slaughteri'g animals.
M.D's only.	Wells 20 to 40 ft.	No ; none	No ; inspected.	No...... .	No	None.
Yes	Wells 10 to 30 ft; no.	No...............	Yes	No..........	No	None.
No	No ; about 50 ft.; no.	No...............	None in the corporation.	No.	No.........	None.
No.........	No ; wells and river ; no.	No ; no	No ; fed to hogs; no.	No	No.........	Tallow melting; slaughter houses.
Yes	Yes ; no	Yes	None in corporation.	Yes	Yes	None.
Yes	Waterworks and wells ; no.	Yes ; no....	None in the corporation.	No	No.........	None.
No	Yes; some wells; 1 case.	No ; no	No ; no	No	No	None.
Yes	Yes	No ; no	None in town...	Yes	Partially ...	No.
No	Wells from 15 to 60 ft ; no.	No; no	No ; boiled and fed to hogs; no	No...	No	None.
No	Wells about 23 ft.; no.	No cases..........	None	No	No,........	None.

	(2)	(3)	(4)	(5)	(6)	(7)
Humberston...	Inspection is made as required.	Diphtheria, 3 cases, 1 death Typhoid, 5 cases ; tuberculosis. 2 cases, 2 deaths.	No ; no	No.........	Not always..	Yes : yes ...
Pelham.........	Yes ; yes....	....	Yes	Yes........	Yes	....
Stamford.......	Yes ; repeated at intervals	Diphtheria, 1 case, 1 death. Tuberculosis, 1 death.	No ; no	Don't know.	No.........	Yes ; no....
Willloughby....	Action on com-complaint.	None	No.............	Yes ; yes...	No.........	No.........
WELLINGTON. Towns and Villages :						
Clifford	Yes ; yes.....	Scarlatina, 1 case ; Diphtheria, 1 case.	No hospital; yes.	Yes ; yes...	No.........	No ; no ....
Drayton........	Once a year & on compl'nt.	None	No.	No cases....	No.........	No.........
Elora	Yes ; every year.	Tuberculosis, 3 deaths.	No ; no	No cases....	No.........	No.........
Erin	General sanitary inspec'n	Scarlatina, 2 cases ; tuberculosis, 3 d'ths.	Yes ; no........	No cases....	Yes...	No ; no ....
Fergus	Yes ; yes.....	Diphtheria, 1 death. Tuberculosis, some deaths.	Yes ; no........	....	Yes.........	No.........
Mount Forest ..	Yes ; yes.....	Diphtheria, 5 cases ; tuberculosis, 1 case	Yes ; no........	....	No	No ....
Palmerston.....	Gen. inspect'n.	....	No ; no	No cases....	No.........	No.........
Townships :						
Arthur.........	Action taken on compl'nt.	Scarlatina, 2 cases ; diphtheria, 4 cases; tuberculosis, 1 death.	Cases isolated as much as possible.	Yes ; yes...	No ; physicians in attendance look after this.	Yes; no....
Framosa	....	Scarlatina, 6 cases.	Yes ; no	Yes ; yes...	Yes.........	No.........
Garafraxa West.	Yes ; action taken on complaint.	Tuberculosis, 5 cases.	Yes ; no........	Yes ; yes...	No ; under instruct'ns of Board.	Yes ; no...
Guelph	Frequently inspected.	Scarlatina, 4 cases ; diphtheria, 6 cases, 1 death ; typhoid, 3 cases, 1 death; tuberculosis,6 cases, 5 deaths.	Yes, in Guelph city.	Very satisfactory.	Yes	Yes; yes; no.
Luther, W	Action taken only on complaint.	Scarlatina, 3 cases ; diphtheria, 1 case ; typhoid, 2 cases, 1 death.	No ; no	No	Yes	No ; no ....

(8)	(9)	(10)	(11)	(12)	(13)	(14)
No.........	No ; wells 10 to 150 ft.; no.	No ; no.....	No; offal buried; yes.	No........	No..........	None.
....	Wells ; s o m e cases fr'm old wells.	No........... ...	Yes	No.........	No.........	None.
Yes	From wells 30 to 40 ft.	Yes ; no..........	Yes; fed to hogs; no.	No.	No	None.
No	Wells 12 to 18 ft.; no.	Yes ; no..........	No..............	No.........	No.........	None.
Yes	Wells are 16 to 40 ft.	No ; no	Only one in vil-lage ; no.	No.........	No	None.
No.........	Springs & wells ; no.	No..............	No ; fed to pigs ; no.	No.........	No...	None.
No	No ; wells ; no.	No; no......	No ; inspected : don't know.	No.........	No.........	None.
Yes	Yes ; 20 to 30 ft.; no.	No ; no...........	None in the vil-lage.	No.........	No.........	None.
Yes	....	No : no..........	....	....	....	
Yes	Yes ; from arte-sian wells ; no.	No ; no...........	Yes ; yes	No.........	No.........	None.
Yes	Wells 15 ft	No.............. .	No ; fed to hogs; no.	No.........	No.........	None.
Yes	No ; wells 15 to 25 ft.; no.	No ; no......	No ; no	No..........	No.........	None.
Yes	No ; wells 20 ft.; a few cases.	No ; no..........	No ; don't know; no.	No...... ..	No.........	None.
Yes........	No ; about 20 ft.	No dairies in Tp .	No ; buried ; no.	Yes	No	None.
Yes	Wells, about 5 ft.	None	Yes ; inspected.	No	No	None.
No	No ; no	No	None in Tp.....	No	No	None.

	(2)	(3)	(4)	(5)	(6)	(7)
Minto..........	No; no; on complaint.	Diphtheria, 12 cases; tuberculosis, 3 deaths.	Yes ; no	Yes ; yes...	Yes	No ; no ....
Nichol	Yes ; yes ; on complaint.	Tuberculo s i s, 2 cases, 2 deaths.	Yes ; no	Y e s, when required.	Yes	None ......
Erin	Action on complaint.	Dipht h e r i a, 4 cases, 1 death ; consumption, 3 deaths.	Yes ; no	No	Yes	No ....
Peel	When c o m - p l a i n t. is made.	Dipht h e r i a, 2 cases; tuberculosis, 2 cases.	No	Yes ; yes ..	No	No . ...
Puslinch	Sanitary i n - spector makes visits.	Scarla t i n a, 20 cases, 2 deaths; tuberculosis, 4 cases, 2 deaths.	Yes ; no	Not in general use.	Yes	Yes ; y e s ; general.
WENTWORTH. City and Towns: Hamilton	General i n - spection and on complaint.	Small p o x. 19 cases ; scarlatina 88 cases, 4 deaths; diphtheria, 93 cases, 25 deaths ; typhoid, 58 cases, 10 deaths ; tuberculosis, 97 deaths.	Yes ; yes........	Yes ; yes ..	Yes	Yes ; no ...
Dundas	Yes, once a year.	Tuberculosis, 6 cases.	Yes ; no...	Yes; yes...	Yes	No ; no ....
Waterdown	Yes ; no ; on complaint.	Typhoid, 3 cases; tuberculosis, 1 case.	No ; no	Yes; yes....	No	Yes ; no....
Townships : Ancaster	Yes, o n c e a year and on complaint.	Typhoid, 3 cases.	Yes, except in c a s e s of typhoid.	Yes; yes....	Under medical attendant.	Yes .. ...
Barton	Action on complaint.	Scar l a t i n a, 4 cases ; d i p h theria, 4 ct ses; t y p h o i d, 6 cases, 1 death; tuberculosis, 5 deaths.	No	Yes; yes....	No	No ....
Beverly	No; no; action on complaint.	Scar l a t i n a, 8 cases; typhoid, 6 cases, 1 death; tuberculosis, 4 deaths.	As well as possible ; no hospital.	Yes; yes....	Yes	None ......
Binbrook	Only w h e n complaint is made.	....	Yes ; no........	Yes; yes....	No	Yes ; no....
Flamboro, E ...	On complaint.	None	Patients isolated at their homes.	Yes; yes....	No	No ; no ....
Glanford	On complaint, or when required.	Typhoid, 1 case, 1 death.	Yes, as far as circumstances will permit; no.	Yes; yes....	U n d e r attending physician.	No ; no ....

(8)	(9)	(10)	(11)	(12)	(13)	(2
To physicians only.	No; wells 10 to 50 ft.; no.	No; no	No; fed to hogs.	No	No	None.
Yes	No; wells various depths; no.	No; no; 2 deaths.	No; boiled and fed to hogs.	Yes	No	None.
No	Wells,10 to 40 ft.	No	No	No	No	None.
No	No; wells, 12 to 100 ft.	No	No	No	No	None.
No	Wells, about 25 ft.; no.	No	No, but inspected; no.	School-houses only.	No	None.
To physician only.	Yes	Yes	None in city....	Yes	Yes	....
Yes	Wells are used; one case from well water.	No; none reported.	No, but are inspected; offal fed to hogs.	Yes	No	Two tanneries.
Yes	No, wells, 15 to 30 ft.; no.	No; no	No	No	No	None.
No	Wells, 10 to 50 ft.	Yes; no..........	No	No	No	None.
Yes	Wells, 12 to 20 ft.	Yes; no..........	No; offal cooked and fed to hogs.	No	No	None.
Yes	No; 20 to 100 ft.; yes.	No; yes..........	No; buried; no	No	No	None.
No	No; 20 ft.; yes..	No; no	No; no	Yes	No	None.
Yes	No; depth of wells 15 to 40 ft.; no.	Yes; no..........	No; buried; no	No	No	None.
Yes	Wells; no	Inspection of milk venders by sanitary inspector; no.	No; no	No	No	None.

	(2)	(3)	(4)	(5)	(6)	(7)
Saltfleet........	Yes; yes.....	Diphth e r i a, 3 cases, 1 death; tuberculosis, 1 case.	Yes ; no........	Yes; yes....	No ; by attending physician.	Yes ; yes...
YORK. *City and Towns :* Toronto	Yes; inspected at intervals, and action on complaint.	Small p o x , 24 cases, 1 death; scarlatina, 452 cases,25 de'ths; diphtheria, 1024 cases, 156 deaths; typhoid, 120 cases,23 deaths	Yes ; yes......	Yes ; results not satisfactory.	Yes	Yes; yes....
Aurora	Yes, and on complaint.'	Diphtheria, 1 case.	Yes ; no........	Yes; yes....	Yes	No ; no ....
Markham	General inspection once a year.	Tuberculo sis 3 cases.	Yes ; no........	Don't know.	Yes	No ; no ....
Newmarket	Annual inspection and repeated at intervals when considered necessary.	Scarla tina, 20 cases, 1 death ; typhoid,1 case.	Isolation is systematically carried out ; no.	Yes; yes....	Yes	Yes ; no....
North Toronto..	One general house to house inspection.	Scarlatina, 2 cases ; diphtheria,11 cases, 3 deaths.	As far as possible ; no.	No	Yes	No ....
Richmond Hill.	No ; no ; on complaint.	Typhoid, 2 cases, 1 death; tuberculosis.1 death	Yes ; no........	Yes; yes....	Yes '......	No ; no ....
Stouffville	Yes, general ; repeated once a year.	Typhoid, 12 cases, but none reported.	Yes ; no........	In some cases fairly so.	Yes	No ; no ....
Sutton	Yes, on complaint.	Typhoid, 1 case.	Yes ; no........	Yes; yes....	Yes; no	No ....
Toronto Junct'n	Yes, by sanitary inspector.	Smallpox,1 case; scarla tina, 4 cases,2 deaths; diphtheria, 51 cases,4 deaths; typhoid, 4 deaths ; tuberculosis, 11 deaths.	Yes ; no..... ..	Yes	Yes	Yes ; no....
Weston	Inspection on complaint.	Scarlatina, 1 case ; diphtheria, 5 cases; typhoid,1 case.	Yes	....	Yes	Yes ....
Woodbridge....	Once a year by order of council.	Tuberculo sis, 2 cases.	....	....	Yes	Yes ....
Townships : Etobicoke	Yes	Smallpox,1 case; scarlatina, 4 cases; diphtheria,11 cases; typhoid, 3 cases ; tuberculosis, 3 deaths.	Yes ; under M. H. O.	Yes; yes....	Yes ; under M.H.O.	No ....

(8)	(9)	(10)	(11)	(12)	(13)	(14)
Yes	No ; wells 15 to 20 ft.; no.	Yes ; no..........	No ; offal boiled and fed to hogs, no.	Yes	No	Slaughter houses.
Yes	Yes, from Lake Ontario in general use.	Yes ; no..........	No; regulated by by-law ; offal removed daily to outside city limits.	Yes	Yes	....
No	Yes; no typhoid.	No	None within the corporation.	No	No	None.
No	No; well 15 to 50 ft.; no.	No	No	No	No	None.
No	Yes	Yes ; no..........	No ; offal fed to hogs ; no inspection.	Yes	No	None.
Yes	Yes ; wells supplied by springs, 6 ft.	Yes ; no..........	Yes ; offal carried away from premises ; no.	Only when required,	No	None.
Yes	——Typhoid not caused o f t e n by wells.	No ; no	No ; inspected.	No ; no	No	None.
Yes	Yes ; not in general ; 15 to 20 ft ; yes.	No	No ; boiled and fed to hogs.	No	No	None.
No	No ; wells about 15 ft.	No	No	No	No	None.
Yes	Yes ; from Lake Ontario.	No	None	No	Yes	None.
Yes	....	No	No	No	No	None.
Yes	Well water , no.	None in village.;..	No ; o ff a l carried away.	Yes	No	None.
Yes	No ; wells from 10 to 20 ft.	No	No ; buried ; no.	No	No	None.

	(2)	(3)	(4)	(5)	(6)	(7)
Georgina . .	Action on complaint.	Scarlatina, 2 cases; diphtheria, 2 cases.	No; no	No	By M.H.O., or attending physician.	No; no ....
Gwillimbury, E.	Action promptly taken on complaint.	Scarlatina, 48 cases; diphtheria, 24 cases, 1 death; typhoid, 8 cases, 1 death; tuberculosis, 4 deaths.	Yes; no........	Yes; yes....	Yes, (by M. H. O.	Yes; no ....
Gwillimbury, N.	No	....	No hospital; premises placarded.	Yes; yes....	No; only by Dr. in attendance.	No ....
Scarboro	General sanitary inspection once a year.	Scarlatina, 12 cases, 2 deaths; diphtheria, 15 cases, 4 deaths; typhoid, 1 case; tuberculosis, 3 deaths.	Yes; no........	Yes; yes....	Yes	Yes; no ....
Whitchurch	Action on complaint.	Scarlatina, 16 cases, no deaths ; diphtheria, 1 case, 1 death.	Yes; no........	Yes; yes....	No	No ; no ....
York	Inspection and monthly report to Board of Health.	Smallpox, 4 cases ; scarlatina, 21 cases, 2 deaths; diphtheria, 34 cases, 7 deaths ; typhoid, 2 deaths ; tuberculosis, 9 deaths.	Yes ; no........	Cannot say.	Yes; M.H.O	Yes; no ....

(8)	(9)	(10)	(11)	(12)	(13)	(14)
No	No ; v a r i o u s depths.	No ; no	No	No	No	None.
Yes	W a t e r f r o m wells.	No ; no	No ; no	No	No	None.
No	Good wells, 15 to 40 ft.	No ....,.......	No	No	No	None.
Yes	No ; no	Yes ; fed te pigs ; no.	No	No	No	None.
Yes	Wells ; 15 to 50 ft.	No	No ; offal fed to pigs ; no.	No ..,......	No	None.
On demand.	Well water, 18 to 90 ft.	No	Yes ; offal sold to Harris' factory and fed to hogs.	No	No	B y consent of council, H a r r i s rendering f a c t ory. C l a p p's tallow factory a n d Blackwell v a r n i s h factory.

CPSIA information can be obtained
at www.ICGtesting.com
Printed in the USA
BVHW041425220219
540923BV00007B/206/P

9 781397 329158